BUILDING THE FUTURE

Social Work with Children, Young People and their Families

Neil Thompson

with a Foreword by Professor Nigel Parton

Russell House Publishing

in association with

LCP learning curve publishing

First published in 2002 by:
Russell House Publishing Ltd.
4 St. George's House
Uplyme Road
Lyme Regis
Dorset DT7 3LS

Tel: 01297-443948
Fax: 01297-442722
e-mail: help@russellhouse.co.uk
www.russellhouse.co.uk

© Neil Thompson 2002

British Library Cataloguing-in-publication Data:
A catalogue record for this book is available from the British Library.

ISBN: 1-903855-13-6

Typeset by TW Typesetting, Plymouth, Devon

Printed by Antony Rowe, Chippenham

About Russell House Publishing

RHP is a group of social work, probation, education and youth and community work practitioners and academics working in collaboration with a professional publishing team.
Our aim is to work closely with the field to produce innovative and valuable materials to help managers, trainers, practitioners and students.
We are keen to receive feedback on publications and new ideas for future projects.
For details of our other publications please visit our website or ask us for a catalogue. Contact details are on this page.

For Anna

The author

Neil Thompson is a Director of *Avenue Consulting Ltd*, a company offering training and consultancy to a wide range of organisations concerned with people and their problems (www.avenueconsulting.co.uk). He is also a Visiting Professor at the University of Liverpool. Neil holds qualifications in social work; training and development; management; and mediation and alternative dispute resolution and has been a speaker at conferences and seminars in the UK, Greece, the Netherlands, Australia, Canada and the United States. He has over 100 publications to his name, including *Stress Matters* (Pepar, 1999) and *Understanding Social Work: Preparing for Practice* (Palgrave, 2000).

Contents

Foreword

The last decade has seen considerable development in relation to social work with children and families in England and Wales. In part, this was initially prompted by the Children Act 1989 and its introduction in October 1991. Not only did this introduce a new legislative framework, but it was also based on a set of principles and philosophies which aimed to change the relationship between state, family and children and young people. There was a real attempt to emphasise family support, partnership and trying to keep court interventions to a minimum. The legislation came at the end of a decade which had seen a number of high-profile child abuse cases which had brought social work with children and families into the public arena. Not only did it seem that social workers were failing to protect children, with horrendous consequences sometimes including death, but in other situations there also seemed to be a failure to recognise the rights and responsibilities of parents, leading to an apparent over-intervention into the privacy of the family, as apparently exemplified in the *Cleveland* affair. While the Children Act had a much wider remit than simply these situations that had received high publicity, there is no doubt these acted to propel changes onto the legislative agenda (Parton, 1991).

However, the 1990s saw a range of other concerns come to the fore. Some of these were particularly around the treatment of children and young people in residential settings, and again there are a number of scandals and public inquiries in relation to these. But also, important research which was published in the middle of the decade (DoH, 1995) suggested that the relationship between family support and child protection was in further need of *refocusing*. What this research was seen to illustrate in particular, was the need to try to re-emphasise a much broader and holistic approach to child and family social work which was not so concerned with narrowly defined child protection issues and a forensically driven approach to practice.

The election of the New Labour government in May 1997 heralded a new political administration which has particular interests around the family, the community, social inclusion and parental responsibilities as well as rights. In relation to the public services it has introduced a major *modernising agenda*, which is having an impact across all health, education and welfare services. More specifically, in relation to social work with children and families, it has invested money through its Quality Protects/Children First initiative and a thorough overhaul of the regulatory and educational expectations of social care workers, particularly social workers.

Two key elements of this are the introduction of a three-year, full-time undergraduate programme as the basic professional qualification for social work as from 2003 in England; and the introduction, initially in 2000, of a new *Postqualifying Child Care Award*. The latter is a major initiative which recognises the need for highly qualified social work staff to work in the difficult and complex area that is child and family social work. The development is very much to be welcomed. At the same time it has posed a major challenge to both local authorities and the higher education sector to try and provide, in a very short period of time, the quality of programme which is both required and expected. It is in this context that Professor Neil Thompson's new book is very much to be welcomed.

While the book is primarily aimed at candidates on such postqualifying programmes, together with those on qualifying programmes, it would be a mistake to see the book as an uncritical set of training materials – far from it. A major strength of the book is the way it locates itself in a set of principles and themes which encourage a critical and reflective approach to practice. Not only does it cover the full range of knowledge that candidates will require for the Postqualifying Award in order to meet the learning outcomes, it also does so in a way which is engaging and is likely to extend and challenge candidates' thinking and practice. From the outset the book is explicitly located in a set of values which takes seriously the ideas around: child-centredness; a critical perspective; partnership; the importance of meaning; reflective practice; being systematic; and the positives associated with being professional. The book will be very much welcomed by everybody involved in the Postqualifying Child Care programmes, whether they be candidates, teachers, mentors, those in agencies, or those who are considering embarking on such a programme. The book provides important signposts throughout as to where readers can gain more detailed knowledge and follow up particular interests, as well as including a number of brief reflective exercises to help the reader engage in the material.

As the most recent Department of Health overview of research carried out since the Children Act 1989 (DoH, 2001) reminds us, while there is clear evidence of progress over the last ten years or so, it is also clear there is a considerable way to go. Research, education and training will play a vital role in this. In many respects the quality of the service is very dependent on the quality of the professionals involved. It is in this context that the book by Professor Thompson is very much to be welcomed and I am delighted to have been asked to provide this Foreword for it.

Professor Nigel Parton,
Centre for Applied Childhood Studies,
University of Huddersfield

Preface

It has long been argued that basic social work training is not enough to equip practitioners with the knowledge and skills they need to face the challenges of life as a qualified social worker. The introduction of the postqualifying award in social work has therefore been a welcome contribution to the development of social work education. In particular, the postqualifying award in child care has been welcomed by many as an important step forward, much needed to bolster learning and professional development to support social work staff in facing the major demands of child care practice.

This book has been developed in response to the needs of staff pursuing the award. It is intended as a basic textbook covering the main elements of knowledge associated with the programme. It should therefore be of value to child care social workers engaged in study geared towards the award, as well as to mentors, assessors and others involved in supporting candidates in their learning. Social work students intending to pursue a career in child care social work will find much of interest and value here too.

Over the years as a practitioner, manager, trainer and consultant in the field of child care social work, I have not only learned a great deal but also gained an enormous amount of pleasure and satisfaction (more than enough to make up for the pain, disappointment and frustration). It is my hope that the publication of this book will help others to share with me in that learning, pleasure and satisfaction. Given the pressures and strains of the work, it is important that we make the most of the positives where and when we can.

Working effectively with children, young people and their families is no easy matter. It is complex and demanding work which requires a great deal of commitment, skill and knowledge. Commitment is, I hope, something you already bring to the job. Some of the skills used in child care social work are basic 'people skills', while others can only be developed through actual practice experience over time. The knowledge, similarly, is partly general life knowledge and understanding and partly specialist knowledge developed through a mixture of practice and study. This book will not give you all the knowledge you need, but it is to be hoped that it will make an important contribution to your understanding and will help to point you in the direction of further study and learning. I hope, then, that this book can play at least a small part in promoting high standards of practice so that children, young people and their families can receive the best possible support and assistance.

Acknowledgements

This book has evolved from work undertaken on behalf of the Postqualifying Child Care Award for Wales. I am therefore grateful to colleagues involved in that programme for the benefit of various discussions and for their comments on earlier drafts. In particular I would like to thank Bryan Isaac of University of Wales Institute, Cardiff and Nigel Thomas of University of Wales, Swansea for their enthusiasm and support.

I am indebted to Malcolm Thomas of the Care Council for Wales for his assistance in relation to the National Occupational Standards. Geoffrey Mann at Russell House Publishing also deserves thanks for his backing in creating the opportunity to convert the original study materials into book form – another example of partnership in action.

As with so much of my work, I am very grateful indeed for the very positive role Susan Thompson has played in so many ways. I am running out of ways of saying how indebted I am to her and how important she is to me. The book is dedicated to our daughter, Anna, and this reflects the pride we take in what a wonderful young adult she has developed into.

Finally, I would like to thank Professor Nigel Parton for not only the Foreword that he has so kindly contributed, but also the important part the quality and depth of his work have played in influencing my thinking and practice over the years.

Introduction

Social work with children, young people and their families is demanding and challenging work. This book will not change that. However, what it can more realistically do is help to ensure that such work is undertaken from a well-informed basis. My aim here, then, is to provide a platform from which to build social work practice based on a sound understanding of some of the key issues that relate to the tasks involved. The book will not tell you all you need to know but it should equip you with at least a major proportion of the basics, with avenues to further development indicated as appropriate.

The book comprises five chapters and this 'scene-setting' introduction. This scene-setting begins with a discussion of values, the important ethical principles that play such an important role in shaping and underpinning our practice in working with children and young people.

Next comes an account of the core themes which will form the 'backbone' of the discussions that go to make up the materials for each of the five chapters. This leads into a more detailed discussion of two of the themes: first, reflective practice, an important concept that has become increasingly influential in social work education in recent years – and one which will feature to a great extent in this book; and second, professionalism, a term with both positive and negative connotations. Its positive connotations will feature significantly in each of the chapters, particularly Chapter 4. This is followed by an account of the theoretical model on which the ideas presented here are based. It is a model which is critical of a great deal of traditional theory and practice in child care social work, and which seeks to present an approach more consistent with a philosophy of empowerment and anti-discriminatory practice. To conclude, I provide an overview of each of the five chapters .

Values

The *National Occupational Standards for Child Care at Post Qualifying Level* (TOPSS, 2000) explicitly identify a number of values which should underpin social work with children, young people and their families. These are:

- Children and young people's best interests shall be of primary consideration in all action affecting them.
- Children and young people are enabled to develop and achieve their full potential.
- Children and young people have the right to express their views and have them taken into account in all matters affecting them.
- Children and young people should remain, wherever possible, within their family and community networks.
- Children and young people are to be protected from and empowered to address all forms of discrimination.
- Children and young people have the right to be given proper care by those looking after them.
- Children and young people with disabilities must be helped to be as independent as possible and to be able to play a full and active part in everyday life.
- Children and young people should have their own identity affirmed through the promotion of their religious, cultural, racial and linguistic background.
- Children and young people in Wales have a right to receive services in the Welsh language.
- Children and young people have the right to services which are free from prejudice.

These values underpin the whole book and are therefore very important even where not articulated directly or explicitly. It should also be emphasised that values are to be seen as concrete influences on practice in 'the real world' and not simply as abstract concepts only to be discussed in classrooms and academic assignments (see the discussion below of reflective practice).

Core themes

Working with children, young people and their families involves a vast and complex knowledge base, and one that continues to grow and develop over time. What is needed, therefore, is some assistance in making sense of this huge body of relevant material. This assistance is provided in the form of a set of 'core' themes – that is, a set of ideas that help to draw out patterns and similarities, and which therefore help us to plot our route through, in terms of both understanding the issues and relating them to practice.

The themes chosen to help make sense of contemporary social work with children and families are the following: child-centredness; a critical perspective; working in partnership; phenomenology and the importance of meaning; reflective practice, systematic practice and professionalism. I shall outline each of these in turn:

1. *Child-centredness.* The notion that 'the child's welfare is paramount' is, of course, very well-established. It should come as no surprise, then, to find that it is a key theme as far as this book is concerned. We shall, however, explore this theme not simply as an expectation of good practice, but also as a challenge to be met – in the sense that attempting to be child-centred (or 'young person-centred') is not always as straightforward or unproblematic as it may initially seem. We should note that the term is ambiguous. It can refer to an objective to be achieved – that is, a desired outcome where the child's or young person's needs are met – or a method of working, an approach to practice which involves focusing primarily on the child or young person. Attempts to act in a child-centred way may conflict with other important issues and considerations. Being child-centred therefore involves managing conflicting interests and seeking a constructive way forward. It is a complex matter.

2. *A critical perspective.* As we shall see below, a great deal of material published in relation to working with children and families can be criticised for being too simplistic or, to use a technical term, *reductionist.* That is, they reduce a complex, multilevel matter to a simple, single-level explanation (for example, poor parenting or insufficient attachment). Such reductionist approaches often neglect broader social issues, such as discrimination and oppression, and are therefore not consistent with anti-discriminatory practice and the underpinning value base. A critical perspective is therefore one that does not take matters at face value and is prepared to take into account wider and deeper issues. This is not simply a question of attempting to be more theoretically sophisticated for its own sake. Rather, it is a matter of ensuring that an oversimplified approach does not neglect important issues and therefore leave us in a situation where our practice may reinforce or at least condone discrimination and oppression (see Thompson, 2001).

3. *Working in partnership.* While the term 'partnership' is relatively new to social work theory, policy and practice, the importance of working effectively together with other key people involved has a very long history and is widely recognised as a firm basis for good practice. However, it can be recognised that partnership has become something of a 'buzzword' and is often used without any clarity about what it means, how it can or should be used or even why it is important. The complexities of working in partnership will therefore feature as an important aspect of the work we engage in as practitioners – recognising that partnership is not only a value but also a highly skilful form of practice. This will involve working in partnership with (i) children and young people; (ii) parents, families and other carers; and (iii) other professionals and communities.

4. *Phenomenology and the importance of meaning.* 'Phenomenology' is the study of perception (a 'phenomenon' is literally something which is perceived, as in: 'That's an interesting phenomenon'). It emphasises the importance of meaning – the fact that

our actions depend not so much on what happens to us, but rather how we *perceive* what happens to us – the meaning we attach to the events and developments in our life. This subjective element of perception and meaning is one that is often neglected in traditional analyses and therefore needs to be given more attention than is usually the case. We need to look at not only what is happening in the lives of children, young people and their families, but also what these events *mean* to the individuals concerned, for it is such meanings that will shape the actions and attitudes that follow.

5. *Reflective practice.* This is an approach to professional practice and learning which is critical of the traditional idea of 'applying theory to practice', as if there were a direct and unproblematic relationship between the two. This is another term that has become something of a buzzword in recent years, and has therefore not always been explored in the depth or sophistication the concept deserves. We return to this topic below, as it is an important foundation of the philosophy of learning on which the Postqualifying Award is based.

6. *Systematic practice.* This is a term used to refer to an approach to practice which emphasises the importance of avoiding 'drift' or losing focus. It concentrates on being clear about what we are trying to achieve, how we intend to achieve it and how we will know when we have achieved it (Thompson, 2002a). As we noted earlier, partnership is a central aspect of good practice in working with children and young people. Systematic practice, with its emphasis on clarity about purpose, direction and focus can be a major help in achieving such partnership – clarity of focus can act as the 'glue' that holds together the efforts and intentions of the various people involved.

7. *Professionalism.* The notion of 'professionalism' is often associated with negative connotations of elitism and privilege. However, we should not allow this to distract us from the positive elements of professionalism, the benefits and positive value that arise from adopting an explicitly *professional* approach. This is a very important foundation stone of good practice, and so it is discussed in more detail below.

The reflective practitioner: integrating theory and practice

Traditional approaches to social work education have been criticised for an unhelpful approach to integrating theory and practice (Thompson, 2000a). This critique of traditional approaches goes under the heading of 'reflective practice', a term introduced in the work of Schön (Schön, 1983; Schön, 1987; Argyris and Schön, 1974).

Schön was critical of what he called 'technical rationality', the idea that theoretical, technical or research-based knowledge could be applied to professional practice, as if practice provided the questions while theory provided the answers. This oversimplified view of the relationship between theory and practice has haunted social work education for a long, long time, with exhortations to 'apply theory to practice' falling on stony ground.

Reflective practice offers a far more sophisticated approach in which it is recognised that there is a need to integrate theory and practice (a two-way, interactive process which recognises the importance of theory *and* practice), rather than apply theory to practice (a one-way process which implies that theory is superior to practice). Reflective practice is therefore offered as a potential solution to the age-old problem of the unnecessarily wide gap between theory and practice (Thompson, 2000a).

Schön described the world of theory and research as the 'high ground', likening it to a hill that gives a clear overview of the landscape below. From here it is relatively easy to develop a picture of what is going on below – to see links, connections, patterns, blockages and so on. However, this can be quite different from the much messier, more complex and uncertain world of actual practice which he described as 'the swampy lowlands'. What is called for, then, is the ability to remember and draw upon the insights offered by the high ground while actually navigating the much more difficult terrain of actual practice. The insights of the high ground are of relatively little use if we ignore them in practice, and a form of practice that cannot see further than the next few metres of bog is also not likely to be of much value! Integration through reflection is the key.

Reflective practice can therefore be likened to taking the cloth of theory, research and the professional knowledge base and cutting it to fit the specific practice circumstances we encounter, rather than looking to theory to provide off-the-peg, ready-made solutions. This has a number of important implications, not least the following:

- There is a set of skills involved in 'tailoring' our professional knowledge base to the specific situation – it is not enough simply to 'know' the theory or be *au fait* with the research, as if this will somehow make us better practitioners.
- We often draw on an extensive knowledge base, perhaps without realising that we are doing so. It is therefore very easy for people to make the mistake of assuming that they are just 'getting on with practice' without reference to theory.

The first point alerts us to the danger of underestimating the role of practice skills. Taking such skills for granted may lead us into complacency or an over reliance on unthinking routines because we do not appreciate how much is involved in the process of, for example, professional decision-making (Sullivan, 1999).

The second point alerts us to the danger of devaluing the role of theoretical knowledge in the process. It is a common mistake for practitioners to assume that what they are doing is based on 'common sense', rather than professional knowledge, theory and research. It is clearly dangerous for practitioners to play down the extent to which their actions have been informed by a professional knowledge base (of human development, social processes and institutions, law, policy, ethics and so on) rather than simply left to the guesswork and unquestioned assumptions of 'common sense'.

Schön drew an important distinction between 'reflection-in-action' and 'reflection-on-action'. The former refers to the 'thinking on our feet' that is part and parcel of day-to-day practice – the highly skilled task of drawing on relevant knowledge and values in the pressurised setting of practice encounters. The latter, by contrast, refers to reflection after the event, the time when we think through what has happened, consider how it went, identify any lessons that can be learned from it and plan the next step. Unfortunately, many people see reflective practice in terms of the latter only, as if it were simply a matter of finding opportunities to think about our practice. Clearly, it *does* involve finding such opportunities but it should also be clear that it involves a lot more than this.

The notion of reflective practice offers a distinctly different approach to social work education, and one that has the potential to be far more effective than traditional methods. The significance of reflective practice should become more fully apparent as we work through the chapters.

Professionalism

The term, 'professionalism' is one that has a mixed history in social work. For many years, the notion of being a 'professional' was regarded with a great deal of suspicion, as if it were simply a way of seeking perks, privileges and status at the expense of the clientele that we serve. Of course, it has to be acknowledged that professionalism can be abused in this way, used as an excuse for self-interest. However, we would see it as a significant mistake to reject the notion of professionalism for these reasons, as this amounts to throwing the baby out with the bath water. Indeed, we see professionalism as a very relevant concept underpinning social work with children and families.

The positive aspects of professionalism that we would wish to emphasise here can be summarised as follows:

- *The use of a systematic knowledge base.* – How much faith would you have in a nurse, police officer or teacher if he or she was relying simply on life experience, with no formal knowledge or training to back it up? We can similarly argue that social work must be based on formal knowledge if we are to gain the credibility and respect of both clients and fellow professionals. This is therefore an aspect of professionalism that is very relevant to social work.

An explicit set of values. – The importance of values has already been stressed. By making such values *explicit*, it is possible to seek to ensure that they are being respected and, where necessary, examining or debating their appropriateness in particular circumstances.

A commitment to high standards of practice. – Professionalism implies a primary commitment to quality of service, seeking to achieve as high a standard as is reasonably possible in the circumstances, rather than simply settling for 'good enough'.

A degree of autonomy and discretion. – Although social work practice is largely governed by the legislative framework, the law does not offer sufficient guidance or flexibility to provide detailed prescriptions for practice. The worker has to exercise a degree of professional discretion, forming judgements on the basis of the particular circumstances encountered – a degree of autonomy is not therefore something to be striven for, but rather an inevitable aspect of working within the framework of law (this will be discussed in more detail in Chapter 4).

- *Accountability.* – As a result of the previous point, we are of course responsible for our actions and thus accountable. We cannot simply say: 'I was just doing what the law required me to do'. The law is rarely that prescriptive. This is an important point to emphasise, as the experience of working in a large bureaucracy can often blunt our sensitivity to such matters – but, while bureaucracy may be problematic in this respect, it makes us no less accountable for our actions, and no less open to legitimate criticism if we can justify why we took a particular course of action.

This theme of professionalism is clearly both an important and complex one. It is therefore a topic that we shall return to from time to time as we work through the five chapters of the book.

The theoretical model

Traditional approaches to social work with children and young people can be described as falling within a 'superparenting' model. That is, it can be seen as amounting primarily to a set of attempts to rectify the deficits in parenting that are encountered in working with families. The social worker in this model, it can be argued, plays the role of 'superparent', helping parents to identify and seek to improve inadequacies in their parenting skills and abilities.

This approach can be criticised for being *reductionist*. That is, it reduces a complex, multilevel phenomenon to a simple matter of individual failing. This manifests itself in two separate but related ways:

- *It is individualistic.* It takes little account of the significance of broader social factors, such as poverty, deprivation, discrimination and oppression. This is not to say that individual factors are not important, but rather that they need to be seen in the context of broader concerns and issues.
- *It is pathologising.* It places parents in a position where they are seen as the main root cause of the problems needing attention. This can cause additional problems in terms of attaching stigma, undermining self-esteem and creating unnecessary barriers between worker and client.

It can also be criticised for being paternalistic – indeed, a form of 'state paternalism' in which social workers are cast in the role of 'parenting the parents'.

Traditional approaches can also be criticised for being *essentialist*. That is, they assume certain matters to be fixed and immutable, rather than socially or psychologically variable. For example, in Chapter 1, we shall examine the notion of children's needs and see why dominant approaches to this topic are far from adequate in so far as they tend to present needs as fairly fixed, as if they are biologically given. We shall argue that such an approach is not only lacking in theoretical sophistication, but also largely incompatible with anti-discriminatory practice, thus creating great difficulties for practitioners who are seeking to draw on theoretical understandings whilst also wishing to promote equality and challenge oppression.

Clearly, such approaches are far from adequate for the task of tackling the complexities social workers encounter. An alternative approach is called for. The model presented here is different from traditional analyses in the following three respects: care, control and rights; user involvement; and empowerment:

1. *Care, control and rights.* There is a long-standing tension between care and control in social work. Social work is, of course, one of the caring professions and therefore very much about care, welfare and social well-being. The radical social work movement of the 1960s and 70s was, however, critical of this notion and argued rather cynically that social work was more about social control than care (see, for example, Corrigan and Leonard, 1978). However, a more realistic approach is to recognise that social work is about both care *and* control:

> . . . it would be naïve not to recognise that there are also significant elements of social control. This is because social work involves promoting and protecting the welfare of not only the individual but also the wider community, a dual responsibility that can often lead to conflicts and tensions . . . Protecting the wider community is an example of caring, but, in relation to specific individuals, the same actions can amount to control.
> (Thompson, 2000b, p. 3)

My approach in this book is therefore based on the recognition of both care and control as significant factors. However, in addition to these two key issues, we would wish to add a third, namely that of *rights*. Again there is a long-standing tension to be acknowledged here, this time between care and rights. However, we would again argue that our task is not to enter into a sterile argument about which is the appropriate path to follow, that of care or that of rights, as it is very much our view that the two can be highly compatible. This is parallel with arguments emerging from the Disabled People's Movement (see Oliver, 1990; Oliver and Sapey, 1999) to the effect that a rights-based approach can incorporate care issues (for example, if we see, say, adequate nutrition as a right rather than a care need), whereas an approach that begins with care

is unlikely to incorporate rights, and is more likely to lead us down the path of the paternalistic 'superparent' model discussed above. These complex issues will be explored in more detail in Chapter 1.

2. *User involvement.* Many client groups have staked a claim for having a greater say in how services are organised, provided, evaluated and so on – basically arguing that the user's voice is an important matter to be considered in carrying out assessment and intervention tasks – the client's perspective is clearly not one to be ignored (a point consistent with the phenomenological approach outlined above). This argument can, of course, also be applied to social work with children and young people. However, we have to acknowledge that a significant barrier to such involvement is the process of 'mirroring' that can go on. Because a great deal of social work with children and young people focuses on parenting issues, it is a very easy mistake for the worker to mirror this by adopting a paternalistic role, rather than a facilitative one. This is a point to which we shall return in Chapters 2 and 3 where partnership issues with children and young people, parents and carers and fellow professionals and the wider community are discussed.

3. *Empowerment.* Unfortunately, empowerment is also a term that has become something of a fashionable 'buzzword' that tends to get used uncritically (Gomm, 1993; Humphries, 1996) by many people. This is a great pity as it is none the less a very important and valuable concept. It refers to the process of helping people gain greater control over their lives. This can be seen to apply at three levels:

- *Personal.* – Improved confidence, raised self-esteem, a greater sense of personal agency and so on.
- *Cultural.* – Challenging myths and stereotypes that can hold us back, undermining taken-for-granted assumptions that can be very discriminatory and obstructive ('women are indecisive'; 'men should not express feelings' and so on).

- *Structural.* – Working towards challenging established power structures which disadvantage certain members of the community (for example, in terms of class, race or gender).

  Empowerment in working with children and families involves, amongst other things, helping people to help themselves, thus avoiding the dependency-creation inherent in the 'superparent' model.

A further important aspect of the book is the attempt to achieve a degree of *vertical* and *horizontal* integration, and it is to be hoped that the theoretical model will help to do this. *Vertical* integration refers to the integration of theory and practice, as discussed above. Through the book I seek to promote reflective approaches to practice as opposed to traditional education and training which attempt to place theory in the driving seat, often at the expense of practice. *Horizontal* integration refers to the integration of the various strands of social work with children and families (family support, substitute care, child protection, children with disabilities, advocacy and rights work and so on), so that what is presented is applicable across the board. That is, the book has been designed to concentrate on common themes and issues which can then be applied and adapted to specific practice contexts, rather than attempt the unrealistic task of trying to cover a number of specialist areas in detail. There is a danger in becoming too narrowly specialist in a particular area of practice and possibly losing sight of the commonalities and foundation stones of good practice in working with children and families.

The National Occupational Standards

The book comprises five chapters, each reflecting an area covered by the National Occupational Standards. Each of these covers a number of important themes and issues relating to social work with children and young people. They are to be studied as discrete areas but, of course, they overlap and interlink in a number of ways, forming what should develop into a coherent whole. The overall study area is, of course, vast and complex.

Dividing it up into discrete subject areas is intended as an aid to 'digesting' this major knowledge base. It is not presented as the only or definitive way of dividing up the material, but simply as one that is intended to be helpful.

The five chapters are as follows:

1. Direct work with children and young people

This chapter revisits the basics of child and adolescent development and reconsiders the established wisdom in the light of a more modern understanding of human development, focusing on i) perception and meaning construction; and ii) the wider social context in general and the significance of discrimination and oppression in particular. The importance of an understanding of child development as a foundation of good practice will be emphasised.

This chapter also examines what is involved in working directly with children and young people. This is based on an exploration of the notion of 'working in partnership'. It addresses the questions of: Why is partnership so important? How can it be achieved? and What obstacles can stand in the way of success?

2. Working with families

The theme of partnership continues into Chapter 2, but this time with a slightly different focus. The emphasis here is on working in partnership with parents and carers. This involves exploring important matters relating to parental responsibilities, parent-child relations, the impact and significance of wider social issues such as poverty and deprivation, power relations between worker and client and clarity about the social work task.

The limits of partnership are also explored. That is, we consider what needs to happen when parents or others are unwilling or unable to work in partnership. This involves the use of conflict management techniques and the appropriate use of statutory powers where required.

Another important theme underpinning this chapter is that of systematic practice, as outlined earlier. This is presented as a basic requirement of good practice in order to avoid the serious problem of 'drift' or a lack of focus – a long-recognised failing of much child care practice.

3. Networking

Multidisciplinary collaboration is, of course, another form of partnership work. As any experienced worker will know, working with children and families involves interacting not only with the children, young people and families concerned, but also with the wider network of professionals and other interested parties, and indeed with community networks. This involves some of the same skills but also others as well – 'networking' skills.

This is a complex topic, but one which has often been neglected in the professional literature. Realistically, we will not be able to address all the aspects of this area of practice, but what is offered should none the less go some significant way towards casting a great deal of light on what is required for good practice and what can go wrong.

4. Law and policy

This chapter concerns itself with issues of law and policy. It owes a great deal to our theme of professionalism, in the sense that it explores how the law and policy both constrain professional practice and make professional judgement and discretion necessary. This chapter also considers the difficulties of maintaining a professional stance in an organisational context that often works against such an approach.

5. Professional development

The final chapter revisits the concept of reflective practice and draws links between its main features and the need for continuous professional development. That is, we look at how reflective practice can be used as a means of ensuring that we continue to learn, that we are open to new ways of thinking and new approaches to practice.

These, then, are the basic elements of the book. Each chapter presents a range of key points and issues, supported by relevant theoretical and research-based material as appropriate. Each chapter also acknowledges the challenges and difficulties of practice within the areas concerned and seeks to form links between theory and practice by considering the implications for practice of the various ideas

presented. In addition, each chapter seeks to encourage reflective practice by ending with sections on 'Points to ponder' (questions designed to provoke further thought, analysis, debate and discussion) and suggestions for further reading to help guide you through a very large and complex literature base.

Conclusion

As noted earlier, social work with children and young people has to be recognised as a demanding and challenging occupation. It makes significant demands at a number of levels:

- *Intellectual.* Good practice relies on a range of skills, including intellectual skills, as the following passage indicates:

  *Dalrymple and Burke (1995) make the point that social work is an **intellectual** activity. That is, high-quality social work practice involves being able to:*
  – gather, sift and process relevant information in order to form an overall picture of the situation;
  – be selective and set priorities;
  – use analytical skills: to recognize significant patterns and interconnections;
  – undertake a critical evaluation: to weigh advantages and disadvantages;
  – marshal a set of arguments to support or justify a particular decision or course of action; and
  – communicate clearly and effectively in writing.
  These skills are basically intellectual or academic skills – much needed for writing essays and undertaking research projects – but, of course, it is clearly very much the case that they are practice skills too. (Thompson, 2000b, p. 155)

- *Emotional.* Social work with children and families involves working in what are often highly charged emotional circumstances, and this can clearly take its toll on us. However, in addition, we have to recognise that our own feelings come into play too. Although we may attempt to live up to Biestek's (1961) value of 'controlled emotional involvement', we should not forget that controlling our emotions in this way does not come without cost. This is clearly an area of practice where emotion is a very significant issue in terms of the demands upon us.

- *Physical.* The pressures of the work can easily leave us feeling physically drained, as if worn out by the exacting demands of what is recognised as a challenging vocation. Social work with children, young people and their families requires a fairly strong constitution!

In view of these demands, we should be clear that the better equipped we are to rise to the challenge the greater the chance of success in terms of achieving desired outcomes – and the lower the likelihood of our suffering harm in the form of stress as a result of the demands of the work outstripping our resources for doing it. This book will not, of course, guarantee that you will achieve success or avoid stress, but we firmly believe it can go some considerable way towards ensuring that you have a good grounding in the knowledge, skills and values required. We wish you well with your studies and hope that you will have a great deal of success in linking the ideas presented to the actual demands of day-to-day practice in positive and constructive ways.

Recommended reading

Reflective practice and the integration of theory and practice are discussed in detail in Thompson (2000a).

Butler and Roberts (1997) provide a good general introduction to social work with children and families.

Hayden *et al.* (1999) include a useful chapter on the history of state child care which is very helpful in setting the scene for present-day practice.

Welsh language issues are addressed in Davies (1994), Huws Williams *et al.* (1994) Siencyn (1995) and Barnes (1996).

Thomas (2000) provides a helpful discussion of involving children in decision-making.

Archard (1993) offers an interesting and thought-provoking exploration of children's rights.

The basics of anti-discriminatory practice are clearly laid out in Thompson (2001) and the topic is explored in more depth in Thompson (1998). Gambe *et al.* (1992) address issues of race and culture in child care.

1. Direct work with children and young people

1. Introduction

In this, the first of five chapters, our emphasis is very strongly on the children and young people who are the main focus of our concern. The material relating to the underpinning knowledge base to be covered in this chapter can be divided up into three main areas. First we shall look in some detail at the very important topic of human development, for, as I shall be arguing quite strongly below, a good understanding of child and adolescent development is an essential underpinning of good practice. Second, we shall explore what is involved in working directly with children and young people. Third, we shall consider some of the policy and practice issues that arise in relation to such direct work.

Having mapped out the important issues under these three headings, we shall then draw links between this material and the demands of actual practice. In this way we are being consistent with the theme of reflective practice in so far as we are placing emphasis on integrating theory and practice, rather than making the mistake of simply presenting the theory and neglecting the linkages with practice.

As with the other four chapters, we conclude with a number of 'Points to ponder' and a 'Learning resources guide' section. Both of these are presented to encourage reflection, debate and thus further learning. You are encouraged to pay attention to these and make the most of the benefits they can offer you, rather than the common practice of 'skipping over' the final sections once you have finished the main substance of the text. If we are to take the challenge of reflective practice seriously, then these two sections have a very important role to play, not only in this chapter but also in the others.

2. The knowledge base

The point has already been made that social work with children, young people and their families is very complex and draws on a vast knowledge base. What could be covered under this heading in relation to human development, direct work and law and policy is therefore potentially vast. In view of this, it would clearly be extremely unrealistic to try and present a comprehensive and exhaustive account of this area in the space available. In addition, of course, we have to bear in mind that the knowledge base is an ever-growing one – new developments are happening all the time. Consequently, we have to accept that our treatment of the issues is necessarily selective and is bound to omit a number of areas. We should therefore be wary of the false assumption that anything that is not covered in this text is not important. What is presented here is, of course, part of a much larger whole.

Human development

In this section I shall present an account of traditional approaches to child and adolescent development, drawing on the work of such well-known figures as Freud, Bowlby and Erikson. I shall consider the strengths and benefits of this traditional, well-established literature so that we can make the most of what it has to offer in casting light on human development and its implications for practice. However, I shall also examine the weaknesses and limitations of this traditional body of knowledge and emphasise the dangers of an uncritical use of some of its basic tenets. In particular, I shall argue that much of the traditional approach is inconsistent with anti-discriminatory practice. I shall then present a number of ideas drawn from more recent and more sophisticated theories of human development in order to show how we are not limited to the use of traditional approaches.

Traditional approaches

A number of theorists have contributed to the development of the traditional knowledge base in this area. We shall explore the work of some of those theorists, beginning with perhaps the most famous of them all, Sigmund Freud.

Freud and psychodynamics

The name of Sigmund Freud is one that is closely associated with the subject of developmental psychology. It is interesting to note that Freud's work has become quite polarised in this respect. That is, while some people have clearly been influenced by his work to a major extent, others have gone to the other extreme and rejected his ideas out of hand. We can also note that Freud's work is widely misunderstood and misrepresented. For example, in my work with social work students and experienced practitioners alike, I have often heard ideas attributed to Freud which are not at all in keeping with what he actually wrote or the spirit of the message he was trying to get across. It is therefore important to be clear about what Freud actually said, what he meant and what implications these have for practice.

Freud's approach is generally referred to under the heading of 'psychodynamics'. This is an important term as it helps to begin to explain where Freud was coming from. 'Psycho' refers to the mind, and so we can see that psychodynamics refers to the interaction of mental forces – specifically the id, the ego and the superego. We shall therefore begin our exploration of Freud's ideas with a discussion of these three key terms.

- *The id.* This term refers to the strong urges we have, the strong psychological drives that are said to influence our behaviour. The id can be divided up into two main such urges: *eros* – or libido, the sexual and creative drives that we have – and *thanatos* - the aggressive or destructive forces within us.
- *The ego.* The ego is deemed to be the more rational force within the mind and has the role of 'regulator' – acting as a balancing measure between the id and the superego, as we shall see below.

- *The superego.* The superego is often referred to as the conscience, as it represents the internalisation of parents and social values. It is the metaphorical voice in our heads that says: 'Don't!'.

The basic idea underpinning this aspect of Freud's theory is that the id, representing the individual's own wishes and desires, comes into conflict with the superego, the controlling element of parental authority and society more broadly. If either of these forces becomes too dominant, problems are likely to ensue. For example, if the id is too strong and can easily resist the 'brake' of the superego, the result may be selfish, uninhibited, anti-social behaviour – perhaps inappropriate sexual behaviour. An example of the converse would be where the superego is too strong and stifles the id, leaving a fairly repressed individual who may, as a result, become quite neurotic (obsessive-compulsive behaviour such as constant hand-washing perhaps).

Now this is where the ego comes in, as it is the role of the ego to regulate the conflicting forces of id and superego – to keep them in a 'healthy' balance, with neither dominating the other. This is how we get the well-known saying in relation to Freud's work: 'Where id was there shall ego be'.

Bocock (1983) makes the point that Freud's theory has *sociological* as well as psychological implications. This is because Freud's ideas can be seen to represent the tension between the individual and society. Organised societies ('civilization', to use Freud's own term) would not be possible if individuals did not curb their individual wishes and desires for the sake of the common good – that is, the existence of society depends on the superego (representing the interests of society) being available to counterbalance the id (the interests of the individual). This can be an important point in terms of child development, as it can help to explain some of the conflict and tensions of bringing up children where parents are charged with the responsibility of helping children develop a degree of social awareness.

Another important aspect of Freud's theory is that of psychosexual development. This refers to the process of developing mature, adult sexuality. It is represented as a stage by stage process, as follows:

- *The oral stage.* This stage lasts roughly from birth to the age of about 1 year or so and is characterised by pleasure derived from the mouth – sucking, eating, drinking.
- *The anal stage.* At quite a young age the child moves into a stage where 'potty training' becomes an issue. This begins the process of curbing our id desires to fit in with (superego) social rules about what is socially acceptable – for example, learning that urination and defecation should only take place in certain places and at certain times. Gradually the sensual pleasure associated with bowel control rivals that of oral gratification.
- *The phallic stage.* Between the ages of 2 and 6 approximately children will go through the phallic stage. It is at this stage that children become aware of their genitalia but without appreciating their full adult significance.
- *The latency period.* This is a period of consolidation, lasting approximately between the ages of 6 and 11. It is very much a stage of preparation for the next, more demanding stage.
- *The genital stage.* From the age of about 11 onwards major hormonal changes begin to occur centred around puberty. This paves the way for genital maturity and a focus of sensual pleasure on the genitalia in preparation for adult sexuality.

Part of the significance of this notion of psychosexual development is that it is possible for individuals to become 'fixated' (or 'stuck' psychologically) at one of these stages. In this way, somebody who is orally fixated is likely to derive excessive pleasure from eating and drinking. Such an explanation could be used in part to explain such conditions as alcoholism.

A common misunderstanding of Freud's ideas on this topic is that he had a 'perverted' view of children and sexuality. It is therefore important to recognise that Freud's references to 'infantile' sexuality were made in a technical sense. Despite common misconceptions, he was not ascribing adult sexuality to young children! If we use the term, 'sensuality' in its place, the whole theory makes far more sense and seems much more plausible.

Exercise 1.1

What are your views of Freud's theories? Which aspects do you find helpful and why? Which aspects do you find unhelpful and why? This is not a test, so feel free to discuss your views with your colleagues. Comparing notes like this can be a valuable form of learning.

What has been described here is only one very small part of a very large and complex theory. We have to be very clear that the accounts given here are necessarily very selective. However, they should be sufficient to begin to paint a picture of the range and nature of Freud's approach.

It is also necessary to stress that the treatment of Freud's work tends to suffer from being taken to extremes. That is, while some people accept his ideas uncritically, others tend to reject them wholesale, dismissing his whole work as being of no value. The reality, of course, is somewhere in between. There is a lot that Freud got wrong, but his work also had some value. I shall therefore conclude this section by outlining some of the strengths and weaknesses of Freud's approach:

✓ *Strengths*

- It explains a wide range of phenomena, such as guilt, conscience, obsessive behaviour and so on.
- It is a *dynamic* explanation, and is therefore well placed to explain changes and developments.
- It is quite a sophisticated theory. Although widely misunderstood and oversimplified, it does offer quite a developed level of understanding.
- It acts as a bridge between the inner world of the individual and the wider social context.

✗ *Weaknesses*

- It contains a number of untested assumptions about gender roles, reflecting the Victorian society from which this theory emerged.
- It emphasises the early years of life and pays relatively little attention to ongoing development.
- It draws on fixed symbolism. Freud's discussion of the unconscious assumes that symbols (in dreams, for example) are fixed in

their meaning. It does not take account of the fact that the same symbol can mean different things to different people (this is an example of essentialism in Freud's work).

- It addresses some aspects of the wider social context but offers little or no understanding of sociopolitical issues like class, race or other such social divisions. This is because Freud assumed his theory to be universal.

Erikson and ego psychology

Erik Erikson is what is described as a 'neo-Freudian'. This is because his work takes Freud as a starting point but builds on it in a number of significant ways. Perhaps the two most significant ways are:

1. *Cultural variation.* Freud regarded his theory as universal – that is, as applicable to all people across all societies. Erikson and the other neo-Freudians parted company with Freud on this and argued instead that the basic theory should be seen to vary according to the cultural context in which it was being viewed. That is, different cultures will develop different ways of dealing with these issues – variations on the same theme.
2. *Lifelong development.* The emphasis on Freud's work is on the early stages of life, what he referred to as the 'formative' years. However, Erikson proposed a view of human development that went far beyond this, incorporating the whole life course. This he described in terms of the 'eight ages of man' (Figure 1).

According to Erikson, these eight stages are 'crises' or turning points in our lives. As we reach each of them, we arrive at a crossroads. For example, at a very early stage in our lives we need to develop a sense of trust (see the discussion of attachment theory below). Once we can achieve this level of trust, we are able to move on in our development, until we reach the next crossroads.

An important implication of this theory is that we should be able to attribute particular behaviours to the success or failure of negotiating one or more of these transitions. For example, the fourth 'age' of industry vs. inferiority can be seen as significant in so far as difficulties in moving through this stage can leave the child lacking in confidence and unmotivated to achieve anything.

---

1. Basic trust vs basic mistrust
The young baby needs to learn to trust first parents and then others.
2. Autonomy vs shame and doubt
The young child needs to learn to think and act for him- or herself, to develop self-control.
3. Initiative vs guilt
The growing child needs to begin to move towards independence and use initiative, albeit in a limited way.
4. Industry vs inferiority
The young school child needs to learn the value and pleasure of achieving tasks.
5. Identity vs role confusion
In the early stages of adolescence, a coherent sense of identity needs to be formed in preparation for adulthood.
6. Intimacy vs isolation
The young adult needs to establish adult relationships and form a new generation of family life.
7. Generativity vs stagnation
Maturity needs to be characterised by a sense of achievement, productivity and fulfillment.
8. Ego integrity vs despair
In the latter stages of life, we need to face up to the reality of death with dignity.

Figure 1: Erikson's 'Eight Ages of Man'

✓ *Strengths*

- It goes beyond Freud's emphasis on the 'formative years' and pays attention to development as a lifelong process.
- It takes account of cultural differences, acknowledging that psychodynamic issues will be played out in a different context, with different emphases across the world. It therefore begins to take account of diversity.
- The notion of crisis or turning point is a very powerful one in explaining many aspects of child and adolescent development, and indeed human development more broadly.

✗ *Weaknesses*

- The theory is sadly neglectful of gender issues. The fact that Erikson writes of the eight ages of *man* indicates how he was relatively unaware of the significance of gender as a factor in human development.

- Erikson's work takes account of cultural diversity but does not go as far as to recognise the impact and significance of racism as a factor in development.
- Much of Erikson's work can be described as essentialist. That is, he sees development in terms of moving from one stage to another in line with biological development, and therefore pays little attention to the enormous variations that can occur as a result of life choices, social or political influences and other such matters.

Attachment theory

The work of John Bowlby has had a major impact on child care social work over the years, with the work of Vera Fahlberg also proving very influential. What these two thinkers have in common is a strong emphasis on the important, indeed crucial, role of attachment in the lives of children and young people.

A central feature of this theory is the argument that psychological 'health' is dependent on forming strong attachments to one or more protective adult figures in so far as we gain a much needed degree of emotional security from such attachments. Conversely, children who do not have the benefit of such secure attachments, it is argued, are likely to grow up with significant problems unless steps are taken to rectify the situation. As Durkin (1995) comments:

Observational and clinical evidence indicated that the absence or serious disruption of the attachment relationship led to severe distress in the infant and sometimes to enduring behavioral-emotional problems. Bowlby became convinced that an attachment between caregiver and child was fundamental to normal development and he drew on Lorenz and others' ethological studies of attachment behavior in subhumans to develop an account of the place of attachment in nature, including human nature. (p. 85)

Central to the theory is the notion of 'maternal deprivation'. This refers to Bowlby's view that children should experience 'a warm, intimate

and continuous relationship' (1953, p. 13) with their mother or mother substitute. Bowlby's thesis was that children who do not enjoy such a relationship will be hampered in their development.

The theory was further developed by Ainsworth and her colleagues (Ainsworth, 1985; Ainsworth *et al.,* 1978) on the basis of experimental work undertaken with young children. She described three different types of attachment relationship (A to C), and Main and Solomon (1990) added a fourth (D) as follows:

A. *Anxious/avoidant.* This is a form of insecure attachment and shows itself in avoidance of contact.
B. *Secure.* This is the basis of 'healthy' development, based on a strong bond with the mother (or mother-equivalent).
C. *Anxious/ambivalent.* A further form of insecure attachment, in which the child is ambivalent about contact.
D. *Disorganised.* Cowie (1995) describes this in the following terms:

. . . a further insecure pattern which is seen most frequently in families where there is parent pathology, child abuse or very high social risk. Here the child appears dazed, confused or apprehensive, and shows no coherent system for dealing with separation and reunion. This behaviour suggests fear/or confusion about the relationship and prompts the label disorganized attachment pattern. (p. 14)

Rutter (1981), however, was less prepared to adopt Bowlby's view of attachment. He argued that there is no direct causal link between early experiences of separation and later problems or distress. What is important, according to Rutter, is the quality of support the child receives during and after a period of separation. It will be this support that will prove crucial, rather than the separation itself. This paves the way for a more sophisticated approach to attachment. For example, Belsky (1984) posited three important sets of factors that are deemed to be significant in relation to attachment. These are:

(a) Personal psychological resources of the parent, including mental health, the quality of internal representations of relationships . . . and their developmental history.

(b) Contextual sources of support, including the social network of support from partner, relatives and friends, and job conditions and financial conditions.

(c) Characteristics of the child, in particular easy or difficult temperament. (Cowie, 1995, p. 27)

It can be seen that Bowlby's work takes account of only the first of these. That is, it tends to neglect broader social factors (something which makes it incompatible with anti-discriminatory practice) and characteristics of the actual child concerned (thus lacking a degree of child-centredness). This means that we have to be very wary of taking on Bowlby's ideas in their original, undeveloped form.

One significant development in attachment theory is to be found in the work of Fahlberg (1988, 1994). She describes what she refers to as the 'arousal-relaxation cycle'. In this the young child expresses a need (for example, crying with hunger). This involves the child experiencing displeasure. When the carer satisfies the need (for example, by providing food), pleasure is experienced until the need is felt again (for example, when hunger reappears later). This cycle thus produces a sense of trust, security and attachment.

Another significant cycle Fahlberg described was the 'positive interaction cycle'. While the first cycle involved the child in initiating contact through an unmet need, this cycle involves the carer in taking the first step. By initiating positive interactions with the child, a positive response can be achieved which further reinforces the carer's behaviour in initiating contact. This cycle produces a sense of self-worth and self-esteem.

In view of these two cycles we can therefore understand some forms of 'unhealthy' development as a failure of either or both these cycles to be carried through effectively. That is, poor attachment can arise if these two cycles are not operating well for the child through one or more carers who promote security through responding to needs and promote self-esteem through initiating positive interactions.

✓ Strengths

- The theory is capable of explaining many aspects of children's behaviour patterns and

indeed many aspects of parenting behaviour also.

- It takes account of the importance of human interactions and relationships.
- It recognises the significance of loss in the lives of children and young people.

✗ Weaknesses

- Gambe *et al.* (1992) point out that much of the work on attachment has tended to assume white, western norms of child-rearing (based on individualism), and therefore has the effect of marginalising or even pathologising families who do not fit into this norm.
- Similarly, the emphasis on an individual attachment object has been criticised for reinforcing gender stereotypes and oppressive expectations of women as mothers (but see Daniel *et al.*, 1999, for a response to this).
- There is a strong emphasis on 'normative development' (Knight and Caveney, 1998), and relatively little attention paid to cultural or other forms of diversity, social and economic conditions and so on.

Exercise 1.2

Take one strength and one weakness from the list above relating to Erikson's theory of human development. Drawing on your own practice experience, give an example of a situation that reflects the strength you have chosen and another situation that reflects the weakness.

Cognitive development

The foremost thinker in relation to cognitive development is clearly the Swiss developmental psychologist, Jean Piaget. Piaget's work has proven to be immensely influential, particularly on teacher education. His theory is based on his own extensive work with children and young people. His work is very complex and extensive and so we cannot hope to do justice to it all here. I shall therefore restrict myself to a fairly brief overview of some of the main tenets of his approach.

Piaget argued that children go through stages of cognitive development. That is, he believed that there was a sequential process of development common to all children. He described four main stages:

1. *The sensori-motor stage – from 0 to 4 years.*
   This is where children concentrate on movement – their own movement in terms of mobility and the movement of other things in terms of being able to manipulate objects (toys, for example). In order to understand such movement children develop 'cognitive schemas', rudimentary frameworks of understanding that help the individual child to make sense of the changing landscape as people and objects move (or are moved) about.

2. *The pre-operations stage – from 2 to 7 years.*
   For Piaget, 'operational' thought refers to thinking that involves linking schemas together, forming a wider network of understanding. This stage is therefore characterised by an inability to link schemas, a tendency to maintain separate (and often incompatible) schemas. This stage is also characterised by, amongst other things, egocentricity and animism. The former refers to the tendency to see things only from their own point of view (this does not mean selfishness in the everyday sense of the word, but rather an inability to put themselves 'in the other person's shoes'). This may be significant at the time of a bereavement. For example, if a grandparent dies, the child may feel guilty and responsible for this as a result of this egocentricity (see the discussion below of loss and grief). The latter refers to the tendency to ascribe consciousness to inanimate objects – for example, a four-year old girl not wanting to clean her teeth may say: 'The tooth brush doesn't like going in my mouth'.

3. *The concrete operations stage – from 7 to 11 years.*
   By this stage the child is starting to think 'operationally' – that is, linking schemas together and thereby developing more rational systems of thought. However, this stage is referred to as the *concrete* operational stage because the child has yet to learn how to think in more abstract terms. That is, they can deal with here and now objects and situations but may not be able to deal with such matters in the abstract or in the physical absence of the objects or people concerned. The ground is being prepared for full-scale abstract thought but that goal has not yet been achieved.

4. *The formal operations stage – from 11 to 16 years.*
   This stage is the culmination of cognitive development, in the sense that young people at this age are learning how to conceptualise and think in abstract and logical ways, thus significantly increasing their cognitive abilities in terms of analysing and understanding complex, multifaceted situations.

Piaget's work has been heavily criticised (see Davenport, 1994), particularly for being too rigid in its approach and for oversimplifying a highly complex set of processes. However, his work remains very influential and few would doubt that, whatever its limitations, his work has considerable value in giving us at least a basic framework for understanding children's and young people's cognitive development. If we are to take seriously the notions of partnership and involving children and young people in decision-making and related processes, then an understanding of their cognitive abilities (that is, what it is realistic to expect them to be able to understand) is a fundamental part of what we need to undertake such work effectively.

A further development from the work of Piaget is represented by the writings of Vygotsky. While Piaget emphasised the internal, psychological aspects of cognitive processes, Vygotsky laid stress on the social aspects. For example, he felt that the support children received was a very important factor. This was because he believed in the importance of what he called the 'zone of proximal development' (ZPD). Vygotsky:

> . . . *maintained that a distinction ought to be made between a child's actual developmental level and his or her potential developmental level. A child's actual developmental level is the level at which he or she demonstrates understanding and the ability to use ideas and concepts competently without help or assistance from another person. When children are operating*

within their ZPD (their potential developmental level), they can work with more advanced ideas and concepts, provided they are receiving the support of someone who already has a more sophisticated grasp of the relevant concepts.
(Faulkner, 1995, p. 241)

This is an important departure from Piaget's work as it introduces more clearly and explicitly a social element – it recognises the significant role of other people and social processes as influences on individual cognitive development. It helps us to avoid the essentialist trap of seeing a child's cognitive development in terms of predominantly internal psychological and/or biological factors by recognising the part played by the social context of development. And, of course, once we introduce a social element, we introduce variation, diversity and change rather than fixity and essentialism.

✓ Strengths

- Piaget's approach helps us to see a meaningful thread of development through the four identified stages.
- It gives us a broad-based 'map' from which to develop a picture of where a particular child or young person is in terms of their development of cognitive skills and processes.
- Vygotsky's theory helps us to appreciate the role of broader social factors in cognitive development and thus to challenge the myth that such development is essentially a narrow psychological/biological one.

✗ Weaknesses

- The stages approach can be seen as too rigid, not recognising the enormous variation across individuals and groups. It should therefore be used as a basic guide, rather than a definitive statement on 'normal' development.
- Piaget's approach takes relatively little account of social factors in shaping development.
- Although Vygotsky's approach introduces a social dimension, it does not go so far as to consider such centrally important issues as class, race or gender.

The ecological approach

The ecological approach is represented by the work of Bronfenbrenner (1986). This approach adapts the geographical term of ecology to apply in a narrower, social sense. In this sense, ecology refers not to the individual in his or her physical environment of climate, flora, fauna and so on, but rather to the human and technical systems that are part and parcel of modern life.

Bronfenbrenner argued that it is necessary to take account of the broader context in which child and adolescent development takes place. That is, he was critical of the view that the key to understanding development was to look narrowly at the individual and his or her carers. He developed a complex model of interacting systems, involving four levels, each embedded or 'nested' within the others like a Russian doll. These are:

- *Microsystem.* This involves the setting of home, school or workplace and so on – that is, the interrelationships between the individual and those aspects of his or her immediate environment.
- *Mesosystem.* This refers to interrelationships among 'major settings', such as family, school, peer group or church.
- *Exosystem.* This refers to wider social institutions that can have a significant bearing on the mesosystem and includes the neighbourhood, the media, government and informal social networks.
- *Macrosystem.* This is, as the name implies, the broad context of social, economic and political systems. It includes two forms: explicit – these are structural factors such as the law and social policy; and implicit – those that act as carriers of ideology and meaning, for example through custom and practice.

This approach offers a systematic basis for identifying particular influences on behaviour and development and can be used as the basis of assessing a particular child or young person at a given point in their development. It therefore offers a potentially useful way of understanding human development.

✓ Strengths

- It places individual development within the context of social factors.

- It recognises and begins to map out the complexities of the social context in which development takes place.
- It is a dynamic and interactive model – that is, it recognises the importance of interaction and change over time.

✗ Weaknesses

- Although attentive to the broader social context, this theory has relatively little to say about social divisions and the role of discrimination and oppression. It has the potential for forming the basis of an anti-oppressive approach but remains undeveloped in this respect.
- It focuses strongly on systems issues but pays relatively little attention to the role of the individual within those systems (for example, the individual is conceptualised as an 'organism' and often referred to as 'it').
- Although the significance of meaning and ideology is acknowledged, the role of meaning and interpretation is given far from adequate attention.

Exercise 1.3

The ecological approach goes beyond the individualism of many other approaches, and this makes it far more compatible with anti-discriminatory practice. However, can you identify any ways in which this approach does not sit comfortably with an anti-discriminatory one?

Children's needs

In trying to make sense of children's needs, theorists in this field have developed various models, based on their particular view of what it is that children and young people are deemed to need. Butler and Roberts (1997) describe some of the main models in the following terms:

Mia Kellmer Pringle (1974)

- *Love and security.*
- *New experiences.*
- *Praise and recognition.*
- *Responsibility*

Christine Cooper (1985)

- Basic physical care: *e.g. warmth, shelter, food, rest and protection.*
- Affection: *e.g. physical contact, admiration, tenderness, patience, companionship.*

- Security: *e.g. continuity of care, consistent patterns of care and daily routine, harmonious family group.*
- Stimulation of innate potential: *e.g. praise, encouragement, educational stimulation.*
- Guidance and control: *e.g. examples of honesty and a concern for others, discipline, to develop socially acceptable behaviour.*
- Responsibility: *e.g. to practise decision-making skills and to gain experience through mistakes.*
- Independence: *at first about small things but 'over-protection is as bad as too early responsibility and independence'* (p. 61).

Margaret Bryer (1988)

- Physical: *e.g. medical care, possessions, shelter, space, fresh air and exercise, physical affection, adequate financial resources, discipline and control.*
- Educational: *e.g. knowledge of culture, knowledge of own background, play and hobbies, holidays, sex education, formal education.*
- Social: *e.g. friends, interest groups, to be a member of the community, to express individuality.*
- Ethical: *e.g. aesthetic sense, sense of identity, values, self-respect, opportunity to practise religion.*
- Emotional: *e.g. trust, praise, individual attention, loyalty, love, security, privacy, understanding, fun and laughter* (p. 25).

While there are clearly differences between these models, we can also identify a significant degree of overlap across them. They clearly have much in common.

However, one element that is generally absent from these formulations of need is a clear understanding of what we actually mean by the term, 'need'. That is, there is a danger that the term is used uncritically. We shall return to this point below when we discuss the criticism of much traditional theory for being 'essentialist'.

Identity development

A further major feature of human development is the significance of identity. Gradually, as we grow and develop, each of us establishes a sense of self, an identity which acts as the basis

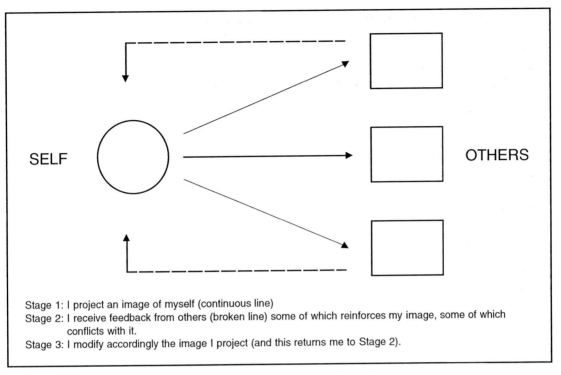

Stage 1: I project an image of myself (continuous line)
Stage 2: I receive feedback from others (broken line) some of which reinforces my image, some of which conflicts with it.
Stage 3: I modify accordingly the image I project (and this returns me to Stage 2).

Figure 1.1 The 'looking-glass self'

of our experience of the world. The self serves as a 'unifier' of our experience. By relating the various 'bits' or strands of our diverse experiences to our sense of self, we are able to make sense of it, to maintain a sense of personal coherence through a variety of settings and circumstances.

Identity formation is a complex issue and the very concept is a contested one – that is, there is much debate about what it means, how it should be conceptualised and how it relates to practice. But, whichever way we conceptualise identity, there can be little doubt that our sense of who we are is a strong influence on our thoughts, feelings and actions.

The sense of who we are (or 'self-concept') is often divided into two main areas, self-image and self-esteem. Self-image refers to how we see ourselves, the picture we have of ourselves. Self-esteem relates to the value we place on ourselves. These two factors are both very significant influences on behaviour. For example, a teenage girl who sees herself as overweight when she is not may fall prey to anorexia nervosa (self-image) while a child with low self-esteem is likely to lack confidence and

be very wary of trying new experiences, thus being less likely to learn.

A helpful model of the self is Cooley's notion of the 'looking-glass' self (Cooley, 1902). This describes an interactive view of the self in which the individual's self-perception owes much to the feedback he or she receives from others – that is, how I see myself will depend, to a certain extent at least, on how other people see me. This model is represented in Figure 1.1.

Strands of development

The concept of 'human development' is often seen to relate primarily if not exclusively to biological development. That is, there is considerable emphasis on 'maturation', those aspects of development that have their roots in our biological make-up. However, as we shall discuss in more depth later, this is both misleading and not consistent with anti-discriminatory practice. It is misleading because it downplays the significant role of other aspects of development – the various 'strands' that we shall explore shortly. It is inconsistent with anti-discriminatory practice because an emphasis on biology distracts attention from significant social and political issues. As we shall note below, biological explanations often indicate the use of ideology – sets of ideas being used to legitimate the status quo of discrimination and inequality by concealing the significance of power relations. This is an example of our core theme of reductionism, a point to which we shall return below.

What, then, are the other strands of development? Generally speaking, these are the psychological, social, political and ontological:

- *Psychological.* This can be divided into two parts: cognitive and affective. We have already considered cognitive development in relation to Piaget and Vygotsky but we should not forget that emotional development is also an important factor, partly in relation to attachment as already discussed, but also more broadly in terms of the fundamental role of emotions in our lives.
- *Social.* The social context in which we grow and develop is a crucial influence on the nature, extent and shape of such development. For example, it can certainly be argued that poverty has a major effect on development. We should also not underestimate the significance of other social factors such as racism (Robinson, 1995).
- *Political.* Children are relatively powerless in the social order but gradually learn how to use what power they have and even extend it. Although not generally recognised as a key issue in traditional texts on child and adolescent behaviour, the development of political awareness and the ability to use power are important dimensions of development.
- *Ontological.* Ontology is the study of being and refers to how we deal with the challenges of living in a changing world with few certainties, and how we make sense of it all. The ontological dimension of development therefore refers to the process of making sense of the world and creating our own place within it – for example, through identity formation, development of values and so on. These are points to which we shall return below.

Exercise 1.4

Think of a child or young person you know (either professionally or in your personal life) and consider each of the 'strands' of development above. For each of these strands can you identify aspects of his or her life that illustrate its significance in terms of development?

These dimensions of development are extremely important, as to neglect these is to undermine the basis of good practice. Consider, for example, the following:

- *Psychological.* A neglect of cognitive development can have serious implications in terms of educational achievement. The *Quality Protects/Children First* initiative emphasises the importance of education in the lives of young people, particularly those who enter the care system and face a number of potential obstacles to a settled and productive experience of education. Emotional development is also something we ignore at our peril. For example, the impact and significance of abuse will depend to a large extent on the emotional development of the youngster concerned, and so to ignore emotional development issues would be to risk working on the basis of a very distorted and inadequate assessment.
- *Social.* It is unfortunate that so much of the literature on child and adolescent development has such a strong psychological and thus individualistic focus. Neglecting the social aspects of development not only weakens the value of any assessment or intervention undertaken in general but also undermines the development of anti-discriminatory practice in particular. A basic tenet of anti-discriminatory practice is the need to understand people in the context of their social location and the various ways in which patterns of discrimination and oppression operate (Thompson, 2001).
- *Political.* Developing an understanding of the workings of power and learning how to play a part in the complex interactions between individuals, groups and institutions are basic ingredients of growing up in complex societies. This is an essential part of working

in partnership with children and young people – helping them understand what rights and power they have and helping them to learn how to use such power responsibly and constructively.

- *Ontological.* Growing up is a confusing and difficult process. Much traditional literature presents it in predominantly biological terms as if so much of what really matters is mapped out for us. Ontology helps us understand just how much of what happens to us depends on wider structural factors (social and political, for example); discourses, ideologies and systems of meaning; and, of course, *human agency* – the fact that we are decision-making creatures who make our own way in the world, influenced by other factors, but none the less still responsible for our own actions.

This section should have helped to demonstrate how complex child and adolescent development is and how we have to be very wary of following much of the traditional literature which tends to paint a fairly essentialist picture of development. It is for this reason that we shall return below to a further discussion of the significance of ontology under the heading of 'reification'.

Crisis, loss and transitions

Children and young people undergo transitions and therefore experience crises and losses. Indeed, we should recognise that these are fundamental aspects of the developmental experiences involved in growing up (and, of course, of continuing our development through the life course). However, it is important to recognise that this area of theory is commonly misunderstood. For example, the term, 'crisis' is widely misused in social work and the related term of crisis intervention is perhaps one of the most misused terms in the social work vocabulary (Thompson, 1991).

A crisis is a turning point in someone's life, a situation where existing coping methods are no longer adequate and new ways of coping have to be found. This is often mistakenly equated with an emergency – that is, a situation that has to be dealt with urgently. The truth of the matter is that crisis and emergency often overlap but they often do not. Consider the following examples:

1. A 15-year-old girl finds that she is pregnant and her parents throw her out of the house, saying that they are disowning her.
2. A single mother with two young children arrives in a social services office late on a Friday afternoon because her benefits giro has not arrived and the Social Security Office is closed. The matter is easily resolved by a loan from an emergency fund that the duty social worker has access to. The mother copes quite calmly with the whole situation, confident that the Department would not let her children go without food over the weekend.
3. A 16-year-old boy who has spent the past three years in residential care moves into an outreach facility as part of a plan that had been agreed more than a year previously.

In the first case we are encountering a situation that is both a crisis and an emergency. That is, it is a turning point in the young girl's life, but it is also a situation that has to be dealt with urgently. The second case scenario represents an 'emergency' in so far as it needs an urgent response – the situation cannot safely be left, but it is not actually a crisis in so far as it does not represent a turning point. (It is interesting to note that a failure to respond quickly to an urgent situation can often lead to a crisis.) The third scenario, by contrast, describes a turning point and therefore a crisis situation, but it is not an emergency – it does not require an urgent response. We should therefore be wary of overusing the terms, 'crisis' or 'crisis intervention' and reserve them for the specific situations where they are appropriate.

Crisis intervention is an approach to practice which recognises that, when a turning point in our lives is encountered (that is, a point where we cannot continue to use our existing coping methods, where we are forced into adopting a new approach), the situation can take a turn in either direction. On the one hand, a crisis can weaken and disempower us, undermining our confidence and self-esteem. On the other hand, a crisis can strengthen and empower us, providing excellent opportunities for learning and development. The role of the worker practising crisis intervention is to do whatever is reasonably possible to minimise the negative potential and make the more positive outcomes as much of a reality as possible (see Thompson, 1991).

This approach can be seen to be particularly significant in relation to child and adolescent development as children and young people encounter a series of transitions and crises as they grow up. Some of these crises are relatively predictable because they form part of the life course (adolescence, for example), while others are far less predictable as they arise as a result of unexpected events (a death, for example).

In addition to crisis intervention we have the related field of loss theory. There is a number of different approaches to the significance of loss, but the two most dominant of these are i) the stages approach and ii) the tasks approach.

The stages approach is associated with writers such as Elizabeth Kübler-Ross and Colin Murray Parkes (see, for example, Kübler-Ross, 1970; Parkes, 1995). Originally conceived as a way of understanding how terminally ill people face up to the reality of their impending death, it was later adapted to explain reactions to loss – that is, the ways we grieve in response to a bereavement. The main stages identified by Kubler-Ross were:

- *Denial.* Not being ready to take on board the reality of the situation, due to the time taken for the information to 'sink in'.
- *Anger.* Commonly a feeling of resentment and injustice, based on the idea of 'Why me? What have I done to deserve this?'
- *Bargaining.* An irrational attempt to 'bargain' a way forward out of the predicament.
- *Depression.* Switching off from the world around us, taking refuge within ourselves.
- *Acceptance.* Beginning to come to terms with the reality of the (impending) loss.

Parkes (1970) followed a similar stages or phases approach in building on Bowlby's work on attachment. He described the process in terms of the following four phases:

- *Shock and numbness.* Similar to Kubler-Ross's notion of denial, this is a phase characterised by an inability to take on board the enormity of the changes brought about by the loss. The sense of 'I can't believe it; it just doesn't seem real' is strongly associated with this phase.

- *Yearning and searching.* Part of the process of coming to terms with the reality of the loss is a process of longing for the person (or thing) lost, and this often involves searching for them, an irrational response but none the less a very common one.
- *Disorganisation and despair.* Our lives can become quite chaotic and overwhelmed by the strength of feeling generated by the loss, leaving us feeling quite literally 'at a loss'.
- *Reorganisation.* This is the process of rebuilding, beginning to restructure our lives by making the necessary adjustments to the absence of the person or thing we are grieving for.

An alternative approach was that of Worden (1991) who described the process in terms of tasks rather than stages. He identified four developmental tasks that we have to achieve in order to deal with the loss we have experienced:

1. To accept the reality of the loss.
2. To work through to the pain of grief.
3. To adjust to an environment in which the deceased is missing.
4. To emotionally relocate the deceased and move on with life.

This approach had much in common with the stages approach but was also significantly different. Its main difference lies in the fact that it presents a more active model of coping. That is, by conceptualising the process in terms of tasks, Worden is painting a picture of an active process whereby we have to achieve certain things before we are able to 'move on'.

We shall consider below some more recent developments in loss theory, but for present purposes it is sufficient to recognise that the stages and tasks models have long been dominant ways of thinking about loss and grief.

Before leaving the topic of loss, it is important that we consider the significance of loss in children's and young people's lives. Consider, for example, the losses involved in abuse situations:

Child abuse can be seen as a phenomenon that is closely related to loss in a number of ways and at a number of levels. For example, Stewart (1994) draws links between loss and the experience of abuse in adults. Such losses associated with abuse are many and various. They include:

- *boundaries;*
- *trust;*
- *hope;*
- *feelings and what they mean;*
- *intimacy;*
- *childhood;*
- *spontaneity.*
- *privacy;*
- *self-respect;*
- *confidence and serenity;*
- *family;*
- *happiness;*
- *identity.*

(Thompson, 1997, pp. 116–7)

When we add to this the range of losses that can be seen to apply when a child or young person has to leave home or move to another placement, we can see that loss is likely to be a significant part of the life experience of so many of the children who come into contact with a social worker. And, of course we can add to this other losses brought about by divorce or family breakdown (Kroll, 1994), illness, disability and so on, painting a clear picture of loss as a major feature of life for some children and young people at least. This is, of course, in addition to the many losses that arise purely as a result of the necessary changes and transitions that are part and parcel of growing up.

A further significant aspect of coping with transitions is the important concept of 'resilience'. This refers to the positive effects of a range of factors that have been identified as helpful in dealing with adversity and the problems many children and young people encounter. Rutter (1985) identified three sets of factors that can be seen to promote resilience:

- *Self-esteem.* High self-esteem can act as a buffer against adversity, helping people cope with confidence.
- *Self-efficacy.* This helps in being able to adapt to changes, as it helps to establish a sense of control.
- *Problem-solving skills.* Having a wide range of problem-solving approaches can help equip children and young people to deal with the challenges they face.

However, we should be wary of adopting too narrow a focus on resilience, as there are other factors which can be seen to have a significant bearing on the development of resilience (Daniel *et al.*, 1999). These include family, friends, school and other such wider social factors.

Taking into account what factors contribute to resilience (and what may undermine it) can therefore be recognised as a significant part of the process of assessment, as it can give us some important insights into how the child or young person copes, how he or she is likely to react to certain situations and so on. However, we should note the danger here of turning resilience into an essentialist concept. That is, we should recognise that we are dealing with a complex set of interacting factors that change over time. 'Resilience' is not an innate essence that forms part of the child's or young person's 'nature' – it is something that can and often does develop.

Milestones of development

A significant aspect of development is the notion that there are identifiable 'milestones' that can be used to assess an individual's development. For example, although different infants will learn to walk at different times, we can identify general patterns. Here we are talking about what is often referred to as the 'broad spectrum of the norm'. That is, we do not expect all children to follow exactly the same timescale, but we can expect a broad pattern.

By being aware of such milestones we are in a position to begin to assess whether or not a particular child is developing well or is perhaps being hindered in some way – experiencing 'developmental delay'. A well-established example of this is the use of the notion of 'failure to thrive' in a child protection context. The Looked After Children (LAC) documents provide a useful 'shorthand' guide for considering developmental milestones, and can easily be adapted to apply to children who are not being looked after by the local authority.

The LAC 'Assessment and Action Records' divide development into seven sections as follows:

- health;
- education;

- identity;
- family and social relationships;
- social presentation;
- emotional and behavioural development; and
- self-care skills.

Chapter 2 of Brandon *et al.* (1998) provides a good introductory overview of the stages of development and what can usually be expected at given ages. This is recommended as a starting point. For more detailed guidance on 'developmental milestones', it is worth making contact with one or more health visitors. This is for three reasons. First, they usually have a very good knowledge and understanding of child development. Second, they may be able to give you access to charts which map out the main 'milestones' of development; and, third, this is a good basis for working in interprofessional partnership (see Chapter 3).

Disability and development

The concept of 'disablism' is one that has now become firmly established in the vocabulary of anti-discriminatory practice. It refers to the various ways in which disabled people can be discriminated against (Oliver, 1990; Oliver and Sapey, 1999). One such form of discrimination is marginalisation. This occurs when the needs and interests of disabled people are pushed 'to the margins' – that is, generally neglected and overlooked. This can be seen to be the case in terms of much of the literature relating to child development which frequently takes little or no account of development issues as they relate to children and young people with disabilities.

One problem is that disability is generally seen in individualistic, medical terms, rather than in broader social terms (see Thompson, 2001, Chapter 6; Oliver and Sapey, 1999). Middleton (1999) makes the important point that:

Traditional explanations of disadvantage experienced by disabled children rest on the medical model of disability which holds that the trauma of impairment is in itself an explanation for the individual's failure to achieve a reasonable quality of life. The 'social model' shifts this emphasis away from pathologising the individual and stresses restrictive environments and attitudes.

It is therefore important that we do not see child and adolescent development in narrow, essentialist terms, as this would have the effect of marginalising and even pathologising those whose circumstances and life experiences fall outside the assumed norm – children with disabilities, for example.

Exercise 1.5
In working with a child with disabilities, what factors would you need to take into account in order to ensure that he or she is given an adequate and appropriate assessment? How might his or her development be significantly different from that of other children?

A critique of dominant approaches to human development

The traditional approaches to child and adolescent development presented here can be criticised in a number of ways. I shall therefore outline a number of criticisms that can be levelled against the established wisdom in this area. However, before doing so, it is important to make it clear that, in criticising traditional approaches in this way, my aim is not to imply that their value is being rejected altogether. It is to be hoped that the criticisms will help lead to a more balanced view of this area, one that recognises both strengths and weaknesses.

Biological reductionism

There is a longstanding tendency amongst commentators on human behaviour to present complex, multilevel phenomena as if they were primarily or exclusively biological. For example, matters relating to *gender* (which is socially and culturally defined) are often dealt with as if they related mainly to the biological category of *sex*. In this regard, many people regard women's roles in society (that is, *social* matters of gender expectations) as biologically determined. Consider, though, the difference between *childbearing,* which is biologically determined as female and *childrearing* which is socially determined. That is, while men may, for biological reasons, not be able to bear children, we have to look very carefully at the question of whether men are able to *rear* children. Clearly, the one-letter difference between childbearing and childrearing has enormous implications for our expectations of what is appropriate behaviour for women and men – we have to be wary of equating the two and thereby confusing biological matters over which we have relatively little control with social and psychological matters which are much more amenable to change.

The tendency to neglect the broader sociopolitical context is clearly a major weakness of many of the theories presented here, as such a neglect renders the theory incompatible with anti-discriminatory practice. This can be seen to apply in the following areas:

- *Psychodynamics.* The focus here is clearly on the individual and what goes on within his or her mind. While social factors are taken into consideration up to a point, this aspect remains relatively unexplored. In particular, the question of gender equality is one that Freud's theory would struggle to address (although see Mitchell, 1974, for an alternative view of this). This is not to say that Freud's work cannot be developed to make it more compatible with anti-discriminatory practice (see, for example, the discussion of existential psychoanalysis in Thompson, 1992), but it does mean that we have to be very wary of using traditional psychoanalytical theory uncritically.
- *Erikson's life stages approach.* Again gender can be seen as the main weakpoint here. The point was made earlier that, while his theory recognised the importance of cultural variation, he took little or no notice of gender issues. The theory is presented from a 'malestream' perspective. The social elements are seen as influences on what is basically presented as a psychobiological process of development.
- *Attachment theory.* The following passage from Daniel *et al.* (1999) makes telling comment:

    > Attachment theory involves the study of human relationships, especially early, formative relationships. Further, the theory asserts that there is a **biological imperative** for infants to form attachments and that they exhibit attachment behaviours to promote attachment. In this sense attachment behaviour can be viewed as survival behaviour. (p. 14, emphasis added)

While it can be argued that attachment theory has some value as an explanatory framework and as a guide to practice, the tendency to root such theorising so firmly in a biological base is clearly problematic. Attachments can be explained in social and psychological terms and do not need to fall foul of biological reductionism.

- *Piaget's constructivism.* Piaget's work was very individualistic in its focus, and it has to be recognised that such a narrow focus can be very misleading, distracting us from the significant role of broader social factors, such as racism (Robinson, 1995).
- *The ecological approach.* One of the benefits of the ecological approach is that its emphasis on interlocking systems gives scope for developing an understanding of power, discrimination and oppression. The ecological approach is therefore not so much inappropriate as undeveloped.
- *Crisis intervention.* Traditional approaches to crisis intervention are firmly rooted in a psychological (if not psychiatric) individualism, with little or no attention paid to the structural or cultural factors that can have a significant influence on crises and how they are experienced. This theory, then, is also one that is not so much inappropriate as undeveloped, although Thompson (1991) goes some way towards making the theory base more consistent with anti-discriminatory practice.

These examples should make it clear that we have to be very wary of adopting theoretical perspectives uncritically. Indeed, it is an important aspect of reflective practice that we should engage critically with theory – that the demands of practice should be used to test and extend theory so that theory and practice influence each other (rather than the traditional view that practice presents the questions while theory presents the answers).

Essentialism

The point was made earlier that the way needs are generally conceptualised reflects a degree of essentialism. That is, they tend to present needs as 'essences' within us, rather than as 'situational' factors, linked with what is known

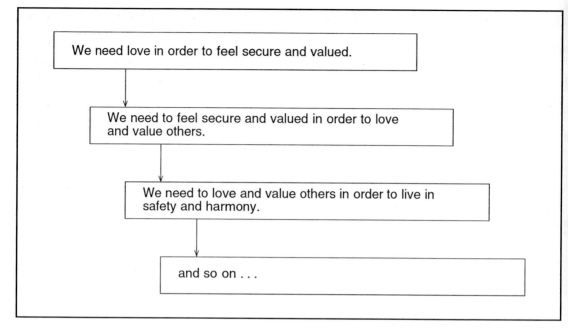

Figure 1.2 Layers of need

technically as 'intentionality'. Intentionality refers to the fact that we are creatures who have intentions – wishes, hopes, aspirations. While many theories seek to explain behaviour in terms of *past* events ('antecedents'), intentionality is a concept that is used to explain behaviour in terms of the *future* – that is, the future we wish to create. Consider your own actions. What motivates you to do certain things? When you think of aspects of the future (for example, what you want to achieve or the destination you want to reach) you are drawing on the concept of intentionality – there is a reason or purpose behind your actions geared towards a desired (future) outcome.

We can apply this notion to needs. Rather than see needs as something internal to us, as if they reflect a given essence (and are therefore relatively fixed and resistant to change), we can see them as linked to particular intentions. This can be seen in terms of linking needs to particular outcomes. The key phrase that helps us to understand this is 'in order to'. For example, when we see that we need food and water, we are not saying this in any absolute sense. Implicit in the statement is the idea that we need food and water *in order to* survive. This may seem quite obvious and unremarkable, but if we change the example, we can see that a

clear picture emerges. Consider the example given in Figure 1.2.

One theoretical 'tool' that can help us deal with needs in a non-essentialist way is what is known as the 'progressive-regressive method', a term drawn from the work of Sartre (1963). The method is:

> . . . regressive because it takes account of the past and the contradictions that have featured in its development. It is progressive because it looks to the future – the goals, intentions, ambitions of people . . . The interplay between the two elements, progressive and regressive, is dialectical. (Thompson, 1992, pp. 61–2)

While the term, 'progressive-regressive method' may be far from user-friendly, it is actually quite a helpful concept. Basically, it refers to the idea that our actions are partly explained by the past (our 'biography') and partly by our future ('intentionality' – what we are hoping to achieve). The present moment is therefore partly shaped by the past and partly by the future.

We can use this method to understand children's and young people's needs and other issues that are commonly seen in essentialist terms. Instead of thinking in terms of fixed 'essences' we can think in more sophisticated terms about the dynamic interaction between past influences and future aspirations.

Exercise 1.6

The object of this exercise is to give you the opportunity to apply the progressive-regressive method to a real-life situation so that you can better understand its significance. Consider a child or young person you know quite well. What important issues from his or her past have played a part in arriving at the present situation? What aspects of his or her future (wishes, fears, aspirations and so on) also play a part in shaping the present situation?

Reification

Sibeon (1999) regards reification as one of the four cardinal sins of theorising. That is, he sees it as a fundamental weakness of some types of theory. He describes it in the following terms: 'Reification . . . is an illegitimate method of analysis that attributes agency to entities that are not agents' (1996, p. 42). Here the term, 'agency' is being used in its sociological sense to refer to the capacity to exercise choice, make decisions, take responsibility and so on:

> *Merely taxonomic collectivities like 'society', 'classes', 'men', 'black people', 'white people', etc., are not actors. They are collectivities that cannot do anything or be held responsible for anything; this is because they are social aggregates that 'have no identifiable means of taking decisions, let alone of acting on them'.* (Hindess, 1988: 105). . . . *To repeat:* **for an entity to be an actor (or agent) that entity must have means of formulating and of acting upon decisions**. (1996, p. 35, emphasis in original)

It can clearly be argued that much of the traditional literature on child and adolescent development falls foul of reification, in the sense that children and/or young people are presented as unified categories, as if generalisations can readily be drawn from a smaller sample. That is, it is assumed that by studying some children or young people we can identify patterns across children or young people in general. This is a dangerous assumption to make as it neglects two very significant sets of issues:

1. It fails to take account of cultural and other forms of diversity. As far as diversity is concerned, reification muddies the water quite considerably as this process fails to take account of significant variations *within* groups of people as well as across them. Reification leads to statements such as 'It is important for children to have . . .' – treating children as a generalised group.

2. It disregards the role of human agency – that is, it does not acknowledge that people are decision-making beings who exercise choice and responsibility and who therefore, in many ways, do not follow standard patterns. It takes little or no account of meaning-making. The question of meaning-making is, as we noted in the Introduction, one of the key themes of this book – the phenomenological dimension in which perceptions and interpretations are recognised as crucial influences on our actions and attitudes. Reification leaves little or no room for meaning and interpretation.

Reification also returns us to our earlier discussion of one of the frequently 'missing' strands of child and adolescent development, namely ontology. Although children and young people may have much in common in some ways, we also have to recognise that each person faces his or her own unique life challenges. It is therefore important that we are not seduced into seeing only the common themes and failing to address the specifics that relate to that individual alone. Brandon *et al.* (1998) make important links between this question of the unique individual and the developmental framework when they argue that:

> *When social workers are observing, talking to, listening to or playing with children, they need to have the knowledge and skills to take into account the developmental processes of childhood and, specifically, children's own changing perspective on their world. The child must be seen as an actor in his or her own life rather than just a passive recipient of parenting and other experiences. From birth, the child will be trying to make sense of the world and will construct a framework for*

understanding and responding to events and relationships. Social workers need to be constantly asking, what is the child's experience of this situation? (p. 37)

We should therefore be careful to avoid over generalising and treating children and/or young people as if they were a unified group. While they may have much in common, this has to be balanced against the significance of social diversity and individual uniqueness.

Developments in loss theory

The traditional approaches to loss outlined above have come under increasing criticism. As Stroebe *et al.* (1993a) comment: 'Much has been written on 'stages' of grief. Most researchers would agree that these are to be taken only as general, flexible guidelines' (p. 463). It is unfortunate, then, that so much store has been set by the assumed stage-related process of grieving. This approach has become a dominant model, proving to be quite influential in professional training and practice, despite its limited value in explaining the complexities of loss and grief.

In view of the limited value of traditional loss theories and the dangers of oversimplifying this complex area (Riches and Dawson, 2000), it is important to explore more sophisticated and developed approaches to understanding loss and its consequences. I shall outline three such developments so that their value in making sense of the practice situations we encounter can be identified:

(i) Dual process theory

This is a theoretical development introduced by Stroebe and Schut (1999). It describes our response to loss in terms of two processes that occur, rather than a single one. They write of two 'orientations': a *loss* orientation which is characterised by intense sadness and other related feelings and a *restoration* orientation which is geared towards rebuilding our lives and moving beyond the loss experience. They argue that we do not go through stages as depicted in traditional theory. Rather, we tend to 'oscillate' between these two orientations. It may be that, in the morning, we feel in acute emotional pain and wonder whether we will ever get over the trauma of the loss – we are firmly ensconced in

loss orientation. However, by that afternoon we may be feeling a bit stronger and may be beginning to consider possible tentative steps forward – we have moved into restoration orientation. By evening, though, we may have lost that momentum and begun to sink back into loss orientation, as the hurt reasserts itself.

It is argued that, over time, restoration orientation will become dominant but the timescale for this will be different for different people in different circumstances. This avoids the trap of reification, of seeing people who are grieving as a homogeneous group, going through more or less the same process.

This approach is different from traditional approaches in (at least) three main ways:

- It raises questions about assessment practices. It warns us of the dangers of basing an assessment on seeing someone when they are in one orientation or another. To get a more realistic picture of their situation we would need to know a lot more about the patterns of their grieving and not simply try to identify what 'stage' they have reached or what 'task' they are working on. A more holistic overview is called for.
- The notion of 'you will get over it in time' is challenged by this theory. While restoration orientation is argued to become the dominant orientation over time, it never 'extinguishes' loss orientation altogether. Consequently, it is possible for loss orientation to reassert itself at any time, especially at such key times as the anniversary of the loss, the birthday of the person who has died and so on.
- Cultural and gender differences are easily accommodated by this theory. This is because characteristic patterns associated with a particular culture or gender can be linked to this model. Consider, for example, gender-related patterns of grieving. It has been argued that men try to cope in more active ways – that is, they are more likely to spend more time in restoration orientation (Thompson, 1995). Similarly, some cultures seek to influence patterns of mourning – for example, by prescribing set periods of grieving (Parkes *et al.*, 1997), thus adding a degree of social legitimacy to loss orientation during that time but placing the emphasis on

restoration orientation after that period has elapsed.

(ii) Meaning reconstruction theory

A further important development in loss theory stems from the work of Robert Neimeyer and his colleagues (Neimeyer *et al.*, 1998; Neimeyer and Anderson, 2002). This theory is very consistent with our phenomenological theme, as it emphasises the importance of meaning-making. Its basic tenet is that when we lose someone or something important to us, we also lose the meaning associated with the person or entity we have lost. That is, after a death, we not only lose a person but also what the person means to us. For example, if I gained a sense of security from the presence and influence of a particular uncle in my life, then his death may also, for a time at least, deprive me of my sense of security and leave me feeling very vulnerable.

According to this theory, then, the process of grieving is not a largely standardised one with identifiable stages, but rather one which depends very much on the individual's circumstances, perceptions and frameworks of meaning – the values, beliefs and other meanings that shape his or her identity, approach to life, actions and attitudes.

(iii) Disenfranchised grief

Kenneth Doka is the theorist associated with this important concept. In a very significant and influential book (Doka, 1989), the key notion of disenfranchised grief was introduced and explored. Grief is said to be disenfranchised when it is not socially sanctioned or approved of. Doka argues that this can occur in three main ways:

- *When the relationship is disenfranchised.* This would apply to a secret relationship (for example, an extramarital affair) or a socially marginalised relationship (for example, gay or lesbian relationships).
- *When the nature of the loss is disenfranchised.* This would include losses through suicide, for example – types of loss that tend to be stigmatised in some way. Although Doka did not discuss losses associated with abuse, we can none the less see that grieving brought about by abuse

may also be disenfranchised (Thompson, 1997).
- *When the griever is disenfranchised.* This refers to groups of people who are assumed not to grieve or at least to be less affected by grief. This includes older people ('They get used to loss and grief'), people with learning disabilities ('They don't understand what is happening') and, of course, children.

What is particularly significant about this concept is that it can apply to children and young people at all three levels – that is, children and young people tend to be disenfranchised *because* they are children or young people, but may also face losses that are disenfranchised because of the nature of the relationship and the nature of the loss. Clearly, then, this concept can be seen to have major implications for understanding how children and young people react to losses, particularly when we remember that this notion applies to *all* types of loss and not just those that are associated with death.

This brief insight into developments in loss theory should help us to appreciate how complex such matters are (and therefore how inadequate traditional approaches are). One clear implication is that, if we are to have an adequate understanding of the development of children and young people, then we need to go beyond traditional models of loss and grief which fall far short of the explanatory power of the three more developed theories presented here. One further important point to note is that the three theories, although arising from different theorists within different schools of thought, are largely compatible and so there is excellent scope for combining their insights within a framework of reflective practice. This offers exciting possibilities.

Drawing on stress theory

The fact that children and young people are subject to stress at certain times in their lives – particularly those who have had need to enter the care or child protection systems – is one that would generally be acknowledged. However, it can also be argued that the significance of stress (and the related concept of depression) has not always been fully recognised in either the literature base or practice. But what is perhaps just as important to recognise, if not more so, is that the awareness of i) what stress is; ii) how it affects people; and iii) how it can or should be tackled, has tended to be at a fairly low level.

Consequently, one way of going beyond the limitations of traditional approaches to child and adolescent development is to take further our understanding (and use) of contemporary stress theory. This is a major topic in its own right (see Thompson *et al.*, 1994a) and so I shall restrict myself to commenting on three aspects of the theory base here:

1. *The three-dimensional nature of stress.* Stress is commonly regarded as the result of pressures overwhelming our coping resources. This is a two-dimensional model, representing a battle between the individual's capabilities and the nature and extent of the pressures he or she faces. A major problem with this approach to stress is that it has the unfortunate effect of pathologising the individual. To experience stress, according to this conceptualisation, is to be weak and personally inadequate, unable to cope with the pressures of the job. A less punitive and destructive model is a three-dimensional one which incorporates the often missing element – that of support (Thompson *et al.*, 1994a). Support can be seen as a crucial factor because it helps to: i) keep pressures in proportion and thus make them more manageable; and ii) enhance coping resources, for example by boosting confidence. An absence of support, by contrast, can have precisely the opposite effect – that is, to make pressures loom larger than they need to and to undermine coping resources. This third dimension therefore makes a huge difference in terms of our understanding of stress as a psychological and organisational phenomenon.
2. *The social and organisational context of stress.* A further major problem associated with the traditional two-dimensional model of stress is that it distracts attention from the organisational context. By focusing almost exclusively on the individual, it fails to take adequate account of the role of the organisation and wider social factors. A more realistic model of stress must therefore explore these wider factors by considering to what extent social or organisational issues have a bearing on people's experiences of stress.
3. *The effects of stress.* It is a pity that stress is often presented as if it were an illness. For example, the very well-known writer on stress issues, Cary Cooper, regularly refers in his writings to the 'symptoms' of stress. The effects of stress can therefore easily be presented in narrow, physical terms (appetite, sleep, effects on health and so on), thus neglecting other aspects of the detrimental effects of stress: undermining of confidence and self-esteem; strained relationships; unwillingness to take necessary risks and so on. We should also recognise that the effects of stress can easily lead to a vicious circle in which low confidence and so on lead to a lower level of coping which leads in turn to a higher level of stress which can then undermine confidence further – and so it goes on into an ever-deepening spiral of problems.

This brief discussion of stress theory can be helpful in casting light on our own experiences as workers in highly pressurised work settings – and this is a theme to which we shall return in Chapter 5 in relation to continuous professional development – but, for present purposes, the important point to emphasise is that this theory can also be seen to apply to children and young people (and indeed their parents and carers). Children and young people are not immune from stress, and yet the links between stress and child and adolescent development are rarely explored or developed. Indeed, stress tends to be seen as a predominantly adult phenomenon, even though there is no real reason for us to make the common assumption that stress and its consequences are not relevant factors in working with children and young people.

Direct work

'Direct work' with children and young people is an ambiguous term. It is used in both a broad and a narrow sense. In its broad sense it refers to any work undertaken directly with a child or young person – that is, those aspects of practice which focus specifically on interactions with the child or young person as the primary client (as opposed to the various other aspects of practice that involve working with parents, other carers and so on). In its narrower sense, it refers to a specific approach to therapeutic work with children and young people. In this section we shall be using it in its broader sense, to incorporate all aspects of seeking to communicate and engage with children and young people as part of an assessment and a systematic plan of intervention (see Chapter 2).

We begin by looking at partnership skills, the various abilities that combine to give us the capacity to work effectively alongside children and young people. We shall then move on to examine the topical and none the less important topic of risk assessment, before considering the dangers of drift and the importance of a systematic approach to practice. Following this we look at the range of issues relating to involving children and young people in decision-making processes and the lessons we can learn from research.

Partnership skills

The role of partnership as a central theme in this programme has already been stressed. We can now begin to see how this works in practice by exploring what is involved in working in partnership directly with children and young people. For present purposes I shall divide this area up into three sections: communication, the think-feel-do framework and needs-led assessment.

Communicating with children and young people

A major feature of this chapter is the emphasis on the importance of appreciating the significance of child and adolescent development. This is particularly important when it comes to communication, as it is vitally important that we communicate at a developmentally appropriate level. For example, if we talk at too high a level to a young child, he or she may comprehend very little and thus become alienated or even distressed by the process. Similarly, to talk to a teenager at too

basic a level will come across as patronising and therefore do very little to promote working in partnership – indeed, it is likely to act as a barrier to such partnership.

Exercise 1.7
How would you decide at what level to pitch your conversation with a child or young person? What factors would you take into consideration? If you were to find you had pitched it at the wrong level, how would you know? What telltale signs would there be?

A further important aspect of communication as part of partnership-building is the need for clarity about what is happening. As Crompton (1990) comments: 'Perhaps the greatest single source of fear for children (and me) is not knowing what is going to happen' (p. 59). This shows the importance of 'setting out our stall', being clear and explicit about what our role is, what we are tying to achieve and so on. Without this clarity, focus and openness come mystique, confusion and misunderstanding – none of which is helpful when it comes to trying to work in partnership.

Of course, a key part of effective communication is the ability to listen. Wheal (1995) offers the following advice to foster carers, but I believe it can also be applied to social workers or indeed anyone working with children and young people:

1. *Never be too busy to listen. Children have important things to say at the most inconvenient time of day.*
2. *Listen to what is being said. Give the child your entire attention.*
3. *Don't anticipate what will be said next. Wait and listen. That way you'll be sure.*
4. *Keep your thoughts to yourself about what is being said. Don't let your mind jump away from the topic.*
5. *Pay attention to both what is being said and how it is being said.*
6. *If you have a question, make a note of it, unless it disturbs the child. Ask the question at the proper time. Don't interrupt or write while the child is actually talking. Asking questions can certainly help but they require careful handling and good timing.*
7. *If you disagree, don't get angry. Wait until he/she is finished. He/she may say*

*something that makes your anger
unnecessary or even embarrassing.*
8. *If the child is continuing for a long time, jot
down a few notes when there is a pause or
when the child has finished speaking. This
will help later on in remembering what was
said.* (p. 86)

Communicating with someone who shares your
cultural background can be complex enough,
but we should also recognise the additional
potential difficulties that can arise in
communicating with someone whose culture is
different from our own. If we are not sensitive to
some of the complications that can arise, then
our communication efforts can fail miserably,
we may actually make communication more
strained in the future, and of course we will miss
the important opportunities for learning from
each other and appreciating different
perspectives on life (note the phenomenological
theme of perception and meaning-making
again here).

Cross-cultural communication is a topic
Guirdham (1999) addresses in some depth. She
discusses the various aspects of
communication in relation to the significance of
culture and shared patterns of meaning. A clear
implication of her work is that it is vitally
important to consider cultural backgrounds of
the respective parties when looking at
communication. In communicating with a child
or young person, then, it is important that we
take account of their culture. If it is a culture we
are not familiar with, then clearly we face the
important task of finding out at least the basics
of that culture, its symbolism, practices and so
on. This is no less true of Welsh language and
culture where a number of differences in
perspective can arise.

The Think-Feel-Do framework

This is a potentially very useful framework that
can help develop good working partnerships
(Thompson, 2002a). This is because it helps us
gain an overview of the situation we are dealing
with and helps to ensure that we do not omit
consideration of an important dimension of that
situation.

The basic idea is that it helps to understand
situations in terms of three dimensions:
thoughts, feelings and actions:

- *Think.* What are my thoughts on this
situation? What do I know? What do I need to
know? What do others involved think about
the situation? What do they know? How do
we analyse or make sense of this situation?
These are important questions to ask, not
only at the assessment stage but also
throughout the whole social work process.
- *Feel.* What are the feelings issues in this
matter? How do the people concerned feel
about the situation? How do I feel about it?
What impact are feelings having on the
situation? What part do they play in its
possible resolution? This is an aspect of the
situation that can often be neglected, as
many people have a tendency to concentrate
on the logical, rational side of things and thus
run the risk of neglecting the crucial
emotional dimension.
- *Do.* What are the key things that have
happened leading up to this situation? What
caused them? What are the key things that
are happening now? How important are
they? How are they helping? How are they
hindering? What do we want to avoid
happening in future? What needs to happen
in the future to make the situation better?

It is not being suggested that practitioners
should mechanistically go through all these
questions, but rather that social workers do
need to have at least some sensitivity to, and
awareness of, this important range of issues.

The think-feel-do framework can be very
useful as a means of checking that we are
looking at the circumstances broadly enough.
That is, we can use it to ensure that we are
addressing all three dimensions and not just
sticking to those that are easier to deal with or
the ones we feel more comfortable with. The
basic argument here is that good practice
depends on being able to address all three
dimensions and cannot rely on a two-sided or
even one-sided approach.

As a basis for partnership, think-feel-do offers
two main advantages:

1. It offers clarity and focus, something that the
consumer research tells us is important to
clients and carers (see Howe, 1987).
2. It helps to build professional credibility and
confidence, important ingredients in making

partnerships work – if others have little respect for you, you should not be surprised if they are reluctant to trust you as part of a good working partnership.

Needs-led assessment

The implementation of the NHS and Community Care Act 1990 has helped to establish firmly the importance of needs-led assessment – and, of course, it is a principle of good practice that is no less applicable outside of the community care field. However, I fear it remains a term that is often misunderstood and shrouded in myth. I shall therefore seek to clarify what is meant by needs-led assessment and what is involved in it before exploring how and why it is an important part of working in partnership.

We have to be realistic and accept that we work in a context of shortage of resources. Demand for services is potentially infinite, while supply necessarily remains finite, and so it is inevitable that, at some point demand will outstrip supply. This situation has, in the past, led to a service-led approach. This involves focusing on rationing scarce resources and therefore tailoring the assessment more to the availability (or otherwise) of the service, rather than focusing on what the client needs. This has a distorting effect in three ways:

- A very narrow picture of the client's circumstances is likely to emerge from this type of assessment, as only those aspects of the situation relevant to the service in question are likely to receive attention. Consequently, significant issues may be missed (we shall return to this point in Chapter 2).
- The client may not be offered the most appropriate service. That is, it may be that, although the client is eligible for a particular service and may benefit from it, there may be another service which is even more appropriate and beneficial, but which has not been considered because the focus was on the first service rather than the underlying need. This may therefore lead to a situation in which scarce resources are not being used to the best effect.
- It masks unmet need. That is, by tailoring the assessment to the service rather than the needs, those needs which cannot be met by

existing services remain unidentified. The assessment process therefore fails to feed into service and policy development and contributes to the maintenance of the status quo, thus potentially blocking the innovative use of resources.

Some people misunderstand the notion of needs-led assessment and see it as unrealistic or idealistic. However, they have failed to appreciate that making sure your assessment is needs-led does not mean that we would then expect all those needs to be met – but at least we have a chance of meeting them if we know what they are, but we cannot begin to address such needs if they continue to be masked by a service-led process of assessment.

Some people also suggest that needs-led assessment is a waste of time. They argue: 'Why identify needs when we know that we will not be able to meet them?' Again this is based on a misunderstanding, as it fails to realise that:

- Identifying unmet need is, as suggested above, an important part of influencing policy and service development and the future allocation of resources (how do we know whether resources are being used to best effect if we do not know what people's needs are?).
- Needs are not always best met by social work services. Identifying a need that the social worker cannot meet may pave the way for other ways forward (remember that social work is a problem-solving activity and not just a question of providing services – see Thompson, 2000b, Chapter 1). Sometimes people are able to meet their own needs, once they are clear what these are.
- A service-led assessment can easily miss key issues that are having a profound effect on the situation and thus result in services being wasted because it is unlikely that they will be effective while the underlying problems are not being addressed. Grief and debt are two clear examples that come to mind. If someone's need to mourn a loss is not recognised and responded to appropriately, it is unlikely that progress will be made in other areas. Similarly debt can undermine all other plans and projects if its significance is not recognised and addressed.

Needs-led assessment involves looking at the situation as it is, identifying what the issues are (strengths as well as problems), clarifying what needs to be done and planning how to do it. As we shall see in Chapter 2, this is a process that is best carried out in partnership.

Needs-led assessment also facilitates partnership in so far as it helps to break down many of the barriers that can exist between worker and client when a service-led approach is adopted. This is because service-led assessments can easily become the basis for battles over the allocation of scarce resources, driving a wedge between the parties instead of bringing them together with the common aim of resolving the identified difficulties. Needs-led assessment, by contrast, involves both parties having a clear focus on identifying the problems and considering or exploring possible solutions. If a service is required and cannot be provided, for resource shortfall reasons, then this can be addressed together, with a broader focus on problem-solving, rather than degenerate into crude negotiation over what resources can or cannot be allocated.

Creating the right environment

The ability to work in partnership is clearly a major feature of high-quality social work with children, young people and their families. However, all this has to happen within a context, and so our ability to succeed in this regard depends to a certain extent on getting the contextual factors right – in particular being able to create the right environment. That is, a great deal of effort and good work can so easily go to waste if there are aspects of the environment in which we are trying to operate that undermine what we are doing. It therefore pays to give some thought to the environmental factors that have a part to play.

Perhaps one of the first things we need to address is: where should our dealings with the child or young person take place. Home is an obvious answer that has a lot of strengths. However, we should also recognise the possible limitations or drawbacks of home, not least the following:

- *Parental influences.* Children or young people may not be willing to talk openly if their parents are present or may be within earshot

– or it may even be that they see home as their parents' 'territory' and therefore feel inhibited about speaking their mind.
- *Abuse experiences.* If home is the location where abuse has taken place, again the child or young person may feel very inhibited in speaking up about issues – 'echoes' of the abuse situation (even where the abuse has ended) may be enough to create a reluctance to work closely with the social worker in a place associated in their mind with betrayal and an abuse of trust.
- *Distractions.* There can be many distractions in the home – television, telephone calls, friends or neighbours calling round and so on. There are ways and means of dealing with these but we do have to acknowledge that they exist and that they can be a problem at times.

So, if we decide to seek an alternative venue, what are the possibilities? A trip to the local burger bar has become a bit of a cliché for many child care workers and is also a mixed blessing. It may be more relaxed than at home and may help make relationships less formal, but there are also clear drawbacks like distractions, possible problems over confidentiality and so on.

Use of the worker's office may be a realistic possibility, but can also be fraught with difficulties, depending on facilities, location and so on. School can be a useful meeting point, but this needs to be used carefully as a visit of a social worker to school can play a part in stigmatising the child or young person concerned.

There are, of course, other options, such as a family centre or other such 'neutral' venues. However, whichever setting we choose to use, we have to make sure that we have weighed up the advantages and disadvantages so that we are sure that we are not making a mistake.

Of course, a primary consideration will be the wishes and preferences of the child or young person concerned. What seems a very good environment for you may be disastrous for them due to reasons you are not aware of, but which are only too painfully clear to him or her.

The physical venue is not the only aspect of the environment that is important. How we make use of that venue can also be very significant. For example, who sits where can be very significant (a form of body language). The setting can be made to be very welcoming or can be inhibiting, so it is important to give some thought to this – what seems comfortable and appropriate to an adult may not be so appealing to a youngster.

Exercise 1.8

How would you decide what is the best venue or setting for interviewing a child or young person? What options are available to you in your current work setting? Compare notes with your colleagues to see whether there are suitable venues available that you do not know about.

Risk assessment

The subject of risk assessment is one that has received a great deal of attention in recent years. It is an aspect of practice that has important consequences, as a failure to undertake an adequate risk assessment can lead to situations in which one or more children or young people are exposed to an unacceptably high level of danger. This topic is explored in more depth in Chapter 2, but for present purposes it is important to stress that working directly with children and young people puts us in a situation where we have to be aware of what risk factors are operating, how significant they are, what protective factors apply and so on. This is not to say that it is necessary to undertake a formal risk assessment on every child or young person we work with, but we do have to make sure that we are alert to risk-related matters. Indeed, I shall be arguing in Chapter 2 that one important skill that we need to develop is the ability to get the balance right in relation to risk – for example, by being sufficiently sensitive to risk issues but without becoming oversensitive and indulging in defensive practice (see Thompson, 2000b, for a discussion of the dangers of defensive practice).

It is important to begin by stressing that risk is an ever present aspect of social work with children and young people. We should be wary of falling into the common trap of assuming that risk is an issue related primarily or even exclusively to child abuse and protection. All aspects of social work involve an element of risk.

A detailed analysis of risk assessment is beyond the scope of this text, and so what is presented here is necessarily selective. You are therefore advised to make use of the 'Learning resources guide' in Section 6 below to identify suitable books for further study of this important topic. For present purposes, I shall restrict myself to making a small number of key points.

Sargent (1999) makes the important point that:

Assessing risk is a mixture of art and science. A scientific approach needs more and better ways of accurately identifying children who are most at risk, and proving that the methods used for identification are both consistent and reliable. The art of risk assessment lies both in the application of available instruments and in the use of practitioners' judgement and experience.
(p. 184)

We should therefore be careful to avoid the two destructive extremes, one of regarding risk analysis as something wholly rigorous, objective and scientific, and the other of seeing it as largely a matter of (educated) guesswork. The reality, of course, is somewhere in between these two unhelpful extremes.

Another possible misunderstanding of risk is what Macdonald and Macdonald (1999) refer to as the 'hindsight fallacy'. This describes the sort of situation where, because something goes wrong, perhaps drastically so, it is assumed that assessments made and decisions taken were in error. As they put it: 'It follows that a bad outcome in and of itself does not constitute evidence that the decision was mistaken. The hindsight fallacy is to assume that it does' (p. 22). One clear implication of this is that, even where we do everything we reasonably can to support sound decision-making, there is no guarantee of a positive outcome.

We should also recognise that risk is not, of itself, a bad thing, in so far as a life without risk would be a very unhappy and distressing one. It follows, therefore, that attempts to create situations for clients where risk is eliminated can be seen as oppressive. We therefore have to be clear, when talking of removing or minimising risks, that we are not doing more harm than good.

We need to be clear, in seeking to protect people from risk, that we understand what we are doing and why. Risk is a complex subject and we can cause a lot of problems by oversimplifying the situations we deal with. Williams (1997) writes of the 'risk of not taking a risk'. That is, he is pointing out that being too cautious or defensive brings with it its own risks – we can never be immune from risk.

Macdonald and Macdonald (1999, p. 32) cite Arnauld's view that 'Fear of harm ought to be proportional not merely to the gravity of the harm, but also to the probability of the event'. This comment provides us with a good framework for considering risk. It involves asking:

- If a particular occurrence were to take place, how harmful would it be?
- How likely is it that this occurrence will actually arise?

By asking these two questions we can gain a useful overview of the situation. Basically, it gives us four possible scenarios:

1. Low harm, low likelihood of occurrence.
2. Low harm, high likelihood of occurrence.
3. High harm, low likelihood of occurrence.
4. High harm, high likelihood of occurrence.

It should be quite clear that we would need to respond differently to each of these different combinations of the two factors. Asking these two key questions can therefore tell us a lot about the situation.

As with any form of assessment, we should not forget that risk situations change over time. What is an unacceptably risky situation now may be quite acceptable in a few days' time, while what was presenting little concern a few days ago may be a major source of concern now. We deal with moving pictures, rather than snapshots and so we have to be very wary of regarding a risk assessment as written in tablets of stone. We have to be sensitive to the extent and pace of change over time.

As well as the problem of the need to keep track of changing circumstances, we also face the potential problem of seeing risk in very narrow terms. Parsloe (1999) makes the following important comment:

Poverty, poor housing and attendant ill health may cause as much significant harm to children as child abuse. Despite all these examples there is no equivalent of the social model of disability to establish the idea that much risk is imposed upon people by social conditions rather than arising from their personal attributes or behaviour. We seem to lack a social model of risk. (p. 12)

Parsloe is right to suggest that much of the research and literature on risk has tended to focus on individual and interpersonal levels, thus neglecting wider social and political issues. Of course, social workers are not in a position to rectify this situation, but what we can do is to try to make sure that our assessment is not too narrow and individualistic. In order for our work to be consistent with the values of anti-discriminatory practice it is important that we see individuals in their social context, and so there is a double imperative to make sure that we do not stop short at the individual level.

In view of these complexities, it should be clear that we need to ensure that we address the following questions:

- When we say that someone is 'at risk', we need to clarify at risk of *what*?
- If we remove or minimise a particular risk, what negative consequences may arise as a result of this (assessing the *balance* of risk)?
- Are we clear about both how likely a particular event is and how harmful its consequences may be?
- Are we being appropriately sensitive to the timescales involved here? Is our information sufficiently up-to-date?
- Are we taking adequate account of wider social factors or are we falling into the trap of seeing risk in narrow, individualistic terms?

Systematic practice

This is a term used to refer to an approach to practice which emphasises the importance of keeping a clear focus on what we are doing and why we are doing it. It is proposed as an effective way of avoiding a long-standing problem in social work with children, young people and their families – that of 'drift'.

Systematic practice can be characterised as an approach based on addressing the following three questions (Thompson, 2002a):

1. What are you trying to achieve?
2. How are you going to achieve it?
3. How will you know when you have achieved it?

The first question helps us to be clear, focused and explicit about our objectives – in other words, about the desired outcomes we wish to work towards. If we are not aware of what it is we are trying to achieve, then clearly we are going to struggle when it comes to trying to achieve it.

The second question builds on the first in so far as it looks at what road we intend to follow to achieve our desired outcomes, what steps we need to take to achieve our aims. Simply knowing what we want to achieve will not tell us what we have to do to achieve it. We still have to face the question of what needs to be done to get us where we want to go.

However, it is the third question that can cause us the most difficulty. This is because answering this question successfully depends on having answered the first two appropriately. If we have been too vague in answering Question 1 and/or Question 2, then we will find it very difficult, if not impossible, to answer this third question. Consider the following example:

1. What are you trying to achieve?   To support the family.
2. How are you going to achieve it?   By visiting regularly.
3. How will you know when you have achieved it?   ???????????????

To be able to come up with a coherent answer to Question 3 (that is, how will we recognise that we have succeeded, what will success look like?), we have to have tackled Questions 1 and 2 clearly and appropriately – that is, in an explicit and focused way that leaves no room for 'drift' or unnecessary ambiguity.

It is important to note that the 'you' used in the three questions is to be read as a plural you. That is, it is not the individual worker who should be addressing these questions in isolation, but rather in partnership with the other people who are part of the process of dealing

with the particular matter – not least the clients concerned, of course.

The major benefits of systematic practice can be identified as follows:

- 'Drift' is far less likely – that is, it is much less likely that we will lose our focus or 'lose the plot' of what we are doing. This is a significant advantage as drift is a common characteristic of situations where people are very busy and perhaps overstretched. In the pressurised world of social work with children, young people and their families, drift is therefore an ever present danger (see Thompson, 2000b, Chapter 7).
- Partnership becomes easier to achieve. A clear focus on what is being done, why, and with what outcomes helps staff, service users, carers and other professionals to work together on the basis of shared goals and shared means of achieving them. Indeed, this notion of identifying shared goals and shared ways of achieving them is a major feature of both partnership and systematic practice.
- The clarity of focus involved in systematic practice can be a major source of job satisfaction and morale – for example, by giving people a clear sense of control. This is an important factor in keeping stress at bay.
- Accountability becomes a much easier matter to handle. For example, in the event of any sort of inquiry, complaint or investigation, a systematic approach makes it far easier to be able to account for our actions and thus be able to justify them if called upon to do so.

Finally, in relation to systematic practice, a point worth emphasising is the importance of time management. When systematic practice is explored in a classroom setting or through reading, it can come across as being very simple and easy to achieve. However, what has to be recognised is that pressure of work often leads people into a vicious circle. Because they are under a lot of pressure, they do not make the time to practise systematically and try to cut corners. This can easily lead to a lack of focus and the problems that often come with this type of 'drift'. This in turn can lead to a lot of wasted time and effort, and can have the effect of sapping morale and motivation. This then adds to the feeling of pressure and work overload, thus establishing a vicious circle. It is therefore crucial that we make the time to be clear about what we are doing and why we are doing it so that we do not get into a vicious circle of drift and demotivation (we shall return to this point in Chapter 4).

User involvement: strategies and obstacles

Involving children and young people in the processes and decision-making that affect them can be seen to be a positive step forward and certainly one that is in keeping with the notion of partnership. However, in developing such an approach it is important to recognise that we are very much swimming against the tide in so far as the dominant ideology is so firmly along the lines of 'children should be seen and not heard' – that is, the idea that children should have an active say in what happens to them is one that is likely to encounter a lot of resistance, in certain quarters at least. As Thomas and O'Kane (1998) comment:

> We live in a society and culture in which children are generally not listened to, consulted or involved in decision-making. Children say very clearly that adults don't listen to children. They ignore them, leave them out, interrupt, re-define or over-ride what they say . . . The Children Act 1989 has been influential in encouraging children to be part of the decision-making process.

Of course, our comments about involving children and young people in decision-making processes has to take account of their level of development, as discussed in the earlier part of this chapter. The idea that we take account of the child's age and level of understanding is a well-established one in relation to child care law, and it would be wise to apply that principle more broadly to our practice.

It is understandable that children and young people, with their limited experience of life, may not understand what is happening, may not be able to make sense of the complexities of the situation and may not have a clear grasp of the roles of the various people involved. What is also understandable is that such a lack of understanding may well generate a lot of tension and anxiety which may, in turn lead to a hostile or uncooperative approach or

withdrawal from the situation. As a bare minimum, therefore, we should be ensuring that children and young people are consulted on such matters, given clear and full explanations of what is going on and given the opportunity to ask questions.

However, it can also be argued that we should go a step further in trying to make sure that children and young people are treated as full partners in the process of work and are therefore encouraged and supported in becoming active participants. This can be seen to include:

- Involving them directly in any process of assessment wherever possible. Their perspective on the situation may be very different from that of their parent(s). We cannot assume that the adults involved are in a position to speak for them.
- Inviting them to meetings, where appropriate, and supporting them in preparing for the meeting and contributing to it.
- Giving them the opportunity to voice their views on all aspects of the work being undertaken, and supporting them in doing so.

There are many reasons why it is important to make 'user involvement' a fundamental part of social work practice, not least the following:

- It is more likely to motivate clients and carers to take the necessary steps to address their problems.
- It makes for better working relationships and a firmer foundation for partnership.
- The perspectives of clients and carers are more fully represented.
- Confidence and self-esteem can be boosted by active involvement.
- It is consistent with our underpinning theme of being child-centred.

Of course, we have to be realistic and recognise that it will not always be possible to involve children and young people in the process, or at least not as fully as we would like. However, we should not allow this to let us become defeatist and not make the effort of trying.

Lessons from research: evidence-based practice

What does the research base tell us? This is an important question to ask and one that many would argue has been neglected over the years (see, for example, Macdonald and Sheldon, 1992). It is perhaps rather worrying that so much of the accepted wisdom in social work has relatively little firm evidence to confirm its validity, value and appropriateness. This is not to say that such wisdom is necessarily wrong or invalid, but rather that we have tended to assume that its benefits are self-evident – we base much of our work on faith and tradition, rather than rigorous investigation and strong evidence.

There are two potential problems that we should be seeking to avoid. The first is where we are using a particular approach which is well-established but which may actually not be effective or appropriate – parallel with current concerns in the health service about the long-standing use of certain drugs which may not have the therapeutic value their manufacturers claim. The second is where there is much to be gained from the lessons we can learn from research but we do not take advantage of this knowledge or the insights for practice development it presents. Everitt *et al.* (1992) argue the case for recognising the importance of what they call research-minded practice. This refers to practice that takes account of the research-based knowledge that is available to act as a guide.

We are fortunate that, in social work with children and young people, there is a great deal of research to draw upon and a number of key texts that summarise and contextualise this research, as the following examples illustrate:

- Child protection – DoH/SSI (1995);
- Creating stability for looked after children – Jackson and Thomas (1999);
- Services for disabled children and their families – Beresford *et al.* (1996);
- Family placement – Sellick and Thoburn (1996);
- Leaving care – Stein (1997); and
- Parenting – Lloyd (1999).

It is therefore clear that there is no shortage of relevant literature, and so the scope for making our practice research-based is no doubt quite considerable.

However, it is important that we should not have too optimistic a view of the role of research in informing practice. Schaffer (1998) acknowledges that there are several limitations to the use of research, and argues that: 'research is by no means immune from value judgements: it has to be conceded that its objectivity is in fact only relative' (p. 7). What is called for, then, is a critical approach, within the context of reflective practice – one which recognises the contribution research can make, but also recognises its limitations.

The question of drawing on research, and indeed the professional knowledge base more broadly, is one to which we shall return in later chapters.

Law and policy

Here we look at a brief overview of some of the relevant sections of law and policy. The aim is to provide the opportunity for you to draw links between the issues we have been discussing so far in this chapter with the underlying law and policy base. This also helps to set the scene for Chapter 4 where there is a major emphasis on legal and policy issues. We shall look at four particular themes: children in need, significant harm, substitute care and the Looked After Children (LAC) system.

Children in need

This is a concept that was introduced in the Children Act 1989. It is defined in Part III of the Act. A child is deemed to be in need if:

(a) he [or she] is unlikely to achieve or maintain, or to have the opportunity of achieving or maintaining a reasonable standard of health or development without the provisions for him of services by a local authority under this Part;

(b) his health or development is likely to be significantly impaired or further impaired, without the provision for him of such services; or

(c) he is disabled. (s. 17 (10))

One potential problem with the concept of children 'in need' is that the term can be seen as one which contributes to a process of pathologising, largely due to the tendency to present such ideas in individualistic terms (as if to imply that any problems are a result of the inadequacy of the individual or family concerned). As such, we can envisage difficulties in aligning this concept with anti-discriminatory practice, with its broader sociopolitical focus. However, we should be wary of oversimplifying the situation. This can be seen to apply in (at least) two ways:

- Guidance and regulations relating to children in need (DoH, 1991a) point out that assessment should take account of strengths as well as problems (a point to which we shall return in Chapter 2).
- Although the term *implies* a narrow, individualistic focus, this does not mean that we cannot use the term more broadly and use it as part of a commitment to anti-discriminatory practice. As Braye and Preston-Shoot (1997) point out, the law is not as prescriptive as people often assume and there is a great deal of scope for adaptation, negotiation and flexibility in the use of legal concepts.

Significant harm

This is also a concept that was introduced in the Children Act 1989. It is not a very precise term, but that is partly what makes it a useful term – it can be adapted to different circumstances. Butler and Roberts (1997) provide helpful comment:

> Note that it is the harm which has to be significant, not whatever act caused it. Hence, a sustained series of privations, not individually harmful, as in the case of neglect, could amount to significant harm as far as the child's development was concerned. Not all harm will be significant, nor will significant harm in one context necessarily be significant in another. Ultimately, it is a matter for the court to determine whether the harm is significant for the particular child in question. (p. 248)

This passage raises a number of issues, the following two in particular:

- Where there is a question of determining what constitutes significant harm, reference must be made to child development – that is, consideration must be given to the circumstances of the child in question in relation to what could reasonably be expected of a child of a similar age.

- The concept is not sufficiently well-defined to allow a 'procedural' or technical approach to the matter. It is therefore a good concept to illustrate the need for reflective practice – to draw upon the concept of 'in need' as the basic cloth to be used, but to have to cut that cloth to suit the specific circumstances by using 'reflection-in-action', as discussed in the Introduction.

Substitute care

A major emphasis of the Children Act 1989 is the importance of supporting families and trying to keep children with their parents as far as is reasonably possible. However, there are many situations where this is not possible and alternative care becomes necessary.

One of the difficulties associated with substitute care is that, given the emphasis on keeping families together, the situation is generally quite far advanced, with perhaps deeply ingrained problems – thus putting a great deal of strain on the placement and the carers involved. This can easily lead to a placement breakdown, thereby putting even more strain on the next placement. Consequently, it is not uncommon for a series of placement breakdowns to occur. The challenge of providing appropriate substitute care can therefore be seen as a very significant one.

Two of the principles of the Children Act 1989 are as follows:

> Wherever possible, children and young people should be brought up and cared for by their own families . . . [and] When a child or young person has no parents, or where parents cannot offer their children adequate standards of care, high quality substitute care must be provided. (Stainton Rogers and Roche, 1994, p. 26)

Both of these principles are quite significant. The 'family first' principle means that substitute care should not normally be seen as an early option. The second principle is significant in the reference to 'high quality' substitute care. The publication of the Waterhouse Report (Waterhouse, 2000) has shown how *un*satisfactory much substitute care provision has been in the past and how important it is that we 'get it right' as far as possible in future.

The LAC system

Part of the challenge of providing high-quality substitute care is the reliance on appropriate practices in assessment and planning (as we shall discuss in Chapter 2). The LAC system was introduced in order to be of assistance in this respect. As we noted earlier, the documents provided by the system can be very helpful. However, they are not without their critics.

Garrett (1999) argues that the LAC system incorporates an element of 'social authoritarianism'. This is consistent with the discussion in the Introduction of the critique of the 'superparenting model', where there is an apparent expectation that social workers 'parent the parents' without taking adequate account of the other factors that can contribute to parenting problems (poverty and/or racism, for example) or the fact that there is no single, definitive type of parenting. Knight and Cavaney (1998) echo this sentiment when they argue that the LAC system is premised on a model of white, middle-class parenthood.

It should be clear, then, that the LAC system, while offering some degree of helpful guidance, should not be used uncritically. As a starting point for reflective practice, the LAC system can be very useful. However, as an alternative to reflective practice, it can be quite dangerous.

3. Tasks and challenges

In this section we begin to examine the implications for practice of the ideas presented here. This needs to be seen in the context of reflective practice. The intention is not to look to theory to provide the answers, but rather to consider both theory and practice together so that the two can be integrated, as discussed in the Introduction. We shall address the practice issues in terms of the three practice requirements associated with this chapter:

A1 Engage with children and young people.

This practice requirement refers to the partnership skills discussed above. If we are to be able to ensure as far as possible that children and young people play a more active part in the decision-making processes that can have such a crucial bearing on their future, then

clearly partnership skills become very important indeed. This is a clear example of the social work values of partnership and being child- or person-centred.

The challenge of partnership and participation is a major one. For many social workers, it involves going against the grain of an established culture that leaves little or no space for 'user involvement'. This practice requirement therefore involves a willingness and ability to 'swim against the tide' in some situations and challenge any assumptions that children or young people should not be actively involved in decisions and processes relating to their care and their lives more broadly.

There are also communication skills involved here – being able to get our message across to children and young people as well as being able and willing to listen to what they have to say. Success in this area also depends on a knowledge of child development in order to be able to pitch our communications at a suitable developmental level – finding the right balance between conversations being 'over the head' of the child or young person concerned on the one hand, and being patronising on the other. In sum, then, this area of practice involves a level of understanding in terms of knowledge, skills and values.

A2 Identify and assess the developmental progress of children and young people, taking into account all main dimensions of development.

If we are to be able to identify problems in children's and young people's development, then clearly we have to know what constitutes 'normal' development. That is, we need an understanding of the 'developmental milestones' associated with human development.

It is not necessary for social workers to be experts in child and adolescent development, but there is clearly a need for practitioners to have a good working knowledge of the main elements. However, simply having the knowledge is clearly not enough on its own. There is also a need for the ability to draw on that knowledge in practice (which is, of course, part and parcel of reflective practice). This involves being able to recognise important aspects of development, the 'telltale signs' that all is not as it should be. There is, then, a need to be able to engage in 'reflection-in-action'.

There is also a need to be able to work in partnership, not only with the children and young people concerned, but also with other professionals who have an understanding of, and professional interest in, child development (doctors, health visitors and so on), and, of course, with parents and carers who will often have a good understanding of their children's development.

Of course, one clear practice pitfall that we should be wary of in this area is the adoption of a mechanistic approach to development, seeing the whole process as simply comparing a child to where he or she should be on a chart. As this chapter should have made perfectly clear, the whole subject matter is far too complex to allow for such a reductionist approach. Understanding developmental milestones can play an important part in the crucial role of assessment, but we should be clear that it is only one part of a much broader and more complex process of understanding children, young people, their rights, needs and circumstances.

A3 Plan, implement and review the outcomes of direct work with children and young people.

Good practice depends on: having a clear plan to work to; making sure that our actions are consistent with that plan; and regularly reviewing it to make sure that it is still appropriate (we shall explore these issues in more depth in Chapter 2).

In this chapter the idea of systematic practice has been introduced. This is a very useful way of staying focused so that this practice requirement can more easily be met. Assessment and planning will feature more fully in Chapter 2, but it is important to stress here that the process of intervention needs to be carefully handled so that drift and a lack of focus on desired outcomes do not allow the efforts of all involved to be misguided or undermined.

Another important theme of this chapter that relates to this requirement is the importance of evidence-based practice. Are we drawing on the insights of current research in planning our work? Are we clear about the outcomes we are looking for so that our work can be evaluated? These are important questions to address and we shall return to them below, in Chapter 2 when we look at the social work process and in Chapter 5, when we explore the question of continuous professional development.

4. Conclusion

Childhood and adolescence are, by their very nature, times of change, growth and development. It should therefore be quite clear that, in working with children and young people, we need a good grounding in matters relating to such development. To undertake such work without appreciating the significance of developmental issues is to engage in a dangerous form of practice in which we may be acting in highly inappropriate ways, given the development of the particular child or young person we are working with at any given time. The discussions in this chapter should have borne more than ample witness to this argument. In working with people we are working with a 'moving target', in the sense that people and their circumstances keep changing.

Many of these changes are unique and unpredictable, part of the rich variety and variability of human existence. However, many such changes have a large degree of predictability associated with them. This is because they are linked to one or more aspects of human development, reflecting some of the patterns we have identified in the first part of this chapter – that is, they fall within what we identified as the 'broad spectrum of the norm'. In addition, we can learn a great deal about certain situations when behaviour or other aspects of people's lives fall outside that broad spectrum for whatever reason. This reflects the Freudian view that the structure of a crystal becomes apparent when and where it is broken. That is, by looking at where a certain established pattern has broken down we can learn something about that pattern and what gives it its potency as an aspect of development. Social work with children, young people and their families can therefore tell us a great deal about human development. This is an important part of reflective practice – practice should inform theory, as well as theory informing practice.

While the significance of child and adolescent development is clearly well-established at a general level across the spectrum of social work with children, young people and their families, we can also see that the issues apply in different ways in different settings. For example, in child protection, the emphasis may be on issues like failure to thrive; in terms of substitute care, there is likely to be a broader focus on health, education and so on. Different groups of workers will therefore clearly have differing agendas when it comes to the use of knowledge about child and adolescent development. It none the less remains the case that such knowledge has a key role in helping us appreciate the circumstances children and young people find themselves in and their perception and understanding of those circumstances.

Effective practice with children, young people and their families also clearly relies on being able to 'engage' with the child or young person concerned, to work alongside them in identifying what needs to be done, how it is to be done, over what timescale and so on (assessment) and in actually carrying out the steps necessary (intervention). As we have seen, this is highly skilled work that requires us to have our wits about us and be very clear about what we are doing.

This chapter has now laid important foundations. Next we move forward to build on these foundations by exploring children and young people in the broader context of their families and personal networks. The focus in Chapter 2 is therefore broader than here, but we should remember that the discussions of these broader factors should be seen as an addition to the points raised here rather than as an alternative to them. There is no point entering into the sterile debate of: which is more important, the individual child or his or her family context? The crucial point to emphasise is that it is not a question of either/or, but rather one of looking at how *both* the individual *and* the family context have an essential role to play.

5. Points to ponder

➤ In what ways are you able to take account of child development issues in your practice?

Can you identify links between particular concepts or issues and aspects of your own work?

➤ It is clear that traditional approaches to development have serious flaws, especially when we consider them in the light of anti-discriminatory practice. How might you reconcile or at least handle the tension between established wisdom in child and adolescent development and the requirements of a more sociologically oriented and critical approach consistent with anti-discriminatory practice?

➤ Partnership is clearly a major part of good practice. Which aspects of partnership-based working do you feel comfortable with and which aspects do you feel you need to develop further?

➤ Systematic practice involves keeping a clear focus on what we are doing and why. What aspects of your current work situation help in this regard, and what aspects may make this more difficult?

➤ This chapter has presented a wide range of concepts and issues. What steps can you take to incorporate these into your practice in order to make reflective practice a reality?

6. Learning resources guide

A clear overview of Freud's work is presented in Stevens (1983). Erikson (1977) is a classic text which is worth consulting, although the criticisms outlined above should be borne in mind. There are a number of useful texts available that provide a good introduction to child development. See, for example: Barnes (1995); Davenport (1994); and Oates (1994).

Howe (1995) and Howe *et al.* (1999) both provide useful discussions of attachment theory and its relevance for social work, with the latter having a strong practice focus.

Daniel *et al.* (1999) is a text that provides a thorough overview of child development issues, which also has a strong focus on attachment theory. Wheal (1998) is a helpful, practice-focused introduction to adolescence. The work of Piaget is addressed in Piaget and Inhelder (1966) and Durkin (1995).

Corr *et al.* (1996) provide a clear, thorough and helpful introduction to the various issues relating to death, dying and bereavement. Smith and Pennells (1995) cover such issues from the point of view of working with children and young people. Thompson (2002b) is an edited collection of readings about loss and grief issues, covering not only death-related losses but also those that apply more broadly.

Stress and related issues are covered in Thompson *et al.* (1994a), Thompson *et al.* (1996) and Thompson (1999).

Working in partnership is discussed in DoH/SSI (1995b) and Jackson and Kilroe (1996). Harrison *et al.* (2002) provide a useful guide to partnership working at the agency or organisational level, but with implications also for the face-to-face level.

The case for listening to children and understanding their perspective is very well made in Thomas (2001) and more fully developed in Thomas (2000) and Ruegger (2001).

Risk assessment and risk management are explored in some depth in Parsloe (1998), Parton *et al.* (1997), Kemshall and Pritchard (1995) and Kemshall and Pritchard (1997). See also Thompson and Thompson (2002) Chapter 4.

Research-based practice is discussed in Everitt *et al.* (1992), Thompson (2000a) and Sheldon and Chilvers (2000). The importance of research specifically relating to work with children and young people is well-covered in Alderson (1995), while Schaffer (1998) provides useful summaries of research relating to decision-making in child care, with some discussion of the implications for practice.

2. Working with families

1. Introduction

While the emphasis in Chapter 1 was on understanding the developmental issues relating to individual children and young people and the importance of developing effective partnerships, this chapter has a parallel but wider emphasis. The focus here is not on the individual as an individual, but rather as part of a family and carer network. We shall therefore explore and examine a range of key issues in relation to that network – for example, by developing our understanding of families and family life.

We shall follow a similar pattern to Chapter 1 by first exploring key aspects of the professional knowledge base underpinning this area of practice. This is, of course, a very large knowledge base, and so once again what is presented here is necessarily selective. We focus on what I regard as some of the key issues, but what counts as a key issue is, of course, a contested matter – others are likely to have different views. Once again you are encouraged to approach the materials critically and reflectively.

We then move on to look at the tasks and challenges that face us in working with families. This leads us into the conclusion, the 'points to ponder' and, of course, the learning resources guide for this chapter.

2. The knowledge base

The knowledge base of working with families for better outcomes, it has to be acknowledged, is a huge one. It is therefore clear that we cannot realistically expect to cover it all in this chapter – our aims must be far more modest. In order to provide an overview of the range of issues involved, I shall present the materials in six sections.

The first relates to the family and explores the complexities surrounding this deceptive term.

Here we consider the dangers of adopting an uncritical, reductionist approach to the family as a social institution and the basis of so much social work practice.

In the second section, we discuss the social work process, looking at the sequence of events that characterises social work with children, young people and their families. The discussion here fits very closely with our theme of systematic practice, with its emphasis on being clear about what we are doing and why we are doing it.

The third section explores the crucially important topic of planning and relates this to our theme of reflective practice. It is argued that effective planning is a highly skilled activity and one that is central to good practice.

The fourth section revisits our theme of partnership, as discussed in Chapter 1, but this time with a wider focus on working in partnership with parents, carers and other family members. While this has much in common with working in partnership with children and young people, there are also significant differences.

The fifth section explores the fundamental concept of parenting. Here we take a critical look at an aspect of child care social work that often goes unexamined, despite the dangers of an uncritical approach to parenting being seriously at odds with the value base of anti-discriminatory practice.

The sixth section addresses the important issue of rights. The rights of individuals can come into conflict within families, and so it is important to explore this complex area.

The family

The term, 'family' is one that is regularly used in social work practice, theory, policy and law, although it is often used in a vague and ambiguous way, with little clarity about what we mean by the term or why it is deemed to be so important. Our task here, then, is to explore some of the complexities surrounding this concept so that we can appreciate the dangers of adopting an oversimplified view which falls into the trap of reductionism.

The first point to emphasise about the family is its diversity. We use the term in a variety of ways. It may refer to a person's immediate family (as, for example, when a woman may speak of her husband and their children) or to our family of origin ('My family is very different from my husband's'). It may also be used to refer to children. For example, in response to the question: 'Do you have family?' may come the reply: 'No, but we are trying for a child'.

The form families take is also quite diverse. Although we tend to think in terms of the dominance of the nuclear family, there are, of course, very many other family forms: childless couples, lone parents, single-person households, gay and lesbian couples. We should therefore be very wary of thinking in terms of *the* family, as if only one form of family exists (or should exist). As Muncie and Langan (1997) comment, the family:

> . . . is not a simple concept whose meaning can be taken for granted. There are families, and certainly most of us experience or have experienced some form of family life, but it is impossible to find a model of 'the family' which is universally accepted. Many people have living arrangements which simply do not fit with dominant models. (p. 1)

Similarly, it is important to note that different cultures have different 'patterns of kinship', which means that there are different rules about what constitutes a relative or family member and how important different family relationships may be. We should be wary of imposing our own idea of what is a family or family network on people whose background is different from our own.

Dallos and Sapsford (1997) make the important point that:

> . . . when we speak of 'the family' we are in reality describing not an object but a process – a social grouping which at any time has a predictable history and a predictable future. The norm to which we refer when we speak of 'the family' progresses from unattached

> young people of opposite genders (themselves emerging from families) via courtship and couple-formation to marriage, the conception, birth and raising of children, the years together after the children have left home, to (probably) years of living alone after the death of one partner. (pp. 136–7)

What this passage indicates is that families follow 'life courses' in similar ways to individuals, as discussed in Chapter 1. We can see how this works in relation to income and vulnerability to poverty. A family in their early stages of formation may have two incomes and no dependants, and may therefore be relatively comfortable in financial terms. A few years later, they may have only one income and one or more children to support. In this situation, their vulnerability to poverty is likely to be far higher. This 'up and down' pattern of income and expenditure is a common one and is closely associated with the 'family life course'.

Other families, however, may be very different from this general trend. For example, the parents of a child with disabilities may find that the costs of caring are much higher than for other families – higher both financially and in other terms – and may last well into adulthood when other children have grown up and left home to establish an independent lifestyle. The idea of a family life course can therefore be seen as a useful one for helping to make sense of family life and where individual families are up to. However, it is also clearly a notion that needs to be used flexibly to take account of varying patterns of family patterns and experiences, so that it is not used oppressively to squeeze certain families into predefined norms.

Exercise 2.1

Think of three families that you are currently working with. Where would you place each of these in terms of a 'family life course'? Are there any patterns or similarities across the three? Are there any clear links between the life course point they are at and the problems they are encountering?

A further important aspect of the family is the need to recognise the importance of what has come to be known as 'disaggregation'. This refers to an understanding of the family as an institution which has different consequences for different members. It is a concept that helps us guard against seeing a family as a unified whole, an entity in its own right. It helps us appreciate that, while life in a particular family may be beneficial for some members, it may be very harmful and destructive for others. Consider, for example, the phenomenon of secondary poverty. This refers to families where the overall income is more than adequate for the family's needs, but where poverty is none the less experienced by some members of that family. An example of this might be a man who earns a high salary but who uses a disproportionate amount of it on his own needs or interests (drinking or gambling, perhaps). We should therefore be wary of falling into the trap of reification – regarding the family as a distinct unit, with standard interests across the board, as this can mask major problems for the less powerful members of a particular family (and thus render our practice incompatible with anti-discriminatory practice).

We also have to be wary of adopting too idealistic a picture of the family as a social institution. while it clearly has benefits for the people within families and for society at large, we should not forget that the families can also be oppressive. This is an important point and one to which we shall return below.

In addition, we should note that the family helps to 'locate' us in society – it slots us into the wider social system. For example, Barrett and McIntosh (1991) comment on the relationship between the family and the class structure of society:

Almost all of us are born and reared in a family. Those who are not raised by their parents in a private household are brought up in institutions that seek to imitate family life as faithfully as possible. What could be more classless than this universal experience? What could be less divisive? In reality, far from being a social leveller, forging bonds that cut across the barriers of class and sex, the family creates and recreates the very divisions it is often thought to ameliorate. (p. 43)

What is called for, then, is a balanced view of the family, one which recognises its strengths and positive contribution, while also acknowledging its drawbacks and problems.

Families are very powerful influences on behaviour. Indeed, we can see that much of our behaviour has its roots in our family patterns and 'rules'. How we see the world owes much to how our family (particularly our family of origin) sees the world – the family provides a rich seam for the meanings we construct as we make sense of the complexities of the social world around us. In this regard, Dallos (1997) writes of 'family myths':

The function of family myths is to preserve the family stability or homeostasis, to avoid the possibilities of disruption or disintegration of the family or relationships within it. It represents a response to real or perceived threats to the family. A family myth can be seen to represent to the family what a defence mechanism is to the individual. (p. 204)

While I have some difficulty in accepting the use of the word 'function', as it implies a pre-existing intention on someone's part (see the discussion of teleology in Thompson, 2000a), this is an important passage, as it highlights the way families can develop their own unwritten rules (a family culture, in effect) which can have a very powerful influence on family members and indeed on others who come into contact with the family concerned (including social workers).

Families also have rituals – established, tried and tested ways of dealing with certain situations, such as transitions. Rituals are institutionalised ways of dealing with situations in relatively standardised ways. Their strength is that they can give a great deal of succour and support at a difficult time (for example, a bereavement), but their weakness is that they can sometimes inhibit necessary change by placing people under considerable pressure to behave in particular ways.

Rituals differ from family to family, and of course from culture to culture. Lau (1996) comments on the significance of rituals in families:

I have found it extremely useful to inquire about the levels of ethnic minority families. Family rituals provide support, continuity with

family, cultural and religious tradition, and affirm membership for participants . . . Family rituals, whether religious or secular, provide opportunities for family members to meet on a regular basis and to communicate. The pattern and regularity is important. Do the family eat together, watch TV together, go out together? Is there a central family dinner time, are there holiday celebration rituals? Has the impact of immigration on the loss of supportive networks led to a loss of cultural rituals, for example celebration of Chinese New Year? All these factors may have a bearing on the meaning and significance to the family of the problem that has precipitated the crisis leading to referral.
(pp. 166–7)

Exercise 2.2

Think of a family you have worked quite closely with. Can you identify some of the myths or rituals within that family, some of the beliefs, assumptions and/or standardised patterns of behaviour that helped shape family life and the actions of family members? How might these have played a part in the problems encountered and your responses to them?

The final point to consider in relation to the family is the danger of pathologising black families. This is a tendency that has been identified by a number of commentators. For example, Robinson (1995, p. 65) quotes Billingsley (1968, pp. 15–22):

There are four tendencies in the treatment of black families in social science scholarship. The first is the tendency to ignore black families altogether. The second is, when black families are considered to focus almost exclusively on the lowest-income group of black families . . . The third is to ignore the majority of black stable families even among this lowest income group . . . and to focus instead on the most unstable among these low income families. A fourth tendency, which is more bizarre than all the others, is the tendency on the part of social scientists to view the black, low income, unstable problem-ridden family as the causal nexus for the difficulties their members experience in wider society.

This passage warns us of the dangers of adopting a stereotypical view of black families, making the mistake of regarding *different* family forms as *deficient* family forms. If we are not careful, we can allow subtle forms of racism to creep into our practice by making unwarranted assumptions about black families. Interestingly, we can also apply this point to the question of working with, for example, Welsh families, particularly Welsh-speaking families: what assumptions might commonly be made about such families, how accurate are they, and how damaging might they be if shown to be inaccurate? These are important questions for us to take into account in our work with families.

The social work process

Having explored some important issues that cast light on the complexity of the concept of the family, it is now time to 'ground' such issues in the practice context. We are going to achieve that by exploring the social work process – the steps we go through (or at least *should* go through) in order to respond systematically to the problems and unmet needs we encounter.

There are a number of versions of what is known as the social work process. The National Occupational Standards for the PQ Award in Child Care (TOPSS, 2000) describe the process in terms of the following stages:

- *assess;*
- *plan;*
- *implement;*
- *review; and*
- *record.*

An alternative approach is to be found in the work of Howe (1987) who describes a five-stage process as follows:

1. *Identification of **problem** or **need**: 'What is the matter?'*
2. ***Assessment** or **analysis** of people and their situations: 'What is going on?'*
3. *Statement of **goals**, plans and intentions: 'What is to be done?'*
4. *The **methods** by which the goals are to be achieved and the problem solved or need met: 'How is it to be done?'*
5. *Periodic **review** and **evaluation** of problem,*

assessment, goals and methods: 'Has it been done?' (p. 7)

Another five-stage process is presented in Thompson (2002a). While this has much in common with Howe's schema, there are also significant differences. For example, Howe's version does not include ending or 'termination' – the significant processes involved in bringing a piece of work to a satisfactory conclusion.

Ending our involvement raises a number of questions and has significant implications for service users in terms of empowerment (as opposed to dependency creation) and for workers in terms of workload management. Ending is discussed in more detail in Thompson (2002a, Chapter 23).

The five stages of the Thompson (2002a) model can be summarised as follows:

1. *Assessment*	This initial stage of the process involves developing a picture of what the problems are, what unmet needs are present, what strengths and resources are available to draw upon and so on. It can be characterised by the following questions: What is the context in terms of race, gender and so on? What are the problems/unmet needs? What strengths/opportunities can be drawn upon? Where are we trying to get to? What steps do we need to take to get there?
2. *Intervention*	This stage involves acting on the assessment, using various methods of intervention to work towards the identified objectives. This also involves drawing on appropriate resources from various quarters, including services provided by statutory, voluntary or even private organisations. The aim, of course, is to attempt to meet the needs identified and/or solve the problems that have come to our attention.
3. *Review*	From time to time it is necessary to review the situation. This involves looking at: Has the situation changed or developed in any significant ways? Was the initial assessment correct, accurate and appropriate in the circumstances?
4. *Ending*	All intervention has to come to an end sooner or later. We should not allow situations to drift and/or allow ourselves to remain involved in situations after we have reached the point where ending involvement would be more appropriate. This involves considering: Is it safe and appropriate to end our involvement yet? How best can we do this to make sure progress is not undermined?
5. *Evaluation*	Evaluation is very much a neglected aspect of social work. Sadly, many people dismiss evaluation with comments to the effect that they do not have time to do it. This problem is based on two misconceptions: i) that evaluation has to be formal, detailed and therefore time-consuming – there are various methods of evaluating work and the process does not have to be a very time-consuming one; and ii) that time devoted to evaluation will not pay for itself. This view fails to recognise just how much time, energy, frustration (and thus morale and motivation) can be saved by taking the trouble to evaluate and thus learn from our experience. Evaluation involves asking: What did I/we do well that can be built on in future? What could have been done better or more effectively? Overall, what lessons can be learned from the work undertaken?

The ending model (Thompson, 2002a)

Exercise 2.3

Think of a piece of work that you have been involved with recently. Try to match the five stages identified above to what has actually happened in the case in question and what you envisage happening in the future. Can you fit the case and the model together to a certain extent at least?

There are (at least) two important points to note in relation to this five-stage process. First, it underlines the importance of assessment. This is because assessment:

- Sets the scene for everything that is to come later. Errors or too superficial an approach at the assessment stage can seriously undermine the quality, value, effectiveness or appropriateness of what comes later.
- Gives us the framework for planning our intervention. What approach to adopt, what steps to take, what pitfalls to avoid can all be indicated by our initial assessment and so on.
- Provides the platform for review. A common mistake is for reviews to concentrate on the present situation, as if starting from scratch without revisiting the initial assessment to establish whether it is still valid and, if it is not, what the revised assessment should be.
- Sets the parameters for decision-making in relation to ending our involvement. That is, decisions about ending our intervention should be made by reference to the initial assessment (and any subsequent revisions to it). Intervention is often terminated because we have achieved the goals we set out to or have decided that they are not really achievable (or are no longer desirable). This is therefore based on our assessment.
- Gives us a framework for evaluation. For example, when we want to know whether or not our involvement was effective in achieving our agreed aims, then we need to be clear what those aims were – again, a reference to the assessment.

Clearly, assessment is a major issue and so we shall return to this subject below.

Second, it alerts us to the fact that our work can go awry at any of the five stages, as the following examples should illustrate:

- *Assessment.* This can be missed out altogether (by trying to find a solution without first working out clearly what the problem is – see below) or can be done very skimpily, perhaps missing out key aspects of the situation or relying on stereotypes or untested assumptions.
- *Intervention.* A common mistake is for actions taken at the intervention stage not to be consistent with the assessment. Even a high-quality, clear, focused assessment can be of very limited value if the subsequent steps taken do not help to achieve the objectives identified.
- *Review.* There are two main ways in which the review stage can be problematic. The first is through its absence. That is, problems can arise because a review does not take place. For example, a significant change occurring two months before a statutory review taking place may necessitate reviewing the situation well in advance of that formal process. It has to be remembered that statutory or other reviews are only one form of review – review is a *professional* process, rather than just a bureaucratic one. The second area of difficulty with reviews is when, as mentioned above, they do not revisit the assessment. For example, one review I had the misfortune of attending simply considered the current situation relating to the child concerned, with no reference back to an assessment or care plan and no consideration of the future in terms of forward planning – it was a review in name only.
- *Ending.* Sometimes a lack of focus can lead to cases continuing to remain open when either what was intended to be achieved has been achieved or it is apparent that it is not going to be possible to achieve it or it was never clear in the first place what the intervention was intended to achieve. Alternatively, cases may be closed when it is not appropriate to do so, perhaps due to pressure of work from other cases or because a key part of the situation has not been taken into consideration. For example, I once came across a case which had been closed by an (unqualified) worker, even though a court order was still in force in relation to the two children concerned.
- *Evaluation.* The two most likely problems here are: First, there is a tendency in many

quarters to omit evaluation altogether, to regard it as a luxury that busy staff cannot afford (rather than an important tool that busy staff cannot afford to do without). Second, we can also detect a tendency to be unduly negative – that is, to focus only on what can be learned from mistakes made, without also addressing the very important learning that can be drawn from looking at what we did *right* (not to mention the morale and job satisfaction to be gained from identifying the positives and successes).

Of course, it should also be acknowledged that practice can go awry by not having any sense of process at all, by simply entering a state of drift and confusion. Sadly, such a tendency to drift is a characteristic of being busy, a common danger faced by people who are under a lot of work pressure:

Motivation can be lost when we 'lose the plot', when we lose track of what we are doing and why we are doing it. Ironically, it seems that it is when we are under time pressures that we are more likely to slide into this unfocused 'drift' in which we have lost sight of what we are working towards. (Thompson, 1999, p. 81)

Finally, in relation to the social work process, we should note that it is an *iterative* process. That is, it is not simply a mechanical process. It can 'loop back' at various points. For example, although assessment begins the process, it is a point that can be returned to later (typically at the point of review). The process should therefore be used flexibly as part of reflective practice, rather than as a rigid formula to be followed in an unthinking, regimented way.

Assessment

It should be clear from the discussion above that assessment can be seen as a crucial underpinning to all the other stages in the social work process. It is for this reason that we are now going to explore it in more detail.

It has to be recognised that assessment is a complex and highly skilled activity. It is also a risky activity, in so far as mistakes in our assessment can prove very costly, and yet it is clearly more of an art than a science. It is therefore important that we learn from our experience and continue to develop our knowledge and skills in this complex area. Clearly, a *reflective* approach is called for in which we can draw on the extensive knowledge base around assessment issues and 'cut our cloth' to suit the circumstances we face.

Indeed, there are dangers in not adopting a reflective approach. Milner and O'Byrne (1998) make the point that it is dangerous for social workers simply to seek to confirm their initial hypothesis of the situation rather than deepen their assessment:

Social workers almost invariably seek to confirm their original hypotheses (see, for example, Sinclair et al., 1995; and Milner, 1996b). This poor practice can sustain prejudice and make anti-oppressive practice rather difficult to achieve. (p. 26)

While the idea of assessment as a precise science is clearly idealistic, we should be very wary of falling into the trap of allowing assessment to become simply a process of confirming our original perceptions, rather than the more critical and reflective process of developing a deeper understanding of the situation. Remaining open to new ideas and perspectives can therefore be identified as an important assessment skill.

Exercise 2.4

How do you approach assessment? Do you have any particular strategies or 'tricks of the trade' that you use? Are there any aspects of assessment work that you feel uncomfortable with? How might you develop your skills in assessment?

The other skills involved include:

- *Information gathering* An important factor in gathering the information is getting the balance right. Too little information can be very problematic if this leads to significant issues being missed. On the other hand, too much information can not only be a waste of time and effort for all concerned, it can also confuse the issue by leading to information overload – and may even amount to a breach of civil liberties if information is gathered unnecessarily. A key question to be asked here, then, is: How do we decide what is the appropriate amount of information?

- *Communication and listening* It perhaps goes without saying that we cannot carry out an effective assessment without communicating clearly and appropriately. Indeed, patterns of interpersonal interaction can be seen as a basic element of the process of assessment – a 'mechanical' gathering of information is clearly doomed to failure. Active listening is, of course, part and parcel of effective communication, a central part of 'making the connection' needed for good practice.
- *Analysis* Assessment is more than simply gathering information. It also involves making sense of it, building up a picture of the situation, fitting together the pieces of the jigsaw, as it were. This entails using analytical skills – being able to recognise patterns and interconnections. This is an important process, as it is often the analysis that adds the extra dimension – that is, the elements of the situation on their own may tell us very little, but an analysis of those elements may give us a picture that we may otherwise not have recognised.
- *Creativity* A further important element of assessment is the ability to identify possible ways forward, to explore options for resolving problems, meeting needs, removing barriers and so on. A clear danger here is that of relying on formula responses, taking a narrow, unimaginative approach to dealing with the situation. A great irony here is that it is often when people are very busy that they find it difficult to relax and think creatively about possible ways forward – and yet, without a creative approach, it is likely that a lot of time and effort will be wasted on unimaginative, 'tramlines' approaches which will tend to be far less effective than alternative approaches would have been.
- *Partnership* Of course, the success or otherwise of assessment will owe much to the social worker's ability to work in partnership. If clients do not feel comfortable and suitably involved in the process, then it is unlikely that they will participate as fully as they might otherwise have done, thereby undermining the quality of the assessment and placing barriers in the way of progress. We shall return below to this important theme of working in partnership.

Clearly, then, assessment is not a straightforward process, as it involves so many demands upon us. In view of this, it is understandable that mistakes in this area of practice are not uncommon. I shall therefore explore some of the ways in which assessment can 'go wrong'.

First, Howe (1995) makes the important point that:

There is a tendency in the practice of many professionals to jump from problem to solution, without pausing to wonder what is actually going on. A failure to reflect on seemingly familiar situations leads to routine responses; professional habits whose origins have become obscured with time. (p. 188)

On paper, this may look a simple problem to avoid, but, of course, in the highly pressurised context of actual practice, it is an easy trap to fall into. This is sometimes brought about by pressure from others. Parents and even other professionals can often expect quick solutions and lead us down the path of 'skimping' on the assessment. It is therefore important that we are able to resist such pressures (and perhaps pressure from ourselves to make a positive difference quickly) so that we can give the assessment the attention it deserves without jumping to premature conclusions about what needs to be done.

Another potential pitfall to be very wary of is that of relying on assumptions and stereotypes. Again, on paper, this may seem fairly self-evident and an easy problem to avoid. However, we have to recognise that assumptions and stereotypes can be deeply ingrained and we often do not realise that they are operating until someone or something leads to our becoming aware of them. This is especially the case in pressurised circumstances where we are not likely to have the time to think things through as fully as we would like.

This raises important questions in relation to reflective practice. As noted in the Introduction, reflective practice can be very helpful in making sure that we do not go down the tramlines of routinised practice and rely on potentially discriminatory assumptions. It is therefore very important that we find ways of developing reflective practice (see Exercise 2.5 below).

Partnership is a topic that we shall explore in some depth below, but it is also relevant here in relation to assessment. This is because an important part of assessment is the significant role of 'seeing it their way' – understanding the perspective of all the people involved, and not simply imposing our own view of the situation. This links in with our phenomenological theme, with its emphasis on perception and making sense of the situations we find ourselves in. In view of this, assessment work needs to take account of the perspectives of the various 'stakeholders' involved, bearing in mind that how we act depends on how we perceive the situation we are in, on what sense we make of it. This is a skilled activity, and therefore one that merits further attention below.

In Chapter 1, the dangers of a service-led assessment were explored and the point was made that assessment should be needs-led. There is little point repeating that discussion here, but it is worth emphasising the importance of ensuring that our assessment practice focuses on needs, problems and strengths, and not simply on available services.

Finally, in terms of assessment pitfalls, we should be wary of the danger of losing a focus on the family. This can easily happen for a number of reasons:

- Focusing on the problem: This is no bad thing in its own right but can distract attention from the family context. For example, child abuse is a major issue worthy of significant attention, but it should not be forgotten that abuse is an issue for the whole family, as well as the child or young person concerned.
- Focusing on the child or young person: Again, this is not a bad thing in its own right, but needs to be seen alongside the wider family context. We have to be wary of allowing too narrow a focus on the individual to mask wider issues that are likely to have a significant bearing on the situation.
- Focusing on our own survival: Defensive practice is a form of dangerous practice (Thompson and Bates, 1998). That is, by concentrating on not getting ourselves into trouble we can, ironically, increase the

chances of things going wrong and landing us in serious hot water. We therefore have to make sure that defensiveness does not prevent us from maintaining a clear focus on the family.

It is important to emphasise that the need to maintain a focus on the family is not based on a notion that the family is more important than the child or young person, or the problems being dealt with, but rather that it is an *essential* part of the equation, a fundamental part of the child or young person's reality – as well as being a major focus of law and policy.

Exercise 2.5
The importance of reflective practice has already been emphasised. However, pressures of work can mean that it is difficult to apply the principles of reflective practice to assessment. The task in this exercise, then, is to identify ways in which opportunities for reflection can be created. What steps can we take to ensure that our assessment work is reflective, rather than rushed?

A further important aspect of assessment that is worthy of closer examination is the introduction of the assessment framework in relation to children in need (DoH *et al.*, 2000). This framework introduces a number of important developments in assessment practice, not least the following:

- *Timescales* It is expected that the following timescales should be adhered to:
  1. Where there is a new referral or new information concerning an open case, a decision as to what response is required must be made within one working day. The decision may well be that no response is required, but that decision should none the less be made promptly. In all cases, the relevant parties should be informed of the decision and the reason for it.
  2. Where it is decided to undertake an initial assessment, this should be completed within a maximum of seven working days.
  3. Where an in-depth assessment is deemed to be necessary, this should be completed within 35 working days.
- *Levels of assessment* A distinction is drawn between a brief *initial* assessment (which is all

that will be needed in many cases) and a more in-depth *core* assessment (where the nature of the case and/or the degree of risk warrants this).

- *Assessment records* Initial assessment record sheets and core assessment records should be used in the appropriate respective circumstances. The latter is consistent with the developmental framework used in the LAC Assessment and Action Records (see Chapter 1).

This approach provides a good foundation for working in partnership. This is because:

- There is clarity about expectations, particularly in relation to timescales.
- Where a decision is made at the initial assessment stage, this decision and the rationale behind it must be communicated to the parents and, where appropriate, the child or young person.
- Where a decision is made as a result of a core assessment, this too must be communicated to the parents and possibly the child or young person also. In both cases, initial and core assessment, the family have the opportunity to record their views and/or ask for corrections to recorded information.

The framework comprises three interrelated elements or dimensions: the child's developmental needs, parenting capacity and family and environmental factors. These are broken down into their component parts as follows:

The child's developmental needs

- Health;
- Education;
- Emotional and behavioural development;
- Identity;
- Family and social relationships;
- Social presentation; and
- Self-care skills.

Parenting capacity

- Basic care;
- Ensuring safety;
- Emotional warmth;
- Stimulation;
- Guidance and boundaries; and
- Stability.

Family and environmental problems

- Family history and functioning;
- Wider family;
- Housing;
- Employment;
- Income;
- Family's social integration; and
- Community resources.

The point was made in Chapter 1 that the LAC approach is a helpful starting point as a basis for reflective practice, but is no substitute for reflection. The same argument can be applied here. The Framework for the Assessment of Children in Need is, in some respects, a development of the LAC approach, and is premised on the same assumptions. For example, it takes account of 'environmental' factors and is therefore an improvement on individualistic approaches which have too narrow a focus. However, it can be argued that the environment, as presented in the framework, does not pay adequate attention to structural factors and their influences on families and individuals.

What is needed, then, is a *professional* approach – that is, one which takes account of the guidelines provided (and the benefits of structure, clarity and focus that they offer), but does not treat them as mechanical procedures to be followed uncritically. As the Government guidance makes clear (DoH *et al.*, 2000), the mistake made by many practitioners in using the 'Orange Book' in a mechanistic way should be avoided:

This Guidance builds on and supersedes earlier Department of Health guidance on assessing children, Protecting Children: A Guide for Social Workers undertaking a Comprehensive Assessment *(1988). That publication (often referred to as the 'Orange Book') has been widely used by social work practitioners as a guide to comprehensive assessment for long term planning in child protection cases. . . . However, over the years, concerns have arisen about the use made of* Protecting Children. *Inspections and research have shown that the guide was sometimes followed mechanistically and used as a check list, without any differentiation according to the child's or family's circumstances.* (pp. xi–xii)

Planning

The point was made earlier that the National Occupational Standards for the PQ Award in Child Care present planning as a stage in the social work process. The approach being presented here differs from this in so far as it holds planning to be a feature of all stages of the process, rather than a stage within it. Part of assessment is the development of a plan of action in terms of what needs to be done to meet the needs identified, tackle the problems and build on the strengths present in the situation. The intervention stage also contains an element of planning in so far as the steps taken should be based on a clear plan of action, working towards future goals and desired outcomes (thus helping to avoid drift, and thereby illustrating once again our theme of systematic practice). The review stage involves revisiting the assessment and therefore considering whether plans need to be amended, extended or abandoned. Termination occurs when plans have either been realised or have been deemed to be unachievable or no longer applicable. And, finally, evaluation involves planning our future actions in the light of lessons learned from the piece of work in question.

Planning has long been recognised by professionals within the field as a fundamental part of good practice in working with children, young people and their families. This is for a variety of reasons, not least the following:

- Children grow and develop, and so we need to anticipate changes and developments so that we are as prepared for them as we can be.
- There is often a number of people involved, and so planning becomes necessary to co-ordinate the roles and contributions of the various parties.
- Planning prevents drift and a lack of focus.
- The structure and focus of effective planning can help create a sense of security, and thus play a part in stabilising an unsettled situation.
- The sense of control and order provided by high-quality planning can help to dispel feelings of helplessness that can contribute to the experience of stress.

One very important aspect of the topic of planning is a recognition of the need to ensure that such planning is partnership-based – that is, based on an approach that goes beyond the medical model of 'the expert knows best'. Reasons for this include:

1. Other 'stakeholders' in the situation have a lot to contribute in order to make sure that plans are based on a sound grasp of the realities of the situation and are actually workable.
2. All involved in the situation have to accept a degree of ownership for the plans and their implementation if the potential for positive change is to be maximised.

The discussion below relating to partnership skills is therefore very relevant to the topic of planning.

In Chapter 1 considerable emphasis was given to child and adolescent development. This is again significant in relation to planning, as it is important that our plans take into account the development and understanding of children and young people to ensure that they are appropriate and realistic. Planning therefore needs to relate to the life course in order to be consistent with the developmental capabilities of the child or young person concerned.

And, of course, children and young people continue to grow and develop and so plans have to take account of their changing circumstances. That is, plans for children and young people cannot be static because their lives are not static. This reinforces the point made in Chapter 1 that it is important for social workers to have a good working knowledge of at least the basics of child and adolescent development. This is not so that we can apply it in a direct or mechanistic way (what Schön, 1983, would call 'technical rationality'), but rather, so that we can draw upon it in a reflective way to guide our decision-making and thus our actions.

Exercise 2.6

What links can you draw between the discussions of child and adolescent development in Chapter 1 and the planning process? Can you think of examples from your own work of where a knowledge of development was necessary to make appropriate plans?

Planning involves adopting a *strategic* approach – that is, one which identifies the objectives we wish to achieve (or 'targets') and the particular methods (or 'strategies') we can draw upon to achieve them. As Egan (1994) comments:

Strategy is the art of identifying and choosing realistic courses of action for achieving goals – and doing so under adverse conditions, such as war. The problem situations in which clients are immersed constitute adverse conditions; clients often are at war with themselves and the world around them. Helping clients develop strategies to achieve goals can be a most thoughtful, humane, and fruitful way of being with them. (p. 278)

The strategic aspect of planning is therefore clearly closely aligned with systematic practice, with both sharing an emphasis on being clear about what we are trying to achieve and how we hope to achieve it. It is through attempting to achieve such clarity that we are able to develop a vision of where we hope to go in our work with families.

A focus on the future is clearly a major feature of planning as a social work activity. Indeed, anticipating the future as far as possible is very much part of the planning process, but, where possible, we should go a step beyond this by actually *shaping* the future:

Forewarned is forearmed is a well-known saying – and, of course, one that makes a lot of sense. If we are aware that something is likely to happen, we can prepare for it, or even try to prevent it from happening. Anticipating the future is therefore an important part of good practice. A less well-known saying but a none the less important one deriving from management education and training is that: 'A competent manager anticipates the future, but an excellent manager shapes the future'. We can adapt this saying from its management context to a social care one, as we would argue that high standards of practice in working with people in a social care context also involves shaping the future – having a constructive influence on what happens and working towards positive outcomes. (Thompson and Thompson, 2002, p. 106)

In many ways, this is what happens as part of everyday practice without any deliberate effort to do so. Our actions play a part in shaping the future context for children, young people and their families – a reflection of the power that accompanies the social work role. However, given this power and the potential for its misuse, there are clear dangers in influencing other people's lives and their futures in an unplanned, unfocused way. An unplanned approach is therefore potentially an oppressive approach. It is not only *bad* practice, but also *dangerous* practice. An approach to practice which is firmly rooted in a clear process of planning is therefore called for:

In effect, this is the essence of planning – being able to use our understanding, skills and experience to anticipate the future as realistically as we can in order to help shape what happens. This can be an extremely important factor in helping to empower clients (that is, to give them greater control over their lives). This is because the positive actions and attitudes of the worker towards the future can be a significant source of motivation, reassurance and support for the client who, as a result of past negative experiences, may feel less than positive about what the future holds or what can be achieved. Our ability to work positively towards shaping the future can therefore be significant in generating confidence and a commitment to change. The lesson we can learn from this, then, is: Our task is not only to anticipate the future but also to shape it – to play an active part in bringing about positive outcomes. (Thompson and Thompson, 2002, p. 106)

A strong, clear focus on planning can be seen as an important part of empowerment – helping people gain greater control over their lives. In order to maximise the potential for empowerment, it is necessary to ensure that planning takes place in the context of partnership – to ensure that all 'stakeholders' play an active part in the process. We shall therefore focus in more detail on the role of partnership in working with families.

However, before turning to the topic of partnership, there are two further points about planning that need to be emphasised. First, comments often made in relation to planning go along the lines of: 'I haven't got time for planning – I'm far too busy dealing with the here and now'. Of course, this is an understandable comment in the context of highly pressurised social work practice. However, this does not make it a valid comment. The flaw in the logic is that it fails to take account of the fact that planning is an *investment* of time, rather than simply a drain on time. Effective planning saves time in the long-run, makes mistakes less likely, strengthens working relationships and thus makes conflicts less likely. It is therefore extremely important that steps are taken to create the space necessary to make planning a central part of everyday practice – an essential, rather than a luxury. See Chapter 5 for a discussion of time and workload management issues.

Second, effective planning involves drawing on what we already know about children and young people, families, loss and separation and so on. That is, planning involves drawing on a professional knowledge base so that we are not necessarily doomed to repeating the errors of the past. High-quality planning can draw upon the extensive knowledge base already available through, for example, published research. As discussed in Chapter 1, the need for evidence-based practice and the use of research is increasingly being recognised. This raises the question of: what do we already know about working with families? There is now a wealth of material available on the subject of outcomes for children and so you are advised to refer to the list of references given in Chapter 1.

Partnership skills

Working with families can be both demanding and rewarding. What can make the work particularly demanding is when families have a negative view of social work intervention, perhaps because of their own previous negative experiences and/or the generally bad press social work tends to attract (Aldridge, 1994). It is therefore important to recognise that working in partnership with families often starts from a weak vantage point and can face major barriers. In view of this, we need to be wary of

the danger of being defeatist, of seeing the major challenge of developing partnership-based practice as an impossible challenge.

Buchanan (2000) demonstrates clearly the difficulties of working in partnership with families when she comments that:

> *Behind the closed door, in the private world of our family, tensions may develop. If the going gets too rough, one of us may break out and leave. The last thing we want is 'help' because now we know we are really 'in the wrong'.*
>
> *So working with parents is like walking on eggs. The challenge is to support parents without fracturing their already fragile confidence. Add poverty, poor housing, racism, and all the other stresses that disadvantaged families face, surviving is hard enough without well-meaning professionals telling parents where they are failing.* (p. 21)

While there are clearly significant demands associated with developing partnership- based approaches, there are also clear rewards in terms of effectiveness. Butler and Roberts (1997) refer to the Department of Health summary of research findings relating to child protection and use this to demonstrate the value parents place on partnership, as the following passage they cite indicates:

> *All family members stressed the importance of being cared about as people. They could understand that the professional has a job to do and that procedures were necessary, but they strongly objected to workers in whatever profession who did not appear to listen, did not show warmth or concern or who only did things by the book.* (DoH, 1995, p. 87, cited in Butler and Roberts, 1997, p. 101)

This is a helpful passage, as it shows clearly that partnership is, or at least should be, a fundamental element of good practice.

An important task for us to achieve here is to establish some clarity about what is involved in good practice in working in partnership. The following are just some of the important elements of working in partnership:

- *Establishing shared goals and shared plans of action*. Working in partnership involves trying to establish agreement about where we want to get to and what steps need to be taken to get us there. This may involve a considerable amount of work in arriving at the point where this sort of agreement is possible. It is none the less important to make the effort to achieve this, as a failure to achieve such agreement is likely to jeopardise the effectiveness of any subsequent interventions. That is, we cannot realistically expect families to work with us if we cannot agree on what the desired outcomes are or what needs to happen to achieve those outcomes.

- *Recognising and building on strengths* The medical model of social work discussed earlier places the social worker in the role of the 'expert' professional. One of the many problems associated with this approach is that it has a tendency to downplay what clients themselves bring to the situation – the strengths and personal resources that they can draw upon. Partnership presents a different perspective, one which emphasises the contribution clients can make to resolving their own difficulties. This emphasis is important as it can have a major effect on boosting confidence and laying the foundations for empowerment.

- *Self-awareness: how do others see us?* The way we present ourselves to other people is, of course, a crucial influence on how they respond to us. If we are to take seriously the challenge of developing partnership, then clearly we have to have at least a basic degree of self-awareness. By developing an awareness of how we come across to people, we place ourselves in a stronger position in terms of developing the necessary working relationships for effective partnership work (see Thompson, 2002a, Chapter 1).

- *Mediation and conflict resolution skills* The ability to work with families effectively will often owe much to our mediation skills – our capacity to help resolve family conflicts by remaining a neutral facilitator. A significant part of this hinges on being able to distinguish between positional and principled negotiation (Fisher and Ury, 1991). Positional negotiation is the traditional approach and involves the 'warring factions' adopting

relatively entrenched positions and resisting having to give ground. This type of conflict resolution is generally accompanied by a lot of ill-feeling and can lead to an escalation of conflict – possibly proving disastrous for trying to settle a very troubled family situation. It is likely to produce a win-lose situation at best, and may in fact lead to a lose-lose situation, with both parties feeling disgruntled with the outcome. Principled negotiation, by contrast, involves looking for the common ground between the parties and seeking a way forward that they can both be happy with. It is a more creative approach, less prone to generating ill-feeling and capable of producing win-win situations. It is therefore an approach that can be helpful in working with families where there are unresolved conflicts.

- *Addressing the emotional dimension* In Chapter 1 we discussed the think-feel-do framework and emphasised the importance of ensuring that all three dimensions are taken into account, including the emotional or 'affective' dimension. Families are complex entities that can and often do generate a great deal of 'emotional heat'. It is therefore important that we are prepared to address these issues – prepared in both senses of the word, both *willing* to tackle complex and sensitive matters and *equipped* to do so in terms of knowledge and skills. This does not mean that all social workers in this field need to be qualified counsellors, but it does mean that we have to have a good understanding of emotional issues and either possess, or be prepared to develop, the skills involved in dealing with such issues sensitively and appropriately.

- *Promoting change: recognising and dealing with obstacles* In trying to work constructively with families, we are, in effect seeking to promote positive change. It would be naive in the extreme to assume that this will be a straightforward, trouble-free process. We have to acknowledge that there will be obstacles to change (for example, resistance brought about by fear of change) and be prepared to deal with these as best we can – removing them, side-stepping them and/or minimising their impact.

Exercise 2.7

Bearing in mind the final point in the above list, think carefully about what obstacles to change you are likely to encounter in working with families. List as many of these obstacles as you can and then try to draw up a list of steps you might be able to take to deal appropriately with such obstacles.

In addition to the 'pointers' for partnership listed above, a list of fifteen essential principles for partnership has been identified by the Department of Health Social Services Inspectorate (DoH/SSI, 1995b). These relate specifically to working in partnership in child protection, although their application is much wider than this:

- *Treat all family members as you would wish to be treated, with dignity and respect*
- *Ensure that family members know that the child's safety and welfare must be given first priority*, but that each of them has a right to courteous, caring and professionally competent service
- *Take care not to infringe privacy* any more than is necessary to safeguard the welfare of the child
- *Be clear with yourself and with family members about your power to intervene*, and the purpose of your professional involvement at each stage
- *Be aware of the effects on family members of the power you have as a professional*, and the impact and implications of what you say and do
- *Respect confidentiality* of family members and your observations about them, unless they give permission for information to be passed to others or it is essential to do so to protect the child
- *Listen to the concerns of the children and their families*, and take care to learn about their understanding, fears and wishes before arriving at your own explanations and plans
- *Learn about and consider children within their family relationships and communities*, including their cultural and religious contexts, and their place within their own families
- *Consider the strengths and potential of family members*, as well as their weaknesses, problems and limitations

- *Ensure that children, families and other carers know their responsibilities and rights*, including the right to services and any consequences of doing so
- *Use plain, jargon-free language appropriate to the age and culture of each person.* Explain unavoidable technical and professional terms
- *Be open and honest about your concerns and responsibilities*, plans and limitations, without being defensive
- *Allow children and families time to take in and understand concerns and processes.* A balance needs to be found between appropriate speed and the needs of people who may need extra time in which to communicate
- *Take care to distinguish between personal feelings, values, beliefs, and professional roles and responsibilities*, and ensure that you have good supervision to check that you are doing so
- *If a mistake or misinterpretation has been made, or you are unable to keep to an agreement, provide an explanation.* Always acknowledge the distress experienced by adults and children and do all you can to keep it to a minimum. (p. 14, emphasis in original)

It is to be hoped that these two sets of guidelines for working in partnership achieve two things:

1. To establish clearly and unequivocally that partnership-based work is complex and demanding – 'working in partnership' is more than a trite, fashionable phrase.
2. To demonstrate that, despite the inherent difficulties, good practice is indeed possible.

The question of partnership can also be connected with the phenomenological theme. This is because partnership involves working towards a consensus about *what* is to be achieved and *how* it is to be achieved. Clearly, in order to develop such a consensus, the perceptions of the respective parties are going to be very significant. If the situation is viewed in wildly different ways by different family members or others in the child's or young person's network, it is unlikely that consensus or anything resembling it will be achieved.

Similarly, if the worker's perspective is vastly different from that of family members, there is a lot of ground to be made up before real progress can be made. This, then, raises two important questions:

- How can we appreciate other people's perspectives on the situation?
- How can we help reconcile differences in perspective?

These two sets of issues are worth exploring in a little more depth, and so it is to these that we now turn.

Understanding other people's perspective

In some ways, this is simply a matter of drawing on our existing interpersonal skills – active listening, reading body language and so on. However, it is also more than this, in so far as it includes other means of identifying the way the person concerned perceives the situation. These include:

- *Sensitivity to language and culture* The language(s) we use play an important part in shaping our perceptions. We therefore have to make sure as far as possible that we are 'on the same wavelength' in terms of the style of language we are using, the vocabulary we employ (jargon can easily creep in without our noticing) and, of course, the actual language we use (English, Welsh, Urdu or whatever) – we have to be very wary of making the mistake of assuming that everybody's first language is English. Beyond language we also have issues relating to culture, the different assumptions and 'mind sets' that tend to go with particular cultures. It is vitally important that we take account of people's cultural background, values, rituals, practices and so on. This is particularly important when we link this with our emphasis on the phenomenological dimension, with its emphasis on the central role of meaning-making.
- *Problem-setting* This is a term associated with reflective practice. It refers to the process of making sure that we have a clear grasp of what the problem is *from the perspective of the person(s)* concerned, before we set about trying to come up with solutions. For example, a social worker

dealing with a poor school attendance situation may see the problems as being the lack of education and the dangers of becoming drawn into offending behaviour while not at school, while the youngster concerned may define the problem as the fact that he or she was caught! And, of course, the parents may have a different perspective again. Problem-setting can therefore help to ensure people appreciate each other's perspective on the situation, and provides a possible platform for moving forward.

Reconciling differences

Once we are aware of other people's perspectives and any differences that stand in the way of progress, our next task, of course, is to attempt to narrow the gap between them where possible. There are a number of ways that this can be tackled, including the following:

- *Mediation* As discussed earlier, the use of mediation skills and processes can be very helpful in tackling differences of perspective and interest in a given situation.
- *Family therapy* There are many differing approaches to family therapy but what they all have in common is a focus on family dynamics and attempts to amend these so that more positive family relationships and interactions can be established where necessary. Basic family work is something that many experienced child care social workers are able to do, but there are also specialist agencies to make referrals to in certain circumstances.

It is also important to recognise that there are limits to partnership – it cannot always be relied upon, as many situations make partnership too difficult a goal to achieve. However, despite these limits, we have to be careful not to be defeatist and simply *assume* that partnership is not possible – initial barriers can often be removed through skilful work on the part of the social worker (for example, through the use of advanced interpersonal skills). A realistic approach to partnership is one which is neither idealistic nor defeatist, but rather explores constructively the positive potential that exists between those two extremes.

Parenting

Parenting is perhaps one of the most important concepts in social work with children, young people and their families. Hoghughi (1998) describes parenting as 'probably the most important public health issue facing our society' (p. 1545, cited in Lloyd, 1999a, p. 116). This emphasises the importance of parenting, but it is interesting to note that Hoghughi describes it as a 'public health' issue, rather than as a moral or political issue – perhaps a reflection of the 'superparenting' model discussed in the Introduction, with the state 'parenting' the parents.

The importance of parenting can be seen to apply in a number of ways:

- Parental behaviour is a major influence on the behaviour and attitudes of children and young people.
- 'Bonding' between parents and children has major consequences for emotional development (see the discussion of attachment theory in Chapter 1).
- Inappropriate parental behaviour is often involved in cases of child abuse.
- The future parenting capabilities of the next generation of parents will owe much to the experiences of parenting they receive.
- The support of parents can help to counter the negative effects of other problems encountered by children and young people, such as bullying, injury, illness or disability.

There are various aspects of parenting that are worth exploring in more detail. We shall begin with the question of gender.

Gender

Parenting is a term that encompasses two others – mothering and fathering. However, we have to recognise that the two are very different. It is clear that UK society is strongly 'gendered' – that is, it is socially structured along quite firm lines in terms of assigned gender roles.

One of the significant elements of this gender division is an ideological assumption, often reinforced by the media and other social institutions, that parenting is primarily a woman's concern. As Wheal (2000) puts it: 'the term working with parents may sometimes be a misnomer. What it often means is working with

mothers' (p. 3). And Butler and Roberts (1997) make a similar point:

> The phrase 'good enough parenting' . . . may well have replaced the 'fit mother' but, on the whole, it is still mothers who are taught parenting skills by social workers, not fathers. (p. 57)

This has major implications for social work practice in this area. This can be divided into two main elements:

1. *Missed opportunities* Families who come to the attention of social workers generally have a number of problems that need to be addressed in relation to the care of children and/or young people. By focusing primarily on the mother's role, opportunities for positive change can easily be missed. For example, a father may have a very positive contribution to make but may feel inhibited from doing so unless encouraged and supported.
2. *Anti-sexist practice* Families can be very oppressive for some members, particularly for women. An important part of anti-discriminatory practice is the need to challenge gender-based oppression. It would therefore run counter to the precepts of anti-discriminatory practice to reinforce or condone such oppression in families. It is therefore important that we do not approach work with families from an uncritical perspective and thus run the risk of adding to the discrimination and oppression already experienced by so many.

In view of these two sets of issues, it is important that our practice should not reinforce stereotypical gender roles. However, this does not mean that we should make our practice a moral crusade against sexism, as that would clearly be too unrealistic a task. It would also involve overstepping our role in many ways. None the less, it remains the case that our work with families needs to be sensitive to the ways in which the 'unwritten rules' of sexism can:

- disempower women and children (and even men to a certain extent – see Thompson, 1995);
- create an atmosphere of tension and disharmony;

- lead to mental health problems, especially depression;
- block opportunities for progress and development;
- lay the foundations for domestic violence;
- legitimate the exploitation of children and thus contribute to abuse; and
- lead to family breakdown.

Exercise 2.8

How can you ensure that your practice with families does not reinforce sexist stereotypes? What steps can you take to promote anti-sexist practice?

Wetherell (1997) warns of the danger of relying on gender stereotypes, particularly in terms of identifying poor parenting:

A bad mother appears to be one who not only experiences but articulates her stress, thus making her work visible, and directly challenging the social construction of motherhood as easy and naturally satisfying. (p. 232)

Reinforcing such gender expectations in this way would clearly be at odds with what is required to develop a truly anti-discriminatory practice.

The term, 'family' is a shorthand for a complex set of interrelationships, roles and sites of power. Gender is clearly a significant part of this complexity and so we have to be careful to avoid the problem associated with traditional forms of practice – that of 'gender blindness', or failing to recognise the significance and impact of gender relationships within families.

Race and ethnicity

Just as parenting varies along gender lines, so too does it vary in terms of culture and ethnicity. As Butler and Roberts (1997) comment:

Parenting also changes across cultures. It is very tempting to understand parenting only in the context of our own experience and our personal construction of family life. However, there is a danger in judging parents according to only one, often very restricted, standard. In some cultures, for example, child rearing is seen as the responsibility of the extended family, indeed of the whole community. Children may be praised and disciplined by others as well as by their parents. Children may have a number of role

models to learn from and may have much greater involvement with their elders. (p. 67)

This passage warns us of the dangers of ethnocentrism – seeing other cultures from the perspective of our own culture and not taking account of, or respecting, important differences. Such ethnocentrism is, in effect, a form of racism, as it implies that one ethnic or racial group is superior to another. While racism is clearly a problem to be addressed in its own right, we also have to acknowledge that racism acts as a barrier to progress for the children and young people who are so affected (German, 1996).

Dwivedi (1996) makes the point that child rearing practices strongly reflect the sets of cultural assumptions that apply to the family, community or society concerned. A two-way relationship can be detected. Child rearing practices can be seen to be influenced by the wider culture while such practices can also be said to influence that culture in the sense that they will influence the upbringing of children and the transmission of the culture from one generation to the next.

What is needed, then, is a degree of cultural sensitivity – a degree of awareness of the central role of culture in influencing patterns of parenting. We need to be wary of falling into the trap of essentialism, of assuming that there is a 'correct' way of parenting. There are, of course, many different approaches and we have to avoid the oppressive mistake of regarding a *different* style of parenting as a *defective* style. We have to tread carefully before forming a view of the appropriateness or otherwise of approaches to parenting.

However, this is a very complex and tricky issue, and one that needs to be handled very carefully. This is because the importance of cultural sensitivity can be distorted in certain circumstances. This is when the notion of cultural variation is used to mask unacceptable forms of parenting. For example, where a child from an ethnic minority background is being abused but the case is not investigated fully because of fears of being accused of racism. In effect, this approach leads to black children receiving a lower level of protection from abuse than their white counterparts – and that, of course, amounts to racism, albeit unintentionally.

We therefore have to ensure that we strike the right balance. On the one hand, we must ensure that cultural sensitivity is not allowed to stand in the way of appropriate interventions that are not only ethically and legally justified but also essential for good practice. On the other hand, we must ensure that we do not fall into the trap of ethnocentrism by judging the parenting associated with other cultures by our own terms and expectations. Cropper (1997) refers to inquiries into child abuse undertaken in the 1980s and comments:

> These inquiries alerted us to the existence of stereotyping within the assessment process and to the problems which have arisen when professionals have assumed universal categories of race, culture, class and gender. In such instances, workers have assumed rather than assessed . . . Sometimes, this has resulted in a failure to protect black children in abusive situations because workers have based their assessments upon cultural assumptions made about particular 'racial' groups. Such assumptions may be punitive or liberal in their perspective, but both are likely to prove dangerous in practice. . . . Ahmed (1989) has also noted the prevalence of punitive and coercive approaches to black families. In some cases, black children have been unnecessarily moved from their families when workers, and not just white workers, have used their own assumptions about family life as a baseline in their assessment, and have thus failed to recognize the strengths of black families. (p. 32)

Cropper goes on to draw out a number of practice implications from her analysis. One of these in particular is worthy of comment, namely the importance of exploring 'areas of misunderstanding and personal ignorance by asking for clarification, and thus avoid making ethnocentric assumptions' (p. 40). This is consistent with the point made earlier about the need to develop culturally sensitive forms of communication as part of the process of developing partnership-based work.

The family is not a fixed 'essence'. It comes in various shapes, sizes and textures – its diversity shows itself across a number of dimensions, not least that of culture and ethnicity. Approaches to parenting are similarly diverse and do not lend themselves to simplistic, reductionist approaches on the part of professionals. The 'family', as noted above, involves a diverse range of styles and so we should be careful not to distort this complexity into a simplistic model of what the family (and its approach to parenting) should be like.

Class

I referred earlier to Barrett and McIntosh's (1991) argument that the family reflects the class structure of society. Indeed, there are many discernible differences between families that can be seen to follow class lines in terms of family patterns, routines and habits. Consider, for example, mealtimes. Do we have 'tea' late afternoon or 'dinner' later in the evening? Such mealtimes, and indeed the vocabulary used to refer to them, follow a mixture of regional and class lines, and so family lifestyle has clear connections with class at quite a basic level. These differences can also be seen to be reflected in parenting practices.

Class is often broken down in the sociological literature into three main components: income, occupation and education. Income is clearly linked to the likelihood or otherwise of experiencing poverty, and can therefore be seen as significant. As Alcock (1993) comments:

> Poverty is not just a state of affairs, it is an **unacceptable** state of affairs – it implicitly contains the question, what are we going to do about it? (p. 4)

While poverty is itself a problem, it can also be seen to exacerbate other problems due to the pressures, stresses and tensions it brings (Donnison, 1998).

Occupation is closely associated with income but is an important issue in its own right. For example, a factory worker may earn roughly the same as a civil servant but there are none the less significant differences between the occupational groups. Pension entitlement and other such financial differences may well be present, but it is again not simply a matter of finance. There are likely to be greater health hazards in an industrial setting (the class differences in health are well documented – see Wilkinson, 1996); the physical nature of factory work may produce a lowering of productivity (and thus earnings) over time while white collar workers are likely to earn more over time due to incremental pay scales; and shift patterns may disrupt family life. The nature of the occupation of one or more family members is therefore likely to have a significant bearing on pressures within that family and the challenges they face.

Education also follows distinct class lines in terms of access to career development opportunities, job satisfaction, occupational mobility and so on (Reid, 1992). These differences can also therefore be seen as potentially very significant in shaping family life and thus parenting.

Exercise 2.9

What class differences are you aware of in relation to parenting? What implications do such differences have for your practice?

Disability

Disability is relevant to parenting in at least two ways. First, there is the question of parenting children with disabilities and the issues that arise from this. Second, there is the question of parents who themselves have disabilities.

In the first case, an important point to note is that 'disability' should not be treated in an essentialist way, as if it refers to a single matter. There are various forms of impairment, with varying effects on the individuals concerned and, of course, not all individuals respond to an impairment in the same way – the phenomenological theme is again relevant here. This is because it is important to move beyond a medical model of disability in which the focus is on the actual impairment. A phenomenological approach would enable us to explore what the particular impairment *means* to the individual and to his or her family. For example, it is often assumed that certain conditions are a 'problem', while the person with that particular condition may not experience it as a problem at all (hence the need to avoid unduly negative terminology, as in 'Tom *suffers* from autism'). Tom may well suffer as a result of his particular condition, but this is not the same as automatically assuming that he

does – suffering is a very subjective matter, and so we should be wary of imposing our own values. We should also bear in mind, as noted in Chapter 1, that disability can usefully be understood in *social* terms – that is, it is the social response to an impairment that generally creates difficulties for disabled people, rather than, or as well as, the impairment itself.

A further important point to note in relation to parenting children or young people with disabilities is that the parents may have needs above and beyond those of parents of non-disabled children. For example, where a child needs very close supervision at all times, the parents may need respite care to be provided to help them cope or to help them offer time to their other children.

Where the parent(s) are disabled, then the matter of the *social response* is once again very relevant. It is particularly important that, as social workers, we recognise the danger of assuming that parents with disabilities cannot be good parents. While we may not overtly subscribe to such a discriminatory assumption, such ideas can none the less influence us, given how dominant they are within the media and popular consciousness. Working with parents with disabilities may involve us in 'unlearning' a lot of the lessons taught to us through the process of socialisation. That is, we may have to dump a lot of the 'baggage' that society imposes on us through various channels.

A common problem identified in relation to working with people with disabilities is the mistake of concentrating on what they find difficult or need help with, perhaps at the expense of the strengths, skills and personal resources that they bring. It is important to remember that 'respecting and valuing uniqueness and diversity, and recognising and building on strengths' is one of the values underpinning this book, and indeed, of good practice more broadly. If due care is not taken, children and young people with disabilities will not have their strengths recognised and built upon.

Lone parenting

The significance of the lone parent has grown enormously in the past decade or so. While, at one time, lone parents were a relatively small minority (particularly those who had become lone parents *by choice*, rather than through bereavement), the situation now is vastly different. While the stigma associated with lone parenthood was once very strong indeed, it would be naive in the extreme to assume that stigma no longer applies at all.

In considering the question of lone parenting, we have to be very wary of simply adopting the 'common sense' (that is, profoundly ideological) view that children need two parents if they are to grow up to be well-balanced members of society. This raises a number of issues in relation to gender and our expectations of parental roles, as discussed earlier. It is therefore important to be sensitive to the question of gender in addressing issues relating to lone parenting.

A prime example of this is the fact that the majority of lone parents are women. This is significant in terms of social expectations of women as carers. There is a danger that we can fall in line with gender expectations and expect women to cope as single parents *because* they are women (Langan and Day, 1992), without taking full account of their circumstances and the pressures they may face. By contrast, when dealing with men as single parents, there may be a tendency to assume that they are in need of support and assistance *because* they are men. The influence of gender-based ideology is very powerful indeed and tends to be successful in shaping actions and attitudes mainly because it is so pervasive – it has achieved the status of 'common sense' and therefore tends to go unquestioned. There is therefore very clearly a need to be sensitive to the subtle workings of gender ideology as a fundamental part of anti-discriminatory practice.

Exercise 2.10

What rewards do parents gain for the time, effort and energy that go into the parenting role? What do you see as the main problems that parents face? How can social workers play a positive role in supporting parents without undermining them or their confidence?

In Chapter 1, I was critical of some traditional approaches to social work with children, young people and their families. This is because much traditional practice can be seen to amount to supervising parents in their role and, in effect, acting in a form of parental capacity towards them. This can be seen to be highly problematic in a number of ways:

- It concentrates on the role of the individual parent and fails to take account of wider social factors, such as poverty and deprivation.
- It has the effect of pathologising parents (seeing them as people who *are* problems, rather than people *with* problems). This can mean that strengths and personal resources are overlooked.
- It is judgemental in so far as it involves making a judgement about parenting capacity without taking into account significant broader factors.
- It can lead to the creation of dependency by undermining confidence and/or removing motivation.
- It places the social worker in a role that is primarily characterised by social control, rather than one which has a primary focus on empowerment.

Essentialism is a major pitfall to avoid here. It is very easy to see people as 'bad parents', as if this were a fixed essence, an essential characteristic of their personality. A more realistic (and more fruitful) approach is to see parenting as a set of behaviours *in context*. Some people would be excellent parents if they did not have dire poverty to contend with, or if they were not subjected to domestic violence and so on. We have to be fair and ask ourselves: If I were in this person's shoes, with their problems, tensions and constraints, how would I fare as a parent?

This is not to say that *all* parental behaviour is understandable and justifiable if only we take the broader circumstances into account. This is certainly not the case. However, it is not safe to assume that what we see as parenting problems are necessarily a sign of poor parenting. These matters have to be assessed carefully and thoroughly if we are to avoid pathologising families and possibly contributing to a vicious circle of stigma, low confidence and low motivation.

Beyond parenting

There are three senses in which it is important to go 'beyond parenting'. First, it is important to recognise that, while parents clearly have a primary role in influencing children's development, behaviour and welfare, other members of the family also have a part to play. Siblings, grandparents, aunts and uncles and so on can all contribute, sometimes very significantly, to the situation. Indeed, it is a mainstay of family therapy that it is the dynamics of the family as a whole that should be the focal point of assessment and intervention. There are clearly dangers, then, in focusing too narrowly on parenting as a central factor in the child care situations we encounter.

Second, in many cases it is not only the family that play a direct role in bringing up children. Foster carers and/or residential care staff are also key players in many scenarios. Indeed, substitute carers can be seen to have a crucial role in the lives of very many young people. This is because their approach to the child or young person may reinforce aspects of their experiences of parenting to date or may conflict with those experiences – either way, the input of substitute carers can be highly significant. I shall not comment further at this point on the role of foster carers and residential care staff as a more detailed discussion of the contribution they make will form part of Chapter 3. We shall therefore return to the topic of substitute care in the next chapter.

Third, in keeping with our critique of the 'superparenting' model and its narrow focus on parenting issues, we should bear in mind the significant impact of broader social factors, such as poverty, deprivation, racism and so on. While we have already noted that such factors can have a significant bearing on parenting, we should also note that they can also have a more direct bearing on the lived experience of the child or young person. That is, the sociopolitical context of each child and young person will also be a major direct influence on their behaviour, development, life chances and so on, and will not simply influence them indirectly through parenting.

Rights

The question of rights is clearly a complex one – claiming a right, even a legitimate right, will not guarantee that we will get what we want or need. However, when we consider the question of rights in families, we can see that it is even more complex. This is because we tend to think of rights in terms of individuals. And, of course, this means that, within families, the scope for one person's rights to clash with another's is quite significant. For example, what a teenager regards as his or her right to self-expression (through playing music at high volume, perhaps) may well conflict with someone else's perceived right to peace and quiet. The territory is therefore clearly a potential minefield. It raises a number of important questions about power relations in families, channels of communication, processes of decision-making and related matters. For example, the question of to what extent a child's or young person's voice is heard within families can be firmly located within this issue of conflicting rights between family members (and, of course, significant power differentials between adults and children).

An important point to recognise from the outset is that rights are not absolute. They are *situational* – that is, they apply only in certain circumstances. For example, my right to personal liberty no longer applies if I commit a serious crime and am duly arrested for it. Family rights issues are therefore often a matter of balancing rights, understanding one person's claim to a particular right in the context of other people's rights – and, of course, responsibilities.

Three important issues arise in this regard:

- *Communication* It is very easy for rights issues to get extremely complicated because conflicts lead to a raised level of tension which can lead to poor communication, which can, in turn, cause more conflicts and thus create a vicious circle scenario. It is therefore important to make sure, as far as possible, that the channels of communication are kept open, and that clarity is sought, for without this, resolving difficulties is not going to be easy.

- *Mediation* The process of mediation involves remaining neutral, not taking sides. It is this neutrality that enables the mediator to be in a strong position to resolve conflicts. The same model can be seen to apply in respect of rights. Where rights come into conflict and have to be balanced, it is important that the social worker remains neutral in order not to be seen as partisan, thus risking an escalation of tension and conflict. Of course, this does not apply in all such situations, as the need to protect a child or young person from harm may make a neutral position untenable in certain circumstances.
- *Assessment* An emphasis on rights is a relatively new addition to social work with children and young people, and so matters relating to rights have not always received the attention they deserve. While a focus on care needs and related matters is understandable, it is important that we do not allow this to be at the expense of a consideration of the rights involved. A neglect of rights can so easily amount to a misuse of power and therefore be incompatible with anti-discriminatory practice.

Working with families necessarily involves working with rights issues, there can be no escaping that. However, to be involved with such issues without realising that we are doing so is clearly a very dangerous undertaking. This means that we need to develop a clear understanding of rights issues and be prepared to incorporate them into our thinking and our practice if we are not to neglect this important dimension of good practice. This becomes even more significant with the implementation (in October, 2000) of the Human Rights Act 1998, which had the effect of bringing the European Convention on Human Rights into the framework of the domestic courts. Under this Act, public authorities are under a duty to ensure that their actions do not contravene any of the rights contained within the Convention – for example, the right of families to be free of any unnecessary invasion of their privacy.

3. Tasks and challenges

In this section we need to consider the implications for practice in terms of the following two practice requirements:

B1 Develop effective working partnerships with those with parental responsibility, carers and significant others in the life of the child or young person.

This practice requirement has been discussed in some detail. Considerable emphasis has been placed on working in partnership with families. The challenge to be met is that of putting these ideas into practice – developing an 'action plan' for building up a partnership-based approach. You are therefore encouraged to establish such an action plan to enable you to build on the foundations you already have. Appendix 1 (p. 122) provides a 'template' for such an action plan. This can be used to guide you in clarifying what steps will be helpful in developing your practice further. You may wish to seek the assistance and guidance of your line manager or other colleague in developing and implementing such a plan.

B2 Contribute to the delivery of services to support the parenting task.

This practice requirement is something of a 'catchall', as it refers to a wide range of activities that could go under the heading of 'contribute to the delivery of service'. Perhaps the strongest emphasis should be on systematic practice, as discussed in Chapter 1, as this is entirely consistent with the use of the social work process as presented in this chapter. The two concepts go hand in hand, in the sense that they are mutually supportive. The social work process can be enhanced by adopting a systematic approach and a systematic approach is made easier by having a clear grasp of the social work process as a framework to guide practice.

Of course, systematic practice is not the only element of good practice, but it can be seen as a fundamental part of it. It provides a clear and focused approach to practice that can inspire confidence in two ways – it can boost our own confidence by giving a structured framework to guide us through the complexities of practice and it can increase the confidence others have in us by enhancing our professional credibility.

In addition to systematic practice, attention must also be given to a number of other significant aspects of good practice:

- Being able to 'read' family dynamics – the complex and very significant interactions among family members and other significant people.
- Being able to recognise family rituals and understand their significance for the family members concerned.
- Having the necessary understanding and skills to be able to plan appropriately and effectively.
- Not falling into the trap of making assumptions about gender roles in families.
- Being sensitive to rights issues and having the required skills to handle the delicate balancing of rights where necessary.

4. Conclusion

Families are an extremely important part of contemporary society in general and of social work in particular. Families are often the source of problems (or at least the context in which problems arise) and are often seen as the solution to certain problems. Considerable social work effort goes into supporting families and/or finding alternative families and even, in some cases, finding alternatives *to* the family (for example, a child needing a group care placement after a number of foster placement breakdowns). In effect, wherever we are in social work with children and young people, family issues are never far away.

Social workers are often perceived as a threat to families, a perception often reinforced by media coverage of social work issues, and so we have to acknowledge that the task of working constructively with families is one that begins 'from a deficit', as it were. That is, we do not start with a level playing field, but rather one which tips the balance against us. This means that we have to be well-equipped in terms of the knowledge and skills we need to meet this challenge and overcome as far as possible any resistance we encounter. It also means that we have to be very clear about the values we are drawing upon in working with families, as it is often these values that will give us the motivation and commitment to carry on in what can often be difficult circumstances.

However, we should acknowledge not only the difficulties and tensions in working with

families, but also the rewards and pleasures. As social workers, we work with families who so often have to endure immense hardship, face considerable deprivation, discrimination and oppression and cope with various sources of loss, grief, pain and suffering. This brings us face to face with people who show immense resilience, spirit and courage. We should therefore be mindful of the privileges of working alongside people with such strong personal resources in the face of adversity. What is needed is a *realist* approach – that is one which takes account of both sides of the equation, the pleasures and privileges as well as the problems and pains.

5. Points to ponder

➤ How has your experience of family life influenced your view of the family and its value and limitations in modern society?
➤ What links can you make between families and such factors as poverty and deprivation; poor housing; racism and other social conditions?
➤ What steps can you take to make partnership a reality, rather than just fashionable rhetoric?
➤ If you are a parent, can you see links between your own experiences of being parented and your own approach to parenthood?
➤ How can we ensure that the rights of individuals are neither overlooked nor allowed to drive families apart?

6. Learning resources guide

Dallos and McLaughlin (1993) provide a good range of debates around the complexities of the family and its part in the wider social network, as do Muncie *et al.* (1997). The gender dimension of families is covered in Fox Harding (1996), Robertson Eliot (1996) and Gittins (1993).

The social work process and related matters are discussed in Chapters 18 to 23 of Thompson (2002a).

Assessment is well covered in Milner and O'Byrne (1998), and the related topic of decision-making is helpfully explored in some detail in O'Sullivan (1999). The assessment framework is explored in Horwath (2001). The more specialised areas of assessment in relation to sexual abuse are covered in Calder (2001a) in relation to mothers of sexually abused children and in Calder (2001b) in relation to children and young people who sexually abuse.

Evaluation is discussed in some depth in Shaw (1996), while Everitt and Hardiker (1996) also offer helpful comment. See also Subhra (2001) for an interesting perspective.

As mentioned in Chapter 1, working in partnership is covered in DoH/SSI (1995) and Jackson and Kilroe (1996). Barker (1994) offers useful insights into partnership work through the use of consultation. Wheal (2000) is an excellent collection of readings on working with parents. Coleman and Roker (2001) offer an interesting set of readings on supporting parents. Hackett (2001) concentrates on supporting parents of young people who have sexually abused.

Planning in child care is discussed in some detail in Bryer (1988), and is also covered at an introductory level in Thompson and Thompson (2002).

Mediation is discussed in Postle and Ford (2000). There is also a large number of books about family mediation available – for example, Lindstein and Meteyard (1996). Moss and Tzilivakis (2002) is a training pack on mediation and conflict management.

Parenting is a topic that carries with it a wealth of literature. Lloyd (1999) is a good starting point. For a discussion of working with parents with disabilities, see Thorpe (2000).

Children's rights are covered in depth in Franklin (2001).

3. Networking

1. Introduction

Chapter 3 now continues and expands the pattern developed in Chapters 1 and 2. That is, while Chapter 2 went beyond the individualist concerns of Chapter 1 to address issues relating to the broader context of the family network, Chapter 3 now widens the net a step further by examining the community and professional networks that can be seen also to have a significant bearing on the lives of children and young people and on the outcomes of intervention.

This means that partnership is once again a central theme, as it is only through effective multidisciplinary collaboration that we can 'plug into' the wider network of professionals and community groups. As with the previous two chapters, we begin with a summary and overview of a number of key issues relating to the underpinning knowledge base. This is followed by the implications for practice in relation to the identified practice requirements, and a concluding section which includes points to ponder and suggestions for further reading.

2. The knowledge base

As with the first two chapters, we are dealing with a vast and extensive knowledge base, and so what is presented here is again very selective, representing only one small part of the overall wealth of knowledge that can be drawn upon. This knowledge base includes a wide range of ideas drawn from sociology, social psychology and management theory as well as from the literature relating directly to social work with children, young people and their families.

This section of the chapter is divided into four subsections. First we address the question of 'understanding organisations' and consider some of the main issues involved in relating to, and interacting positively with, people, systems and structures within our own and other organisations. Second, we consider the topic of multidisciplinary collaboration and explore what is involved in working to good effect with other professionals. Third, we apply the lessons to be learned from multidisciplinary collaboration to the important question of working effectively with substitute carers, whether foster carers or group care staff. Finally, we look at the complexities of seeking to draw upon community resources and working to best effect with the various individuals, groups and organisations that form part of the local community.

Understanding organisations

A common expectation expressed or at least assumed by 'raw recruits' to social work is that they are going to be spending a large proportion of their time in direct face-to-face contact with clients. Of course, it does not take too long for them to realise that, in reality, much of their time is spent on what can loosely be described as 'organisational matters' – for example, time spent in meetings or otherwise communicating (orally or in writing through forms, reports and so on) with members of one's own organisation or others in the multidisciplinary network. It is perhaps surprising, then, that so much attention is given to the knowledge and skills involved in working with clients and carers and yet relatively little is given to the perhaps equally important roles and tasks of dealing with organisational matters.

The National Assembly for Wales' *Working Together to Safeguard Children* document (NAW, 2000) makes the important point that:

Promoting children's well-being and safeguarding them from significant harm depends crucially upon effective information sharing, collaboration and understanding between agencies and professionals. Constructive relationships between individual

*workers need to be supported by a strong
lead from elected or appointed authority
members, and the commitment of chief
officers.* (p. 2)

This basically places two sets of duties on each
worker. First, there is a duty to use our
professional skills to work effectively in the
context of a multidisciplinary partnership (this
will be discussed in more detail below). Second,
there is a duty to contribute to the broader
managerial and organisational agenda by
bringing matters to the attention of the
appropriate personnel in senior positions. In this
way, we are playing a *professional* role, making
sure we play our own individual part and also
contributing to the broader organisational
endeavour in the best interests of the children,
young people and families that we serve.
Professionalism involves making the necessary
decisions to undertake our duties, rather than
simply waiting to receive instructions from
above. It involves taking responsibility for our
actions and seeking to influence others in ways
that are consistent with our professional aims in
promoting high-quality social work practice.
The process of engaging with and influencing
the organisation that employs us can therefore
be seen as an important one, especially when
the organisation's actions are, in some
circumstances, not consistent with the best
interests of the children and young people
concerned. It is therefore to this topic that we
now turn.

The organisational operator

In considering the organisational context of
social work practice, an important concept to
explore in this regard is that of the
'organisational operator' (Thompson, 1998).
This refers to the type of employee who is able
and willing to use his or her knowledge of
organisational dynamics and his or her
interpersonal skills to influence the organisation
in a positive way:

*'Organisational operator' is a term I use to
describe the role an individual can play in
seeking to have a positive influence on the
organisation in which he or she works,
particularly in challenging discrimination and
oppression.* (p. 200)

Of course, it would be hopelessly unrealistic to
expect every individual employee to have a
major influence on his or her employing
organisation. However, we should be very
careful not to go to the other extreme and
assume that no-one can have an influence.
Indeed, such a defeatist attitude can be a major
obstacle to progress. The reality of the situation
falls somewhere in between these two
extremes, with each employee having some
degree of influence, although much will depend
on his or her i) position within the organisation
and the power that goes with that position (we
shall return to the question of power below); ii)
professional credibility and respect and iii)
interpersonal and strategic skills and abilities.
This introduces another very important issue to
consider – that of the role of influencing skills.

Influencing skills

It is perhaps ironic that social work education
over the years has paid relatively little attention
to the skills involved in influencing individuals,
groups and organisations, even though these
matters can be seen to be a significant feature
of the landscape of social work practice. Space
does not permit a detailed exploration of
influencing skills, but the following brief
overview should none the less prove a helpful
start for considering the issues.

As I have previously argued:

*Success in social work depends to a large
extent on others. The ability to influence
individuals, groups and organisations is
therefore a central part of the successful
social worker's repertoire. Having little or no
influence can leave the social worker
frustrated, ineffectual and en route perhaps
to major problems in the future. The ability to
influence without coercing or exploiting is
therefore an important one to develop.*
(Thompson, 2000b, p. 100)

The final sentence from this passage is
particularly significant. It is important to
emphasise that influencing does not amount to
coercing or exploiting. It certainly does not
mean trying to get your own way at all costs.
Influencing skills are part and parcel of the
process of empowerment, while coercion and
exploitation are clearly more akin to oppression.

How, then, can we have an influence on our organisation or others within the multidisciplinary network? What is involved? The full list of possible methods and strategies would be a very long one indeed, but the following can be seen as some of the most significant:

- *Effective communication* It perhaps goes without saying that we cannot influence others if we are not able to communicate effectively. The basic social work skills of communication should therefore be put to good effect in the pursuit of influencing organisations. Being clear about what is to be communicated, when and to whom, is all part of the skill base of influencing organisations.
- *Clarity of focus* Organisations are often confusing places, and it is not uncommon for individuals, groups or even whole organisations to lose their way. The ability to retain a clear focus can therefore be a distinct advantage, particularly at times of major change. The advantages of a clear, focused, systematic approach are just as applicable in this arena as they are in any other aspect of practice.
- *Knowledge of law and policy* Organisations are, of course, obliged to abide by the law and their own policies. However, it is not at all uncommon for breaches of the law to occur, often because managers do not realise that certain organisational practices are not in keeping with legal requirements. A knowledge of the law and policy can therefore prove very influential at times (although this needs to be handled tactfully – see below).
- *Negotiation skills* The assertive use of negotiation skills can be very helpful in terms of influencing others. An understanding of what is involved in effective negotiation can be a distinct advantage. This is discussed in more detail below (see also the 'Further reading' section below).
- *Tact and diplomacy* In attempting to have a positive influence, we are of course running the risk of making matters worse – for example, by alienating people or otherwise causing ill-feeling. It is therefore extremely important that we make sure that we are

tactful and diplomatic in our endeavours. A sensitive approach is far more likely to be effective than a crude, insensitive one. Indeed, the latter can be highly counterproductive.

Underpinning the question of influencing skills is, of course, the very important concept of power, which is a central feature of organisations. Much of this power is 'official', in so far as it is part of the formal structure of the organisation itself. However, it is also important to recognise that power can also be seen to operate at informal levels. For example, it is not uncommon for a head of a department to be designated as the person with formal power, while it is his or her deputy who really 'pulls the strings' – the 'power behind the throne', as it were.

A significant part of becoming skilled in influencing is therefore a good understanding of the workings of power and the ability to use these positively. One factor that may hamper the development of such skills in using power is that social work still has an unfortunate legacy from some of the crude forms of radical social work of the 1960s and 70s. This legacy takes the form of a mistrust of power or even an assumption that the exercise of power is in itself problematic or even oppressive. Indeed, it has been a great pity that the development of emancipatory practice has led some people to make the mistake of assuming that the exercise of power is in itself oppressive (Thompson, 1998). Such people have failed to understand the crucial distinction between the legitimate use of power in the pursuit of ethical and professionally appropriate goals (authority) and the deliberate abuse or unwitting misuse of power (oppression). We therefore have to be very wary indeed of oversimplifying the highly complex notion of power.

Power and influence are, in part at least, also linked to personal and professional presentation – that is, how we come across to others. One aspect of professional presentation is, of course, the use of the written word – for example, in the presentation of written reports. Our ability to express ourselves clearly and effectively in writing can have a significant bearing on how others see us. In order to influence others we have to win their respect; in order to win their respect, we need to be able to communicate appropriately. A poorly written report can undermine our credibility while a clear, well-written one can enhance that credibility. The skills involved in effective written communication are therefore very important at a number of levels – and the time and effort devoted to developing those skills is clearly a worthwhile investment of personal resources (see Thompson, 2002a, Chapter 12).

One final point to note about influencing skills is the importance of what has come to be known as 'elegant challenging'. This term refers to being able to challenge discriminatory or other ethically unacceptable comments, actions or attitudes in a way that does not:

- cause offence or ill-feeling;
- lead the person or group being challenged to become defensive; or
- allow the issue to become trivialised or sidetracked – for example, by making the person doing the challenging appear dogmatic or unreasonable.

Seeking to influence others is a skilful undertaking and needs to be handled sensitively and cautiously. An uncritical, insensitive or poorly thought-through approach can do more harm than good. A fair amount of caution is therefore called for.

Exercise 3.1

What avenues are available to you for influencing i) the organisation you work for; and ii) other organisations in the multidisciplinary network?

Can you think of any ways you might be able to increase your level or scope of influence?

Effective meetings

Another important issue as far as organisations are concerned is the use of meetings. It is generally recognised that meetings can easily become unproductive, if not actually counterproductive. In terms of resources, meetings are very expensive. For example, a 90-minute meeting involving ten people is the equivalent of two full days of an individual worker's time. If that meeting achieves little or nothing by way of positive outcomes, then that is the equivalent of a worker wasting two full

days of his or her time. Clearly, therefore, we should make every effort to ensure that meetings are as effective and fruitful as possible. The following pointers should help in this regard:

- Are you clear about the purpose and focus of the meeting?
- Are other participants clear about the purpose and focus?
- Is the status of the meeting clear (for example, does it have the power to make decisions or only recommendations?)
- Have you undertaken any necessary preparation?
- Do you actually need to be there?
- Is the agenda realistic for the time available?
- If not, how can the agenda be prioritised?
- If clients or carers are to be involved in the meeting, have they been adequately prepared and supported?

This is not an exhaustive list, but it should be sufficient to paint a picture of what is involved in trying to make sure that meetings are as successful as possible. Of course, you may wish to argue that many of the above pointers are the responsibility of the meeting's chair, rather than yours. However, I would argue that a meeting is an example of partnership in action, and that *all* participants share a responsibility for making the meeting work, although clearly the chair has extra responsibility above and beyond that of the other participants.

The final point in the list above is particularly significant. Where children, young people and/or parents and other carers are to be involved, it becomes even more important to make sure that time is not wasted and that efforts to improve the situation are not lost in bureaucratic confusion or unfocused discussion. Badly-run meetings that involve clients and/or carers can seriously undermine the professional credibility of the people concerned and therefore have a very negative effect in terms of partnership, as a great deal of confidence in the partnership can be lost.

Using supervision

Of course, we are not alone and unsupported in the organisation – or at least we should not be.

Employing organisations have a legal and moral duty of staff care. Under the Health and Safety legislation, employers have a responsibility to safeguard their staff from undue hazards – and it has been established through case law precedent that stress is just such an 'undue hazard' covered by the legislation (see Earnshaw and Cooper, 1996). There is therefore a pressing imperative for employing organisations to take seriously the challenge of keeping pressures and stress within manageable limits. Of course, one very important mechanism for social work organisations to ensure that they are safeguarding their staff from the hazard of stress is that of supervision – a long-standing form of professional support.

Supervision should be about more than just ensuring that staff are undertaking their duties appropriately (the accountability function of supervision). It should also have a focus on helping staff to learn by developing their knowledge and skills (the staff development function of supervision) and of course a significant role in ensuring that staff are coping with the pressures and demands they face (the staff care function). Managers therefore have a legal duty to offer supportive supervision. If you are not receiving such supervision, you will need to consider whether to raise this as an issue with your employer or seek support elsewhere (from colleagues, for example) – or indeed pursue a mixture of the two. The important point to emphasise, however, is that you should not go without supervision if at all possible, as there are clear dangers and destructive processes that can develop over time if workers in child care are not supervised appropriately (see Morrison, 1997, 2001).

Another important point to note is that supervision is a two-way street. That is, both the supervisor and the supervisee have a shared responsibility for making it work (it is, in effect, another form of partnership). It is therefore important that an atmosphere of openness and trust is established at as early a stage as possible – and, of course, both parties have a part to play in setting the tone and creating the atmosphere in supervision. Staff also have other responsibilities in terms of making supervision work (undertaking any

necessary preparation, keeping the time free and so on – see Thompson, 2002a, Chapter 7).

In view of the significant role of supervision, it is important that you consider carefully the nature and extent of the supervision you receive. Is it sufficiently helpful for you? If not, is there anything you can do to improve the situation? For example, does your employing organisation have a policy on supervision that is not being adhered to? Are there other people in the same boat? Can you work together to deal with the issue tactfully and constructively? Or can you at least support each other in the absence of good supervision?

Working together

Of course, some individuals have 'charismatic' qualities and are able to have a significant bearing on the organisation in which they work. However, for most people, influencing the organisation in which we work is mainly a collective matter. That is, it is through like-minded people working together with a common agenda to promote positive change that constructive organisational change is more likely to take place. For example, an individual who is seeking to bring about some form of change is likely to be in a much stronger position if he or she raises the issue at, say, a team meeting and obtains the backing of the whole team, rather than simply dealing with it as a personal issue.

Of course, it does not automatically follow that a team will support an individual's concerns or that, if they do, their efforts to promote change will be any more successful than the individual's. However, what it does do is to increase the chances of success – it makes a positive outcome more likely but certainly does not guarantee any such positive outcome.

Working together within one's own organisation can be a fruitful way forward, and can be very significant in terms of morale. For example, even if a particular effort to promote positive change is not successful, there is much motivation and job satisfaction to be gained from being part of a shared professional endeavour geared towards positive change. This can be a significant factor in fending off defeatism, cynicism and, ultimately, burnout (Thompson, 1999). However, in addition to the benefits of working together within one's own organisation, we also have the benefits of working together across disciplinary and professional boundaries – and it is to this important topic that we now turn.

Multidisciplinary collaboration

The importance of working effectively in partnership with others in the multidisciplinary network should not need too much emphasis. Good working relationships are clearly a central plank in developing effective forms of social work with children, young people and their families. In this section, we look at those factors that can be seen to play a positive role in promoting effective multidisciplinary collaboration and those that are likely to act as a significant hindrance to it. We begin by outlining a number of the 'helps' before moving on to consider some of the 'hindrances'.

Helps

There are, of course, various factors that we can identify that can be seen to act as positive helps in making successful multidisciplinary collaboration a reality. The following list is not exhaustive, but should serve well its purpose of providing an introduction to some of the key issues.

Communication and engagement

The importance of effective communication has already been commented upon. Murphy (1995) shows how multidisciplinary communication has been a very significant feature of success and failure in child protection work:

> One of the central themes in the Colwell Inquiry was that it was the failures in multi-disciplinary communication and cooperation that were to blame for 'at risk' children being identified and afforded protection. The report referred on numerous occasions to failures in communication: 'the fatal failure to pool the total knowledge of Maria's background, recent history and physical and mental condition' (DHSS 1974, p.53).
>
> Repeated inquiries into child deaths were to emphasise the crucial role of multi-disciplinary communication in the

> prevention and recognition of child abuse. Lack of coordination and communication was frequently cited as a key contributor to children's deaths through physical abuse. (p. 12)

The role of clear multidisciplinary communication in child protection has received considerable emphasis as a result of the inquiries to which Murphy refers. However, we should note that it is not only in relation to child protection that such effective communication is so important. As the following passage from Hayden *et al.* (1999) indicates, the case for needing to extend this focus on effective multidisciplinary communication to *all* forms of child care practice is a strong one:

> Inter-agency cooperation and partnership (or rather the lack of it) underpins some of the difficulties of looking after children in the care system. The Audit Commission (1994) highlighted the need for social services departments and education departments to address the issue of the education of looked after children and also found a disappointing lack of collaboration between social services and health authorities in strategic planning for children. On the other hand, where cooperation is mandatory or strongly recommended, as in child protection, greater progress has been made. Subsequently, the requirement of services to take the lead in a number of areas which require multi-agency input via the production, for example, of Children's Services Plans has at least created a situation in which communication is positively promoted across agencies. (p. 203)

The impetus towards more and better communication across disciplines is therefore a significant one.

Knowing what, when and how to communicate is clearly a basic ingredient of effective partnership work in the multidisciplinary network. However, we should also note that what have received far less attention are the questions of *why* communicate and what *not* to communicate.

One problem with working in a complex, multidisciplinary system is that there can be so much information available to us that we have difficulty in deciding what to communicate and what not to. The danger of information overload is a very real one (Etzel and Thomas, 1996). One implication of this is that we have to be clear about *why* we are communicating certain points of information – what purpose are we intending to serve by relaying particular information? Asking the question, 'why?' can be a useful device for making sure we are communicating all that we need to but without overloading people with unnecessary information. That is, we can determine what it is helpful to communicate and what will not be helpful. This is because information overload is dangerous – 'flooding' people with unnecessary detail can lead to important information being missed (Burgoon *et al.,* 1994).

Systematic practice

The point made above about being clear about why we are communicating information is part and parcel of systematic practice – being clear about the focus of our work. However, we can also see that systematic practice more broadly is likely to be a major feature of successful partnership work. This is because the clarity of focus which is a hallmark of systematic practice can be helpful in a number of ways:

- *Highlighting differences* Where there are differences of perspective or desired outcome, a systematic approach can help to identify these. A vague approach characterised by drift and ambiguity can mean that key differences do not emerge, potentially holding back progress and/or creating ill-feeling or a sense that 'it just isn't coming together'.
- *Joint planning* The explicit focus on objectives ('What are we trying to achieve?') and strategy ('How are we going to achieve it?') can play a significant role in providing a very firm foundation for joint planning. The explicit focus on identifying the criteria by which work can be evaluated (How will we know when we have achieved it?) also offers a strong platform for planning how the joint work can be evaluated.
- *Motivation* Clarity can be a source of motivation, in so far as it avoids the demotivating effects of confusion, ambiguity and disorder. Having a clear sense of direction is likely to motivate people to work

together in that direction. Morale is likely to suffer if there is a confusing, frustrating and disheartening lack of clarity or focus.
- *Time management* An absence of clarity and focus can lead to a lot of time and effort being wasted. There can be a number of false starts and dead ends if there is no clear focus to guide our actions. This can also be related to the point above, as motivation is an important factor in terms of the most effective use of time and resources.
- *Influencing others* The point was made earlier that being able to have a positive influence on others involves having a clear focus. Being systematic is therefore also a help in developing our influencing skills.

These points combine to confirm the value of a systematic approach as the basis of multidisciplinary collaboration.

Reflective practice

Reflective practice, as we have noted, involves avoiding routinised or mechanical approaches to our work. This is no less applicable when it comes to working in multidisciplinary partnerships. By using the artistry or craft involved in reflective practice, we are able to look for creative ways of working together – for example, by exploring different options for dealing with situations, rather than relying on standard practices. This more creative approach can be very beneficial in working with different groups, as it is often the differences that can be a source of creativity.

A recognition of difference and diversity as a spur to creative, reflective practice can be contrasted with approaches to practice which try to ignore or downplay differences between groups, as if attempting to brush differences 'under the carpet'. Clearly, a reflective approach has far more to offer multidisciplinary collaboration than one which denies or devalues diversity.

The major question of differences between the respective partners within the multidisciplinary network has long been recognised as a significant one. As Murphy (1995) comments:

It is presumed by some within the British system that the presence of procedures and procedural guidance will be sufficient to produce cooperative multi-disciplinary effort. But procedures on their own are clearly not enough: 'Inter-agency work brings professionals with very different values, perceptions and work conditions together; procedures often appear to ignore these differences or assume that they will somehow be accommodated' (Stone 1990, p. 50).

Skaff (1988) comments that 'most child protection systems in the United States are characterised by fragmentation, overlapping and duplicative services, minimal interagency contacts and agency role confusion' (p. 218). 'Although the British ACPC system has been in existence for a considerable time, there are still many blocks to good inter-agency work.' (p. 41)

Non-reflective approaches, with their tendency towards routinisation and uncritical practice, are therefore likely to stand in the way of effective partnership. Reflective practice, by contrast, is far better equipped to recognise the differences across professional groups and seek creative ways of addressing them as positively as possible.

Exercise 3.2

In what ways can reflective practice be brought to bear in relation to multidisciplinary partnership? What steps would you need to take to draw on the insights of reflective practice in seeking to promote effective multidisciplinary collaboration?

Openness

Openness and honesty can readily be acknowledged as basic building blocks of effective working relations. They are clearly required if any substantial basis of trust is to be developed. These can be closely allied with reliability as a further factor that promotes trust.

Perhaps it would be naive to expect complete trust across different professional groups or even within the same professional group. However, the various steps that can increase and strengthen trust are clearly important ones to take.

Sometimes it is a matter of having the courage to raise difficult or contentious issues, rather than attempt to sweep them under the carpet. This makes a partnership very similar to a strong friendship, in the sense that a strong friendship is generally recognised not as one which is free of any disagreements or conflicts, but rather as one which is able to deal with such difficulties without the relationship being undermined. In effect, we could say that partnership is not about naively seeking complete consensus, but rather being able to work effectively together to deal with conflicts and disagreements.

Assertiveness and negotiation skills

The importance of having the ability to use assertiveness skills in processes of negotiation has already been commented upon in relation to influencing skills. The same argument can also be applied to multidisciplinary collaboration more broadly. That is, well-developed negotiation skills can be helpful in resolving conflicts, identifying areas of common interest and generally serving the purpose of oiling the wheels of collaboration.

The discussion in Chapter 2 of the differences between positional and principled negotiation is also very relevant here. Adopting an entrenched position and trying to 'do battle' to defend that position is not really helpful when it comes to multidisciplinary collaboration. What is much more likely to be effective, of course, is a principled approach in which partners seek constructive ways forward by i) identifying common ground and trying to make the most of it; and ii) identifying areas of disagreement and seeking creative ways of handling these as constructively as possible (or at least amicably agreeing to disagree).

As mentioned above, partnership is premised not on an idealised notion that all partners will agree on everything, with no conflict or tension. Rather, it is premised on the ability to work constructively with tensions and disagreements and find a positive way forward. It is partly for this reason that we can make a very strong link between partnership and professionalism. This is because inherent in the notion of professionalism is a commitment to doing what is right by the client and being prepared to make all reasonable efforts to tackle whatever obstacles stand in the way of realising that commitment. Where individuals 'plough their own furrow' at the expense of the wider good, then clearly this is not consistent with professionalism in general and professional accountability in particular. The ability to handle conflicts well and retain a focus on the professional task is therefore a major asset when it comes to meeting the important challenge of developing multidisciplinary collaboration.

Hindrances

Alongside the various factors that can be regarded as helpful, we must also consider the hindrances that can stand in the way of positive working relationships. There are very many such obstacles, not least the following.

Stereotypes

It is very easy to adopt the lazy approach of relying on stereotypes and making assumptions about people, rather than taking the trouble of listening to them and getting to know them. However, such an approach is clearly in conflict with the tenets of anti-discriminatory practice in particular and the social work value base in general. It is an example of *essentialism* – dealing with people as if they represented fixed 'essences', rather than conscious beings who make choices and are subject to change over time.

Murphy (1995) points out that stereotypes are a block to communication, for example when:

> . . . the practitioner addresses the stereotype or the cognitive map rather than the information and the reality that the other worker is bringing. Instead of helping to decode information, the stereotype prevents crucial pieces of that information from being fully appreciated . . . This is the true role of dysfunctional stereotyping – to protect ourselves from a message we do not wish to hear: 'We hide behind the defences of stereotyping so we can feel safe in the positions we hold' (Moore 1992, p.165). (pp. 46-7)

We can see, then, that stereotyping is not only discriminatory, and therefore not in keeping with the social work value base, but it is also counterproductive and therefore a dangerous form of practice. However, we should not underestimate the power of stereotyping and the ease with which we can be 'seduced' by stereotypical assumptions. It is a constant danger and therefore something that we have to remain vigilant about. This is one of the ways in which high-quality supervision can have an important if not essential role to play. This is because a line manager may be able to see things we cannot see because we are too close to the situation – and stereotyping may well be something that a skilled supervisor can help us to deal with (Morrison, 2001).

Hidden agendas

There are two types of hidden agenda, both of which can be very detrimental as far as multidisciplinary collaboration is concerned. The first is an agenda that is deliberately kept hidden, where one or more partners in the collaboration is knowingly trying to achieve a certain end, but without wishing others to know that he or she is doing so. For example, someone may be using collaborative arrangements to exclude one or more people from a particular situation or playing some other such power game. It may be, for example, that there is a weakness in someone's practice capabilities and he or she is trying to avoid this fact coming to light.

However, an agenda can also be hidden unwittingly. That is, a partner may be acting in a way that serves particular ends, but does not realise that this is happening. For example, as a result of a particular anxiety, he or she may be resisting taking a course of action that would actually be in the interests of the wider group – although he or she may not realise that this is what is happening. This can lead to some very complex group dynamics, and may be very unhelpful by holding the group back.

None the less, however the hidden agenda comes into being, it remains a significant obstacle to effective working together and therefore needs to be tackled. Dealing with hidden agendas once they have arisen can be a very difficult matter. It is therefore much better to prevent them from arising in the first place wherever possible. One key element of this is the retention of a focus on the well-being of the child or young person. That is, an emphasis on child-centredness can help to avoid the development of hidden agendas.

Differences in values

Social work has an explicit value base which acts as an ethical underpinning to practice. Other professional approaches also have ethical or value statements that have a bearing on the activities and views of members of that particular professional group. To a large extent, there is a significant overlap across the value positions of the various professional groups involved in working with children and young people, but there are also notable differences. For example, the need to address discrimination and oppression is generally given more attention in social work than it is in other groups (Thompson, 1998).

It is understandable that health professionals will place a lot of emphasis on health issues, and that educational staff will stress education issues. This is not to say that social workers have little or no interest in health or education, but rather that it is a question of emphasis. Indeed, it could be argued that it is part of the social worker's role, particularly where he or she is acting *in loco parentis*, to have an overview and seek a balance, in order to ensure that the child's or young person's needs are seen from an holistic point of view, rather than just from the point of view of the most dominant professionals.

In recent years social work has been criticised for neglecting wider aspects of the child's or young person's circumstances. The Children First initiative in Wales and its equivalent in England (Quality Protects) are based in part on a recognition of some of the inadequacies of earlier attempts to work to best effect with children, young people and their families. Mather *et al.* (2000) discuss the importance of health issues for looked after children, adding weight to the criticisms of social work practice with children and young people in the care system tending to neglect such issues. The following passage is quite telling in this regard. It describes the views of young people consulted in a research study (Mather *et al.*, 1997):

The young people seemed to lack basic health care information. They wanted information about diet, eating disorders and exercise, confidential contraceptive guidance and advice on drugs. Most found it difficult to access the information. Although they had some knowledge about these issues, they got it mainly from television, magazines and from each other. Communication with their carers about such matters seemed to be mainly about the rules regarding what they could and could not do. There was a real lack of opportunity for discussion and debate about the impact of risk-taking behaviour. They said those who cared for them were too embarrassed to help them think through the issues. (cited in Mather *et al.*, 2000, p. 10)

The *Working Together to Safeguard Children* document (NAW, 2000) stresses the importance of clear roles and responsibilities and agencies working effectively together. Social workers need to be aware of what other agencies can offer and make every effort to work constructively together, despite any differences of values, priorities or perspectives.

Lack of trust

The importance of openness and honesty in developing trust was emphasised earlier. A lack of trust can therefore be seen as a problem to be overcome wherever possible. Trust can be absent for a variety of reasons, not least the following:

- *Unfinished business* It may well be that there is a history of mistrust, either between existing partners or between their respective agencies, with the legacy of this mistrust being carried forward into the present day and present partnership arrangements. Today's partners may well be the victims of yesterday's squabbles and feuds.
- *Misunderstanding* It is very easy for misunderstandings to develop. One slight misunderstanding can be magnified by subsequent events, which in turn can lead to resentment or ill-feeling and a further spiral of misunderstanding and mistrust.
- *Perceptions of (in)competence* If one partner perceives one or more of the other partners to be lacking in competence, then it is not surprising that he or she may well be very reluctant to place any trust in that person. And the important term here is *perception*, as the mistrust can arise even where the person

concerned is actually perfectly competent but for some reason has come to be seen as incompetent.

- *Playing one off against the other* Partners may occasionally fall victim of clients playing one off against the other, perhaps seeking to gain some sort of advantage or benefit by creating conflict between two or more partners in the multidisciplinary network.

It is therefore important to be aware of these dangers and take whatever reasonable steps are possible in order to avoid falling foul of them and thus allowing good working relations to be undermined.

Exercise 3.3

What factors can you identify that i) contribute to building trust; and ii) undermining trust? What steps can you take to maximise the development of trust in multidisciplinary partnership work?

Inappropriate use of language

All professional groups develop their own jargon, specialist terminology that acts as a shorthand in order to save time and effort. When used appropriately, jargon is a very useful timesaving device. However, where it is used inappropriately, it can easily become more of a hindrance than a help, for example by causing confusion or making people feel excluded or alienated.

The danger with jargon is that we become so used to using it that we may well forget that particular forms of language are highly specialised to our professional setting and may be meaningless outside that circle – or perhaps worse still, may mean something entirely different in another professional context, thus causing confusion, misunderstanding and possibly a lack of trust. It is therefore very important that we are very conscious of our own use of specialist terminology and do not use this inappropriately in the multidisciplinary arena.

A lack of understanding of roles

Some years ago I was involved in running a postqualifying course in child protection. The participants were a mixture of social workers and health care workers. A recurring theme throughout the whole programme was the amount of learning the respective groups achieved in relation to understanding each other's roles. It was very significant indeed that a lot of contact between the various professional groups was necessary before the participants felt they had developed a sufficiently good grasp of each other's roles.

We therefore have to recognise that there is a very strong danger that multidisciplinary collaboration will be seriously undermined if respective partners do not have at least a basic understanding of the roles of the other professionals involved. Some areas tackle this potential problem through joint training events. But, however the issue is dealt with, it remains clear that the danger of a lack of understanding of other people's roles is a very real and significant one.

Blurring of roles

A related problem to that of a lack of understanding of each other's roles is that of a blurring of those roles. While there may well be an overlap of skills used, knowledge drawn upon and values adhered to, this does not alter the fact that different professionals within the multidisciplinary network have different roles. Difficulties can arise when professional boundaries are fudged. This is for three main reasons:

- There is a risk of duplication. Different people may end up undertaking the same duties, leading to a waste of time and resources.
- Conversely, certain tasks may fall between two stools. While one professional assumes that someone else is going to undertake a particular task, the other person may be thinking it is not his or her role to do so, and so the net result is that something crucial does not get done.
- Partners may find themselves undertaking tasks for which they have had no training or other opportunities for learning and therefore for which they are not particularly well-equipped.

Ironically, the problems of blurred boundaries can often arise as a result of partners being keen to work together and wanting to support each other. While this commitment to partnership is very much to be encouraged, we should none the less remain aware of the danger of role blurring that can be created in some circumstances.

Clearly, then, there are very many helps and hindrances to effective working together on a multidisciplinary basis. The challenge we face, of course, is to maximise the helps and minimise the hindrances and to support our partners in doing the same. This is not necessarily an easy challenge, but it is none the less a very important one, as it gives us the opportunity of playing a very positive part in making effective partnership work a reality.

Working with substitute carers

Field social workers working with children, young people and their families will often come into contact with people who come under the broad umbrella term of 'substitute carers'. The two main groups who come under this heading are, of course, foster carers and residential child care staff. Unfortunately, the history of relations between fieldwork staff and both these groups is not, on the whole, a very positive one. For example, Waterhouse (1992) reported the concerns of foster carers:

> Foster carers perceived themselves as having low status and little information or influence; many respondents did not perceive themselves as part of an active team working together with social workers and parents to find a satisfactory outcome for a child. This was borne out in the way contact plans and decisions were made by the agencies with little involvement or nurturing of the foster carers. (p. 43, cited in Sellick and Thoburn, 1996, p. 52)

It is clear, then, that we have to be very careful to take the necessary steps to make sure that foster carers are adequately supported and valued. If we are not, we run the risk of losing a very valuable resource as a result of foster carers withdrawing from the service.

The Code of Practice for Foster Carers (NFCA/NAW, 1999) lists the following reasons foster carers have given for leaving:

- *inadequate support*
- *inadequate allowances or the need to seek alternative employment*

- *task confusion (i.e. carers thought the task was different from what it turned out to be)*
- *role confusion (carers expected to be treated as professional colleagues but were not)*
- *inadequate information about the children being placed*
- *impact on carers' own children*
- *the difficulty of the task* (p. 46)

It is interesting (and perhaps instructive) to note that the term 'role confusion' is used to describe a failure on the part of certain individuals to treat foster carers as professional colleagues. It seems to beg the question: Is it role confusion or is it unacceptably poor practice that leads to foster carers feeling undervalued as professional contributors?

This can be linked to one of our key themes, that of the importance of perception and meaning – the phenomenological theme. It can be argued that working effectively with foster carers depends in part at least on being able to appreciate their perspective, to be able to have at least some understanding of the pressures they face, the impact of the situation on their family and their lives and so on. Foster carers may well be a valuable resource, but we should not forget that they are a *human* resource. A failure to appreciate the significance of this point can lead to a lot of ill-feeling and, ultimately, a breakdown in partnership.

Johansen (1999) argues that it is not only the approach of individual workers that can shape working relationships with foster carers, but also the approach of the local authority concerned. She comments:

> The process of building genuine and constructive partnerships with carers depends on the individual workers but also on the approach of the authority. Each agency or authority will have its own views on where carers sit in the hierarchy and how they should be managed. Often such views are quite covert and the mind set may have passed from worker to worker unquestioned.
>
> Happily, some authorities treat their carers as a very valuable resource, a partnership to be worked on and looked after. Carers are sensitively and appropriately assessed, trained, involved, consulted and the development of the carers seen as important.

> *This approach motivates carers and allows them to feel really part of a team.* (p. 171)

Johansen is painting the positive side of what can happen in terms of how foster carers are treated. However, as we have seen, we also have to recognise that relations with carers can equally be very negative and problematic. Good communication and being prepared to listen to foster carers can therefore be seen as essential components of good practice. In this regard, it is worth examining the findings of research into what foster carers want from social workers. These are summarised by Sellick and Thoburn (1996) as follows:

- *Link workers and children's social workers who combine professional competence with a number of personal qualities (Sellick, 1996b).*
- *Social workers who are well informed, purposeful, accessible and reliable and who establish a trusting working relationship, build rapport with foster carers and fully acknowledge the personal costs to them and their families (Sellick, 1992, 1996b; Bradley and Aldgate, 1994; Department of Health, 1995 a and b; Pugh, 1996).*
- *Link workers who use their working relationship to develop foster carers' practice. (Sellick, 1992; Triseliotis et al., 1995).*
- *Link workers are also valued by carers when they liaise on their behalf with others, including children's social workers. Temporary foster carers, especially those who provide very short-term placements, often come into contact with several different social workers with whom they have not established the same kind of working relationship (Sellick, 1992, 1996b; Department of Health 1995a).*
- *Children's social workers are valued by carers when they provide immediate placement-related support. The need for alternative points of contact in the absence of the link or child's social workers especially outside office hours is routinely mentioned by foster carers (Sellick, 1992; Waterhouse, 1992; Fry, 1994).*
- *Relevant practice based training is welcomed when it is provided as a result of the foster carers' own expressed wishes and when*

foster carers and social workers are trained alongside one another (Department of Health, 1995a and b; Sellick, 1996b).
- *The opportunity to participate in support groups and informal networks of foster carers is welcomed to enable foster carers to share experiences and tackle common problems together.*
- *Children's workers and link workers who work together to ensure that respite facilities for foster families are available which offer choice and flexibility. Placement Agreements must offer an opportunity to build in respite support from the start. Shared care arrangements with other foster carers and residential establishments, day care provision and specially recruited 'teen sitters' are examples of this method of support.*
- *Link workers and children's social workers who ensure that expert and accessible specialist advice is available, especially from local health, education and psychological services.*
- *A foster care management which provides a reliable, realistic and fair income (Rhodes, 1993; Ramsay, 1996) as well as efficient systems for compensating foster carers for damage to themselves, their homes and possessions and those of others such as neighbours. This should include the provision of legal defence costs for carers.* (pp. 50–1)

This is a long and detailed list, but careful study of it should make it clear that it is a reasonable set of expectations for a group of people who undertake a very challenging and demanding set of tasks and who are committed enough to give up a proportion of their family peace and privacy in order to do so.

Exercise 3.4
What steps can you take to ensure that foster carers are adequately supported and valued? What do you see as the most important elements of positive working relationships with foster carers?

Residential child care staff are another group who regularly come into contact with field social work staff. It is therefore worth investing some time and effort in considering the implications of the interrelationships between field social workers and residential staff.

Utting (1991) makes the important point that:

> *Scrupulous assessment and review, requiring co-operation between a number of public agencies, is the basis of child care work. Children should not be placed in residential homes, even in emergencies or for assessment, without careful consideration of the alternatives, and a positive decision that the residential placement is the best. Children should be asked to live in residential homes on the basis that this is a positive and jointly considered choice.* (p. 9)

An emphasis on 'family values' has tended to produce a view that residential care is an option of last resort – that is, something that should be considered only when all other family-based options have been exhausted. This causes (at least) three sets of problems:

1. By the time children or young people are admitted to residential care, it is likely that they have already experienced a number of 'failing' family situations. Residential care staff are therefore faced with an extremely challenging job in so far as they are being asked to work positively with people whose experiences of the care system to date are likely to be anything but positive.
2. Residential care becomes stigmatised as the place where the 'worst' cases are dealt with, the 'end of the line', as it were. This adds extra burdens for those who are admitted and extra pressures for the staff who work with them.
3. Children and young people whose needs may be better served in a residential setting may not get the opportunity of a placement in a suitable setting or may only get that chance after they have been through one or more painful or even traumatic experiences in other, family-based placements.

It is therefore important that we do not slide into the stereotypical view of residential child care as simply the 'last resort' for 'hard to place' children and young people.

Adams (1998) comments on the importance of adequate staffing in residential care:

> *Many of the questions about whether quality care is possible return to fundamental issues such as the inadequacy of staffing levels and shortcomings in the training of staff* (Millham, Bullock and Hosie, 1980; Stewart, Yea and Brown, 1989). *Staffing weaknesses in residential child care include failures of management to address such issues as staffing levels, staff training, support and supervision and staff burnout, sickness rates and turnover* (Beddoe, 1980). *Moreover, when problems such as suspected or actual abuse of children arise, the inspectorial systems external to residential child care establishments in particular are not always strong enough to be capable of addressing the difficulties.* (p. 163)

Indeed, the publication of the Waterhouse Report into abuse in residential child care establishments in North Wales in the 1970s and 80s made similar comments about the need to make sure that adequate managerial and support systems are in place (Waterhouse, 2000). Without such systems, residential child care is unlikely to fulfil its potential as a positive resource for children and young people and will also continue to cause problems for staff employed in this sector.

Corby (2000) points out that child protection services in the late 1980s and early 90s became very bureaucratic and proceduralised, an approach which was criticised by government-sponsored research (DoH/SSI, 1995a). He goes on to argue that:

> *It would be a great pity if residential work were to make similar mistakes. Thus, for instance, it is important that:*
>
> - *Recruitment of staff to residential posts is not entirely taken over by procedures designed to weed out potential sex abusers.*
> - *Training is broad-based and focused on the needs of children rather than on non-abusive means of controlling them.*
> - *Complaints be managed in a way that ensures non-defensive and speedy reactions rather than becoming long drawn out and heavily proceduralised affairs.*
> - *Managers of residential care be involved in problem-solving alongside staff rather than seeing their tasks purely and simply as measuring outcomes and dealing with complaints.* (p. 14)

These are important words of counsel for a branch of social care which has experienced major problems not only in recent years, but also going back decades. While there are clearly significant efforts currently being made to address these difficulties, it is important that field work staff are aware of these difficulties so that they can help and support in whatever ways they can – or, at the very least, make sure that they do not make the problems worse through insensitivity or a lack of understanding.

Exercise 3.5

What role do you believe field social workers have in working alongside residential staff? What responsibilities do you feel are associated with this role?

If you have the opportunity, it would be a very valuable exercise for you to discuss this situation with one or more residential child care staff: how do they see their role? How do they see your role? Are there any conflicts or contradictions between their views and yours?

One final point worthy of emphasis in relation to residential care is the importance of the relationship between field and residential staff and the need for both parties to work together in partnership. As Hume *et al.* (2000) comment:

> One of the ironies of current social work practice is that social workers have the statutory powers, responsibilities and duties with regard to looked-after children, but spend little time working with or developing real relationships with them. When the purchasing role is added to the social workers [sic] statutory keywork duties, it seems to produce an unbalanced power relationship with care providers. One deleterious consequence of this situation is that the field social worker often comes to see provider services as accountable to them for their practice and never the other way round. Developing a mutually respectful and joint approach to looked-after children with shared accountabilities is obviously essential, but is still not a common reality. (p. 39)

Accessing community resources

So far in this chapter we have concentrated on interprofessional relations. However, another important element in the partnership equation is the role of the wider community. This is partly because children, young people and their families are part of the communities in which they live and will therefore be influenced (in terms of local cultures, assumptions, patterns of behaviour and interaction and so on) and partly because the community can be a significant source of help at times.

'Community' is a term that is very easy to use but much more difficult to define. Broadly, it can be seen to encompass the role of individuals and families in the local area (the neighbourhood) and therefore incorporates the notion of 'neighbourliness', as well as the role of organisations, such as voluntary groups and associations.

Communities vary enormously in terms of how much activity goes on and how effective such activities are in supporting the well-being of that community and its members. Many areas have received state input in terms of community work (or community development work) – a range of activities geared towards solving community problems and enhancing community resources and functioning. Francis and Henderson (1992) define community work in the following terms:

> Community work is a process of helping groups in the community to develop, in order to tackle their needs, disadvantage or inequality. Community work helps people to identify their needs, to come together in a group, to be supported in the action which they decide to take in order to achieve their goals. It is a learning process, encouraging people collectively to improve their skills, confidence, awareness and understanding, in order to acquire resources and influence. Often, the issues may span a number of different fields, such as health, social services, education, housing, employment, the environment, recreation, the arts. Community work is also concerned with making the services of statutory, voluntary and private organisations more flexible, relevant and responsive to people's needs and demands. (p. x)

While there are clearly some points of overlap between community work, as described here, and social work, it is clearly totally unrealistic to expect social work staff to engage in community work in addition to their existing heavy workloads. A realistic move towards community-based forms of social work requires, in most cases, far more of a culture shift in terms of how services and work responsibilities are organised and the priorities that are given to competing areas. However, this is not to say that we cannot move at all in the direction of a higher degree of community involvement.

Barber (1991) argues that we can and should go 'beyond casework', to encompass a broader understanding of people and their circumstances. Similarly, the systems theory literature (see Payne, 1997, Chapter 6) emphasises the need to move beyond a narrow focus on the individual and/or family and to take on board the wider systems at a macro-social level. Similarly, the radical social work movement of the 1960s and 70s criticised traditional social work for its individualist focus and its lack of awareness of broader social issues (see, for example, Corrigan and Leonard, 1978). This critique formed part of the roots from which modern anti-discriminatory practice has developed (Thompson, 2001). However, it was also partly from this critique that a stronger focus on the community developed, although interest in the community context of social work has tended to wax and wane over the years. These issues, of course, raise the question of *how*? How can we develop a stronger community dimension to our work with children, young people and their families?

This is far too complex a set of issues to offer a simple formula for developing community-based approaches. However, the following ideas should be helpful in raising awareness of what needs to be done and therefore acting as a starting point:

- *Community knowledge* It is not uncommon for social work staff to be so busy working within communities that, ironically, they have little opportunity to learn about that community, what it has to offer and so on. It is relatively easy to become engrossed with specific cases and thereby lose sight of the broader context. However, there is no

substitute for having an adequate knowledge of the community context in which we are working – see the discussion below of 'community profiling'.
- *Community involvement* This works in two directions. First, staff can play a part in being involved in community activities, for example by serving on particular committees. This comment may raise objections along the lines of 'I haven't got time for that sort of thing', but these can be countered by the argument that time devoted to such activities is likely to save a lot of time and effort in other spheres due to the benefits to be gained from a closer community liaison. It is also important to note that it is not necessary for all workers to be involved in this type of activity. Second, members of the community can be involved in professional fora. Citizen representatives can be encouraged to become involved in planning and other such processes – see Beresford and Croft (1992) for a very helpful and informative discussion of the value and practicalities of 'citizen involvement'.
- *Community context* This refers to the value of remembering that every case we deal with has its roots in some way in the local community. We therefore need to keep coming back to the question of: What is the community dimension to this situation?

Exercise 3.6
What other steps do you feel you may be able to take to bring a greater community dimension to your work without overloading you? You may find it helpful to discuss these issues with colleagues.

An important issue to consider in relation to community-based approaches is the role of community audit. Hawtin *et al.* (1994) describe in detail what is involved in what they refer to as 'community profiling'. They explain its significance as follows:

many local authorities, faced with a rising tide of poverty, disadvantage and inequality in their areas together with diminishing resources with which to address such problems, have used social audits or community profiles to inform decision making about the allocation of resources. Some local authorities are also using community profiles to inform strategies for the development of decentralized and comprehensive service delivery. Others have recognised their use in developing baselines which can then be used in the monitoring and evaluation of policies and programmes. Increasingly, too, statutory agencies are interested in ways of obtaining feedback from their 'customers' reflecting the new emphasis on the needs of the customer as opposed to those of the producer. (pp. 1–2)

This raises two important questions:

1. Do you have access to relevant community profile information that can be used to guide and inform practice?
2. If not, what possibilities exist for such profiling work to be undertaken?

As far as 1. is concerned, it is sometimes the case that such information is available, but it has not been disseminated adequately, and so staff may well be unaware that the information has already been collated. In relation to 2, this may be something that needs to be raised through a team meeting and fed into higher management fora in order to try to effect the development of such profiling. It is also worth noting that a small-scale community profiling exercise can be a useful learning experience for a student on placement if assigned as a project.

Another aspect of the community dimension is pointed out by Butler and Roberts (1997) when they comment that, in order to comply with the Children Act 1989: 'The local authority is required to "facilitate the provision by others" of support services (s.17 (5))' (p. 92). This reflects the movement away from the state as a major provider of services towards a greater emphasis of facilitating, regulating and purchasing or commissioning services. There is an expectation, then, that Social Services Departments will play a role in supporting the provision of services by the voluntary and private sectors – for example, through the provision of grants to relevant voluntary bodies or community associations. There should already be, then, links between the statutory and independent sectors to act as a potential foundation for further development.

It also has to be recognised that an understanding of the role of the community has to be premised on an appreciation of local cultures and their influence on individuals, families and organisations. In Wales this is particularly significant in relation to Welsh language and culture. There is a clear danger in seeking to understand the community context of social work with children, young people and their families without taking account of the cultural focus of that community, its linguistic make-up and so on.

Indeed, the importance of language issues should not be underestimated. Just as the language or languages a person speaks are very much part of his or her identity, so too can we see that the languages spoken in a community are very much part of the identity of that community. An important point to recognise in this regard is that languages do not coexist alongside each other in a relationship of equality. Languages follow the general rules of society and fit in with the social power hierarchy to be found in the community at large. In Wales, this means that, despite legal equivalence, the Welsh language occupies a less powerful position than English. This can have a number of implications for Welsh speakers, not least a negative attitude towards the Welsh language. As Davies (1994) comments:

Negative attitudes towards the language:

- *influence the speaker's self-image*
- *affect their confidence and willingness to use it*
- *prevent bilingual people from speaking their chosen language.* (p. 48)

A lack of awareness of the significance of language within communities can therefore be a significant barrier to working in partnership with a given community.

Partnership with local communities is, of course, also fraught with other difficulties for social workers. This is largely because of the 'bad press' that social work tends to receive (Aldridge, 1994), often leaving local communities with stereotypes of social workers as 'child snatchers', or at least as less than competent 'do-gooders'. This means that we often have an uphill struggle, in the sense that we start from a position of deficit – with many members of the community expecting us to be more of a problem than a solution. As I have argued previously:

In view of the established negative image of social workers and the social work profession, it is important that we acknowledge that we are, in effect, starting from a deficit. That is, we may well be seen as not very competent or useful before we have even begun to get involved. (Thompson, 2000b, p. 157)

A further important issue in relation to community links that flows from this is our presentation of self – both personal and professional, as discussed earlier in relation to multidisciplinary collaboration. That is, how we come across as individuals (and as representatives of our professional group) can be an important determinant of how people perceive us and thus how they respond to us. This can be an important part of overcoming the 'deficit' of the negative image that so often plagues our encounters with others. The skills involved in effective self-presentation can therefore be seen as important elements in helping to develop good community links.

Finally, in relation to the role of the community in social work with children, young people and their families, it is worth commenting on the important concept of welfare pluralism. This is a term used to refer to the recognition that, although we have what can broadly be described as a welfare state, it is not only – or even primarily – the state that provides welfare (Johnson, 1987; 1990). Indeed, welfare provision can be divided into the following main categories:

- *the statutory sector* – state services provided through local government, the NHS and so on;
- *the voluntary sector* – charitable bodies, community associations and so on, ranging from small-scale local organisations to major, national bodies, such as the NSPCC;
- *the private sector* – provision of services by profit-making enterprises, such as private children's homes and fostering agencies; and
- *the informal sector* – assistance and support from family, friends, neighbours, colleagues and so on.

It is important to be clear about these four sectors and the range of problems and solutions they encompass, as it is very easy to

have a narrow view of welfare as primarily, if not more or less exclusively, a matter for state provision. If we allow ourselves to adopt this narrow view, we will not appreciate the significance of the wider context or what it potentially has to offer. The term welfare pluralism is therefore one that we would do well to bear in mind.

Exercise 3.7
Consider your current workload. In the range of situations you are called upon to deal with, what roles do the other sectors play? Can you identify any ways in which you could develop or enhance the part they play? Consider this both as an individual worker and more broadly at a collective level – for example, in terms of the team or work group of which you form a part.

3. Tasks and challenges

In this section we consider the implications for practice in terms of the relevant practice requirements for this chapter:

C1 Work with children and young person's networks and communities to achieve optimal outcomes.

Each individual can be seen as part and parcel of a network of significant people who, in various ways, play a variety of roles. Children and young people are no exception to this. Although, in working with a particular individual, we are indeed working with a unique individual, we are none the less dealing with someone with a complex web of interconnections with other individuals, groups and communities. We ignore this network at our peril, as it is clearly a major factor in shaping each child and young person's life experiences and therefore their attitudes, values and actions. It is also, potentially at least, a major source of support and valuable resources that can be drawn upon to help solve problems, meet needs and enable progress to be made.

For many children and young people, the network of which they form a part takes on a new significance when family arrangements break down and substitute care needs to be arranged. The role of substitute carers (both foster carers and residential staff) is therefore clearly a major one. This lays down the challenge for us of being able to work closely and effectively with foster care and residential care colleagues. Phenomenology features significantly here, as it is important for field social work staff to have an appreciation of the pressures substitute carers experience and the skills and resources they bring to the task. We must be wary of projecting our own views of the situation on to others. This is certainly no substitute for listening carefully and with respect.

Similar comments could be made about working with the broader community. We need to aware of:

- the community context – the significance of local culture, facilities and resources, as well as problems, tensions and gaps;
- the significance of the community for the individuals and families we are dealing with – what that community or particular aspects of it mean to them (the phenomenological dimension);
- the need to incorporate a community dimension into our actions and our plans – the community is not going to go away, and pretending it is not there is clearly an unwise approach to adopt.

Of course, we have to be realistic in terms of what can be achieved as far as community links are concerned. The community is vast and complex and so we cannot tackle all the aspects. We have to be selective about how and when we interrelate with various sections of the community, but one thing remains quite clear – we do have to interrelate with the community.

One practical implication of the community dimension is the role of the duty social worker or the intake system more broadly. When members of the community approach a social work agency, then clearly first impressions are very important. If they feel they have been 'fobbed off', not listened to or dealt with disrespectfully, then those impressions can last a long time and do a lot of harm. It is therefore vitally important that initial contact between community members and the agency are handled very well, with clear systems and processes and well-trained and well-prepared staff. This is an important point to emphasise, as difficulties at the duty or intake stage can have major repercussions further down the line, as well as leaving members of the community with a very negative impression of social work and social workers.

C2 Liaise and work with other professionals and agencies to achieve optimal outcomes.

Working with a multitude of others in trying to promote the best interests of the child or young person is not a simple or straightforward task. In that case, perhaps the first point we should acknowledge in relation to practice is that we are going to get it wrong from time to time, we are going to fail to form a coherent partnership that works to best effect. We have to be careful not to saddle ourselves with unrealistic expectations as these are problematic in terms of both their demotivating effects and the possibility that they can lead to stress. The important implication of recognising the difficulty and complexity of multidisciplinary work is that it presents us with excellent opportunities for learning.

The demands of working within a multidisciplinary network have been clearly delineated in this chapter. There should be little doubt, then, that such work needs to be of a highly skilled nature if it is to have any realistic chance of success. What workers face is clearly a major challenge, with a wide range of practice implications.

At base, it means being able to do two main things:

- *Think in broader multidisciplinary terms*. It is very easy to get caught up in the pressures of our own organisation or profession and thereby to lose sight of the 'bigger picture' in which other individuals and agencies feature. We therefore have to train ourselves into thinking in multidisciplinary terms, if we have not already managed to do so.
- *Act in broader multidisciplinary ways*. We must remember that, at all times, we are part of a wider multidisciplinary network. We must bear in mind that what we do may have significant consequences for one or more of the other partners in that network – and that what they do may have a very significant bearing on us, our actions and our plans.

Communication is clearly a major feature of success in this area, but we should be wary of oversimplifying the situation – communication is a very broad and complex set of issues, as we have begun to unravel in this chapter. None the less, it remains a vital part of good practice and therefore one that merits a lot of time and attention. The following questions should therefore be important ones for you to continue to address in relation to every case you deal with:

- Have I communicated appropriately with others so far? For example, have I pitched my communications at the right level?
- Have they communicated appropriately with me, or do I need to chase anyone up?
- Am I clear about who I need to communicate with and why?
- Am I clear about what needs to be communicated (and what does not)?
- What is the best form of communication in each case? (What needs to be in writing?)

Social work necessarily involves dealing with people, and this brings a mixture of joys and frustrations. The challenge of multidisciplinary collaboration is to be able to maximise the joys and minimise the frustrations by drawing on the various skills we have as human services professionals.

4. Conclusion

In this third chapter we have broadened the question of partnership beyond the notion of working effectively with children and young people (Chapter 1) and their families (Chapter 2) to explore the significance of working within the multidisciplinary network, with substitute carers and within the context of the local community.

As with the previous two chapters, what we can see here is that we are dealing with very complex issues. What is needed, then, is a set of concepts that can help us make sense of these complexities and provide a meaningful frame of reference for tackling the issues in practice. In keeping with the spirit of reflective practice, what I have sought to present here is not a set of simple prescriptions for practice, but rather the foundations for a fuller understanding so that the challenges of

practice in this area can be tackled in an informed way.

There are many points that could be emphasised by way of conclusion but I shall restrict myself to two in particular. First, we are once again in the domain of partnership. Good practice in working with multidisciplinary and community networks is premised on partnership, and so a great deal of what has been discussed in this chapter builds on material covered in the earlier two chapters. Second, we need to be wary of the tendency to adopt a narrow focus and lose sight of the wider dimensions of multidisciplinary and community networks. It is understandable that, at times, the pressure of work can lead us to focus very narrowly on the specifics of a particular case without seeing them in their broader context. At these times we run the risk of working on the basis of a distorted and oversimplified view of the situation, and may therefore easily find ourselves in difficulties. The ability to shift focus, to 'zoom out' to the wider context when we need to is therefore an important skill to develop.

5. Points to ponder

➤ What sort of organisational person are you? Do you get fully involved in trying to influence your organisation positively? If not, what is it that holds you back? Is there anything that can be done about any such barriers?

➤ How do you feel about working in collaboration with colleagues from other agencies? What benefits do you perceive for yourself as a worker in working closely with others? What problems does multidisciplinary partnership pose for you?

➤ If you were a foster carer, how would you want to be treated by the social worker working with the child or young person you were fostering? What would your expectations be in terms of the social worker's attitude towards you and his or her relationship with you?

➤ If you have experience of having been a residential child care worker, what do you feel you learned from that experience that can be helpful to you in working with residential staff? If you have no such experience, how would you want to be treated by a field social worker if you were employed as a residential worker?

➤ How much does knowledge of the local community influence your practice? What are your main sources of knowledge of the community? How could you find out more?

6. Learning resources guide

Organisational issues are covered in various textbooks, such as Mullins (1996) or Hucsynski and Buchanan (2001). Chapter 6 of Thompson (1998) discusses the concept of the 'organisational operator' and the organisational context more broadly. Influencing skills are discussed in Lambert (1996) and Thompson (2002a) Chapter 14.

Negotiation is discussed in detail in Kennedy (1998) and Godefroy and Robert (1998). See also Isaac (1991) for a discussion of negotiation in the context of working with children, young people and their families.

Multidisciplinary collaboration is thoroughly explored in Murphy (1995). Although the focus is on child protection, Murphy's analysis has a lot to offer the broader field of multidisciplinary collaboration. Mather *et al.* (2000) provides a very useful guide to health issues affecting looked after children. Harrison *et al.* (2002) address issues of partnership at the wider agency level. Lupton *et al.* (2001) discuss the difficulties of maintaining partnership working in child protection

Working with substitute carers has a fairly substantial literature base to support it. This includes, in relation to foster carers, Wheal (1995) and Wheal (1999); and, in relation to residential work, Burton (1993), Kahan (1994) and Crimmens and Pitts (2000). 'Kinship' care is covered in Broad (2001). A broad overview of 'state' child care is provided in Hayden *et al.* (1999).

Community work in rural communities is discussed in Francis and Henderson (1992). Community audit is the topic of Hawtin *et al.* (1994). Mayo (1994) provides a useful discussion of 'communities and caring'.

4. Law and policy

1. Introduction

This chapter addresses law and policy and emphasises the crucial role that these play as an underpinning foundation of practice. It also stresses the role of practitioners in *contributing to* law and policy, challenging the common misconception that law and policy are, in effect, tablets of stone, with no scope for change, influence or development.

This chapter also seeks to go beyond a technical or mechanistic understanding of the law and policy by exploring phenomenology, meaning and power, thus allowing us to adopt a more critical perspective on this important topic.

The chapter has three different aims:

1. To revisit law and policy and consider them afresh, as it is very easy for such matters to fade into the background and become 'part of the furniture' – taken for granted because they are so much a part of our everyday experience.
2. To explore law and policy at a more advanced level – not simply in terms of the detail of the law, but rather the overall philosophy of professionalism which has its roots in law and policy.
3. To consider ways in which, as a practitioner, you can seek to influence policy and practice – for example, by having a say in whatever fora are available to you.

As in previous chapters, our major focus is on the knowledge base underpinning the topic concerned, in this case, the significance of the legal and policy context and the potential for practitioners to influence or shape it. Having explored the knowledge base, we then move on to examine the practice implications, specifically in relation to the elements of competence that apply to this chapter.

2. The knowledge base

A major feature of the knowledge base underpinning this unit is the emphasis on law

and policy as *processes,* rather than simply fixed entities. We begin to explore this notion of process by examining the relationship between law, policy and practice before moving on to consider how law and policy relate to social work values. Following this we explore some recent developments in the legislative base, focusing in particular on the implementation of the Human Rights Act 1998. This leads into a discussion of professionalism as a key issue and the organisational context as another significant factor.

An exploration of children's services plans and policy factors relating to their development and implementation comes next before we move on to consider the range of skills involved in making a contribution to the development of policy and therefore of practice. Once we have explored the skills involved in influencing policy, we are then in a position to review some of the policy initiatives that are currently of great significance. In particular we shall focus on Best Value and Quality Protects/Children First.

The relationship between law, policy and practice

An important debate that has been going on in social work for a very long time relates to the thorny question of 'What is social work?' While many people would frame their answer in terms of the law (that is, social work is what the law requires social workers to do), I would not wish to go that far (or oversimplify to that extent), but I would certainly want to recognise the significance of the law as a major factor in shaping social work practice.

The report into the death of Jasmine Beckford (London Borough of Brent, 1985) contained a comment from Louis Blom-Cooper to the effect that he saw the law as social work's 'defining mandate'. That is, he saw the law as the primary defining feature of social work. It is perhaps not surprising that someone from a legal background should see social work in these terms, but we do need to put this in context by recognising that there are other forces at work when it comes to defining the nature and purposes of social work, not least the aspirations and values of social workers as a professional group (see Thompson, 2000b). Social work is a contested entity, in the sense that there is no single defining feature, but rather competing definitions and perspectives. However, regardless of what perspective is adopted, it is clear that the law has a central role to play.

This central role, though, does not mean that the relationship between law and practice is a direct one. A key concept to take into consideration is that of *interpretation*. The law does not provide formula solutions for us to adopt, but rather provides a framework or set of parameters in which we must decide how best to operate – see the discussion of professionalism below.

The role of interpretation is described in the following passage:

> *Although the law is often specific and explicit about what can and what cannot be done, there is none the less considerable scope for interpretation. This can be seen to apply at four main levels:*
>
> 1. Statutory guidance *The Government . . . will often issue guidance on how particular pieces of legislation should be applied.*
> 2. Local policies *Local authorities or other social work agencies will develop their own policies and procedures in line with their interpretations of the law and its requirements.*
> 3. Precedent *. . . the law develops through 'precedent', the interpretation of law in specific court cases setting the baseline from which future decisions will be made.*
> 4. Direct practice *The law does not dictate precisely how professionals should act in all situations, and so professional discretion is a further stage of interpretation of the law.*
> (Thompson, 2000b, p. 34)

Exercise 4.1

Consider the role of the law in influencing your practice. Give at least one example of how the law has influenced your practice. Did you find the role of interpretation empowering? If so, in what ways?

Interpretation is clearly a key term when it comes to the relationship between law, policy and practice. The legal mandate is in some ways our starting point, but it would be a significant mistake to fail to take account of the wider issues that have a bearing on the use of the law in practice situations. This is because the law offers some guidance but this is only one small part of the constellation of complex factors that shape our actions in working with children, young people and their families.

In many respects it is the key role of interpretation that offers such a major challenge to social workers. This is because we cannot simply follow the law in a mechanical way – we have to take the law as our starting point and as the set of parameters that govern our work. However, within those parameters, what specific actions we take depends in large part on how we interpret the law, how we interpret the situation we are dealing with, our role within it and so on.

The importance of interpretation reinforces the phenomenological theme, with its emphasis on perception and meaning. Social reality is not 'given' in any direct sense. It has to be constructed through the interpretations of individuals and the wider cultural context of the discourses in which individuals operate. This brings us back to the important issue of power, particularly power at the cultural level of shared meanings through discourse (Thompson, 1998).

Power is commonly seen in oversimplified terms as a form of commodity that some people have and which others do not. However, a more sophisticated understanding of power involves recognising that it works at different levels and is something that all people can exercise. Michel Foucault is the theorist most closely associated with a fuller understanding of power. He emphasised the importance of what he called power/knowledge – the inevitable intertwining of power and knowledge:

> *There is no power relation without the correlative constitution of a field of knowledge, nor any knowledge that does not presuppose and constitute at the same time,*

power relations. (Foucault, 1977, p. 27, cited in Hall, 1997a, p. 49)

For Foucault, power is everywhere, a dimension of all our interactions. This is because, where one person, group or institution is able to wield power, those who are subject to it are able to resist such power to a certain extent at least. And any such resistance is, of course, a form of power in its own right.

This model of power helps us to move away from the traditional view of power which associates power primarily with institutional position. While it is clear that the law is a major site of power, we should not allow ourselves to be distracted from the fact that power also operates at other levels (that is, personal and cultural as well as structural). To see only the structural power of the law as a major social institution is to neglect the scope for influence and change within its broad parameters.

In sum, yes, the law is very powerful in shaping policy and practice but it is not all-powerful and is subject to other forms of power and influence.

Law, policy and values

While it is clear that the relationship between law, policy and practice is indeed complex and multifaceted, we should also note that the addition of values to the combination of factors makes it yet more complex. However, in order to wrestle with this complexity it is important to spell out what roles values play in relation to law, policy and practice.

The first point to emphasise is that the law is a *political* product – that is, it emerges from the political machinery of government. It is therefore likely to reflect the values of its political originators. For example, consider the significance of the Children Act 1989 in relation to the (then) Conservative Government's stance on family values (see Exercise 4.2 below). We could even go so far as to say that the law is in some ways an *expression* of political values, in the sense that the law is a tool that politicians use to meet their political ends – and these ends are, of course, driven by values.

However, this is not the end of the story as far as values are concerned. As noted above, the law becomes translated into policy at a more local level. Social work agencies (such as Social Services Departments, for example) do not simply 'apply' the law in a direct fashion. There is also the question of how law drives policy at this level and therefore how the implementation of the law through policy is again shaped by values – this time by the values of the organisation responsible for policy development.

The values of an organisation are very much a part of its culture, as discussed in Chapter 3 and revisited later in this chapter. These, then, will have a bearing on how the broad parameters of the law become narrowed down in the course of policy development. Consider, for example, the law relating to children with disabilities. As Cooper and Vernon (1996) comment:

The legal structure within which services are provided for children with disability is both complex and confusing. The Children Act 1989 establishes local authority social services departments as the lead agency responsible for co-ordinating social services, education and health care services from a number of different providers according to the assessed needs of a disabled child. The provision of services for a child with special educational needs takes place under the terms of the Education Act 1993; health care services are provided under a number of statutory structures including the National Health Service Act 1977 and the National Health Service and Community Care [Act] 1990. Social services for a disabled child are organised under the Children Act but may be provided under a number of statutory provisions such as the Chronically Sick and Disabled Persons Act 1970, the Disabled Persons (Services, Consultation and Representation) Act 1986 and the Children Act itself. (p. 237)

This web of legal complexities clearly presents major challenges for the development of a clear and coherent framework of policy. Without a clear 'policy steer' from the legislative base, the scope for organisations to adopt their own specific approach to the needs of children with disabilities is quite considerable, as the legal complexity creates a far from clear framework to guide policy and practice. We should not be surprised, then, to find many criticisms of social work organisations failing to pay adequate attention to the needs of disabled children (see, for example, Westcott and Cross, 1996).

Even when we go beyond the level of policy to actual practice, we still do not leave the question of values behind. Implementing law and policy is not simply a mechanical process of following rules. It necessarily involves forming judgements, making decisions and so on, and so we are once again back in the domain of values.

The role of values in shaping decision making is a fundamental part of *professionalism* and so we return to this topic under that heading below.

Exercise 4.2

The point was made above that the Children Act 1989 reflected a commitment to family values. For this exercise, you are asked to consider the following questions:

- What are the 'family values' enshrined in the Children Act 1989?
- How do these values manifest themselves within the Act? Try to give concrete examples.
- Is there any (actual or potential) conflict between these values and the values underpinning anti-discriminatory practice?

Developments in the law

The law is, of course, not a static entity. It changes and develops over time. In this section, therefore, we explore one of the recent developments in the legal base, namely the implementation of the Human Rights Act 1998 – one of the most significant developments ever in the UK legal system.

The Human Rights Act 1998

This important new act was implemented on 2nd October, 2000. In essence, it makes the European Convention on Human Rights (ECHR) part of UK law. That is, those situations involving breaches of human rights which previously needed to be taken to the European Court of Human Rights in Strasbourg can now, for the most part, be addressed in the domestic courts across the UK. The Act applies to 'public

authorities', a term broadly defined to include any organisation which fulfils a public function and therefore clearly applies to those organisations which employ child care social workers, whether in the public, private or voluntary sectors. The term also applies to any court or tribunal.

However, this is not simply a step to make the task of addressing human rights issues more convenient. It is also intended that a philosophy of human rights should become part of the culture of the UK legal systems and even of UK society more broadly. As Crompton and Thompson (2000) comment:

> *The Government's broad aim in introducing the Act is to make a major contribution towards creating a society in which people's rights and responsibilities are balanced. As Straw (2000) puts it: 'A proper balance between the rights of the individual and the needs of the wider community lies at the heart of the ECHR'. The Act seeks to import that European commitment into domestic law.* (p. 2.35)

This is an ambitious aim but one which has received a lot of government support. One very important way in which the Act seeks to influence the overall culture of law and society is through its effect on other pieces of legislation. The important point to note here is that the Human Rights Act 1998 does not only operate directly as an Act of Parliament, it also has an influence on other acts. This is because other pieces of legislation must be interpreted in ways that are compatible with the Human Rights Act. That is, where there is more than one way of interpreting a law, the interpretation chosen must be compatible with the requirements of the new Act. In other words, where there is a possible conflict between an existing piece of legislation and the new Act, the human rights perspective must prevail. If necessary, in some cases Acts of Parliament will be changed to bring them into line with a culture of human rights.

The provisions of the Act are quite wide-ranging but Singh (1997) captures the central core when he argues that:

> *The concept which lies at the heart of human rights is that of equality. The idea of equality*

also provides the link between democracy and human rights, since democracy rests on the essential equality of human beings, no matter what their differences in birth, wealth or education. (p. 2)

We can therefore see the Human Rights Act 1998 as an important development in anti-discrimination legislation, and therefore an important underpinning of anti-discriminatory practice. It is beyond our scope here to provide a comprehensive overview of the Act and so we shall restrict ourselves to highlighting some of the key provisions.

The Act, as noted above, is based on the ECHR, and therefore refers to the 'articles' which form the building bricks of the Convention. The following are some of the articles that are likely to have major implications for working with children, young people and their families:

Article 3

No one shall be subjected to torture or to inhuman or degrading treatment or punishment.

The Waterhouse Report (Waterhouse, 2000) provides us with very many examples of how children and young people can be subjected to degrading treatment and punishment. While we are collectively as a profession seeking to take on board the lessons of the Waterhouse Inquiry and other such investigations, the Human Rights Act 1998 clearly adds extra weight to the need to avoid degrading or inhuman approaches to dealing with children and young people.

Article 5

1. Everyone has the right to liberty and security of person. No one shall be deprived of his [or her] liberty save in the following cases and in accordance with a procedure prescribed by law:
(a) the lawful detention of a person after conviction by a competent court;
(b) the lawful arrest or detention of a person for non-compliance with the lawful order of a court or in order to secure the fulfilment of any obligation prescribed by law;
(c) the lawful arrest or detention of a person effected for the purpose of bringing him [or her] before the competent legal authority on reasonable suspicion of having committed an offence or when it is reasonably considered necessary to prevent his [or her] committing an offence or fleeing after having done so;
(d) the detention of a minor by lawful order for the purpose of educational supervision or his [or her] lawful detention for the purpose of bringing him [or her] before the competent legal authority;
(e) the lawful detention of persons for the prevention of the spreading of infectious diseases, of persons of unsound mind, alcoholics or drug addicts or vagrants;
(f) the lawful arrest or detention of a person to prevent his [or her] effecting an unauthorised entry into the country or of a person against whom action is being taken with a view to deportation or extradition.

2. Everyone who is arrested shall be informed promptly, in a language which he [or she] understands, of the reasons for his [or her] arrest and of any charge against him [or her].

3. Everyone arrested or detained in accordance with the provisions of paragraph I(c) of this article shall be brought promptly before a judge or other officer authorised by law to exercise judicial power and shall be entitled to trial within a reasonable time or to release pending trial. Release may be conditioned by guarantees to appear for trial.

4. Everyone who is deprived of his [or her] liberty by arrest or detention shall be entitled to take proceedings by which the lawfulness of his [or her] detention shall be decided speedily by a court and his [or her] release ordered if the detention is not lawful.

5. Everyone who has been the victim of arrest or detention in contravention of the provisions of this article shall have an enforceable right to compensation.

This clearly has implications for those situations where children or young people are being held against their will for a variety of reasons. In any such situation it will therefore be necessary for considerable care to be taken to ensure that the steps taken are consistent with this article and its various sub-clauses.

Article 8

1. Everyone has the right to respect for his [or her] private and family life, his [or her] home and his [or her] correspondence.

2. There shall be no interference by a public authority with the exercise of this right except such as is in accordance with the law and is necessary in a democratic society in the interests of national security, public safety or the economic well-being of the country, for the prevention of disorder or crime, for the protection of health or morals, or for the protection of the rights and freedoms of others.

In many ways this article reinforces the Children Act 1989's emphasis on the importance of the family, placing particular weight on the need for privacy to be respected. Where there is a need to act against the privacy of the family (in respect of child protection inquiries for example), due care will need to be taken to ensure that privacy is only breached where there is sufficient concern to justify such action. A balance will need to be struck between the welfare of the child or young person and the right to respect for family life and privacy. This in effect gives a legal dimension to what has long been a dilemma or balancing act of professional practice.

Article 9

1. Everyone has the right to freedom of thought, conscience and religion; this right includes freedom to change his [or her] religion or belief and freedom, either alone or in community with others and in public or private, to manifest his [or her] religion or belief in worship, teaching, practice and observance.

2. Freedom to manifest one's religion or beliefs shall be subject only to such limitations as are prescribed by law and are necessary in a democratic society in the interests of public safety, for the protection of public order, health or morals, or for the protection of the rights and freedoms of others.

The importance of ethnically sensitive practice is something that has been recognised for a long time. However, it can be argued that its implementation as a principle of good practice has been very patchy indeed. This article raises it above the level of an expectation of good practice and makes it a legal requirement – and therefore what should become part of standard practice.

Article 10

1. Everyone has the right to freedom of expression. This right shall include freedom to hold opinions and to receive and impart information and ideas without interference by public authority and regardless of frontiers. This article shall not prevent States from requiring the licensing of broadcasting, television or cinema enterprises.

2. The exercise of these freedoms, since it carries with it duties and responsibilities, may be subject to such formalities, conditions, restrictions or penalties as are prescribed by law and are necessary in a democratic society, in the interests of national security, territorial integrity or public safety, for the prevention of disorder or crime, for the protection of health or morals, for the protection of the reputation or rights of others, for preventing the disclosure of information received in confidence, or for maintaining the authority and impartiality of the judiciary.

Again this is something that has long been recognised as an essential part of high-quality practice, but which must now become part of standard practice – a legal requirement rather than simply an exhortation to good practice. This article can be seen as a basis for partnership – listening to children and young people, giving them opportunities to express their wishes, feelings, concerns and so on. It is also a fundamental part of child-centred practice.

Article 2 of the First Protocol

No person shall be denied the right to education. In the existence of any functions which it assumes in relation to education and to teaching, the State shall respect the right of parents to ensure that such education and teaching in conformity with their own religious and philosophical convictions.

As we shall note below in relation to Quality Protects and Children First, the importance of education is something which needs to be given a higher profile. This article not only adds extra weight to this but also emphasises the need to make sure that such education is well-suited to the religion and philosophy of parents. This again lays stress on the importance of both ethnically sensitive practice and working in partnership, this time working with parents.

The Human Rights Act 1998 clearly has major implications for social work with children, young people and their parents – and we have not seen the whole story, as there are other aspects of the Act that are significant too. As mentioned above, the discussion here is necessarily selective.

Exercise 4.3

What difference is the Human Rights Act 1998 likely to make to your practice? Consider the points made above (plus any other information on the Act you may have come across), and identify what changes are likely to be needed.

The Human Rights Act 1998 has major implications for managers, policy-makers and organisations as a whole and so the implications extend far beyond simply our own individual practice. It is likely that, for the foreseeable future at least, organisations will need to wrestle with the implications of this profound change in the legal system and keep a close eye on developments as the new law 'beds down'. This is an important point to which we shall return below when we consider the question of how practitioners can influence policy development and implementation.

A further point to note is that the advent of the Human Rights Act 1998 can be seen as a useful lever in the development of a rights-based approach to social work with children, young people and their families as part of a movement away from the superparenting model discussed earlier in the book in which control can feature more than it needs to and care can lead to dependency creation.

Professionalism

The theme of professionalism has been an important one throughout this book. This is partly because, however constrained we may feel at times, we none the less remain accountable for our actions, and so we have to ensure that our actions can be justified. Such justification has to be in *professional* terms – that is, in relation to:

- the professional knowledge base
- professional values
- the law and policy context governing professional practice

It is this third point which concerns us for present purposes. A common misunderstanding (or at least misrepresentation) is to be found in the view that a social worker has little or no professional autonomy because he or she is primarily 'following orders' in the sense that the law and related policies give little or no room for manoeuvre. Professionalism, so the argument goes, is a myth because the task is basically to follow the strong lead given by the law and policy.

The fallacy of this view can be recognised at (at least) two levels:

- *Interpretation.* As noted above, the law does not provide detailed prescriptions for action – even its basic requirements call for some degree of interpretation.
- *Accountability.* In the event of a serious service breakdown or other such problem resulting in an inquiry, investigation or legal action, 'I was only following orders' would clearly not be an acceptable comment for a professional practitioner to make in his or her defence.

It therefore has to be recognised that being a professional involves understanding the requirements of the various legal provisions that apply and the related requirements of policies, procedures, guidelines, codes of practice and so on, but also understanding what needs to be done in each unique practice situation. The legal and policy requirements may well be a significant part of the story, but they are not the whole story – in fact, in many ways they are just the start of the story and it is what the professional practitioner does within the parameters of those requirements that really counts.

The law is therefore not a barrier to reflective practice – indeed, the nature of the law and its relationship with practice makes reflective practice a necessity. If the legal mandate is, as described above, only one part of the overall range of factors, then there are clearly various other issues that can be seen to have a bearing. Reflective practice can help to equip us to address these, in the sense that reflective practice enables the integration of theory and practice. Reflective practice lays the foundations for an holistic approach which guards against a narrow focus on any one aspect – including an aspect as important as the law. The law offers some degree of guidance but does not take away responsibility for the professional task and the decision-making involved. As Cull and Roche (2001) comment:

> *The law does not and cannot provide an answer to the complex human questions that lie at the centre of the social work task. . . . The law thus provides authority and a structure for decision-making, rather than solutions; it provides the framework within which social workers have to act.* (p. xiii)

Exercise 4.4

In what ways can (an understanding of) the law be used to develop and support reflective practice?

The organisational context

In Chapter 3 we began to explore the significance of the organisational context as a factor (or set of factors) in shaping practice. We return to this topic here to emphasise its significance in relation to law and policy in general and professionalism in particular.

As we have seen, the law is 'filtered' through the level of local policy-making machinery and through the actual day-to-day implementation of such policy. All this is undertaken within an organisational context. That is, it does not occur in a vacuum, uninfluenced by the organisation in which the filtering is taking place. An important element to consider here is the role of organisational culture – the shared ways of seeing, thinking and doing that form the

unwritten rules of an organisation or part of an organisation ('the way we do things around here'). As Schein (1992) comments:

> *Organizational culture is the **pattern of basic assumptions** that **a given group** has **invented, discovered, or developed in learning to cope** with its **problems of external adaptation and internal integration**, and that have **worked well enough to be considered valid**, and, therefore, **to be taught to new members** as the correct way to **perceive, think, and feel** in relation to those problems.* (p. 237, emphasis in original)

Organisational cultures are clearly powerful in shaping the behaviour and responses of the staff who work within them. The development and implementation of policies can therefore be heavily influenced by an organisation's culture. For example, some organisations can have a very defensive culture in which risk-taking is heavily discouraged, and supposedly safe approaches are valued and reinforced. In such cases, the translation of law into policy and of policy into practice can be quite narrow and limited rather than imaginative and progressive. The irony here is that a defensive culture in which risk-taking is frowned upon can actually produce lower standards of practice and thus increase the likelihood of things going seriously wrong (see the discussion of defensive practice in Thompson, 2000b).

The comments of Bate (1992) are significant in this regard:

> *People in organizations evolve in their daily interactions with one another a system of shared perspectives of 'collectively held and sanctioned definitions of the situations' which make up the culture of these organizations. The culture, once established, prescribes for its creators and inheritors certain ways of believing, thinking and acting which in some circumstances can prevent meaningful interaction and induce a condition of 'learned helplessness' – that is a psychological state in which people are unable to conceptualize their problems in such a way as to be able to resolve them. In short, attempts at problem-solving may become culture-bound.* (p. 214)

As Bate's comments make clear, a negative culture characterised by 'learned helplessness' can be a serious barrier to developing high standards of practice if it discourages innovative, empowering forms of practice.

Indeed, there are many aspects of organisational culture that can stand in the way of good practice. Our discussion in Chapter 3 of the 'organisational operator' is one that is very relevant here. If we wish to move away from any negative effects of organisational culture, then our ability to intervene at a cultural level to influence the organisation becomes even more important.

An important point to note in this regard is that, in many cases, the influence of a culture can in itself undermine the role of the organisational operator. That is, a defensive culture is often also a defeatist culture characterised by what I would call self-disempowerment. Staff working in such a culture may have internalised learned helplessness in the form of a 'there's nothing I can do' attitude as part of the culture itself. Indeed, this is often how such cultures manage to sustain themselves – by incorporating one or more such self-protective mechanisms.

This adds an extra degree of importance to developing the skills of being an effective organisational operator, as such skills are necessary to counter the influences of cultures which discourage openness, change and development.

Exercise 4.5

How would you describe the culture of the organisation in which you are employed? Is it defensive or progressive? Is it characterised by openness or are there many hidden agendas? Is there a degree of 'learned helplessness'? How well-equipped do you feel to challenge even in some small way any negative aspects of your organisation's culture? What steps do you need to take in order to become more influential?

Returning to our important theme of professionalism, one important aspect of developing such professionalism is the recognition that the demands of our profession should be rated more highly than the demands of our employers. This is a very important point,

although one that can be very difficult to realise in some organisations or at some times. For example, some organisations lay little store by professionalism and prefer to rely on issuing bureaucratic commands as far as possible. Such organisations present a major challenge for making professionalism a reality rather than simply a rhetorical assertion. However, this does not take away the fact that, as professionals, we are indeed accountable for our actions. As we have noted, professional accountability is not something to be worked towards – it is something that is an inherent part of our practice. We could not avoid it if we wanted to. The danger of simply following orders should therefore be perfectly clear, and so we have to be very careful to avoid and resist those aspects of organisational culture which promote a model of social work practice as a form of bureaucratic rule-following. Payne (2000) argues that contemporary social work is characterised by high levels of bureaucracy and the organisational inflexibility that goes with such bureaucracy. He contends that anti-bureaucratic forms of practice need to be developed in order to promote high-quality practice in general and anti-discriminatory or anti-oppressive practice in particular.

The role and significance of children's services plans

A key feature of policy in relation to social work with children, young people and their families is the part played by children's services plans. The need for local authorities to prepare and publish children's services plans has its roots in the report of Sir William Utting on children in public care (DoH, 1991) where the recommendation for such plans was made. In 1992 this recommendation was endorsed by the Secretary of State in an official circular which advised local authorities to draw up such plans.

This was subsequently turned into a requirement rather than a piece of advice through the implementation of the Children Act 1989 (Amendment) (Children's Services Planning) Order 1996. This came into effect on April 1st, 1996. This amendment had the effect of obliging local authorities to assess the need for Part III services, consult with relevant bodies and produce plans accordingly. It also required local authorities to publish their plans – that is, to make them available as public documents.

This development was highly significant for (at least) two reasons:

- It emphasised the importance of planning at a *corporate* level. That is, while the quality and consistency of plans for individual cases can be seen to vary enormously from area to area and from worker to worker, the need for an overall corporate plan adds an extra dimension and provides at least a baseline to work from and an overall context for individual plans.
- The process through which children's services plans are developed necessarily involves consultation with 'stakeholders' and was therefore a major step in the direction of a more participative approach.

The plan for a particular local authority is therefore a very significant policy document. It is important as a basis for current practice but it is also not a fixed entity. That is, planning is a process that carries on over time, leading to revised plans over a set timescale. The participative nature of the process means that practitioners, individually and collectively can at least have the potential for having a say in what develops and thus influencing the outcome.

Exercise 4.6

Do you have a detailed knowledge of the children's services plan relating to your area? If so, how does this guide the direction, tone or emphasis of your practice? If not, how can you find out more about what the plan says and what its implications are for you and your colleagues and the clientele you serve? What can you do to influence the process of review and revision of the plan?

Skills

This unit should by now have made it clear that the world of law and policy is a complex one but one that is not beyond the reach of influence of the professionals working within its parameters. Being able to make a difference in terms of policy and practice is an important and worthwhile goal, but clearly not a simple or straightforward one to achieve. Indeed,

achieving such a goal is likely to depend upon being able to draw upon a number of important skills. Here we identify some of these key skills and explore how they can be used as part of an overall strategy of seeking to shape the broader policy context of our work.

- *Reading policy*
  By this, of course, I do not simply mean the ability to read a policy document. Rather, I mean the ability to think at a policy level above and beyond the level of individual cases. This is, in a sense, the ability to think holistically, to see patterns and interconnections rather than simply a series of individual problems to be tackled or cases to be managed. This is closely associated with the notion of the 'sociological imagination' (Mills, 1970) – the ability to think in broader social terms, a characteristic that has received a great deal of attention in connection with the development of anti-discriminatory practice.

- *Reading organisations*
  In Chapter 3 and again earlier in this chapter we encountered the idea of the 'organisational operator', someone who is skilled in influencing the organisation in which they are employed. The skills involved in being an organisational operator are very important in playing a part promoting anti-discriminatory practice. They include being able to 'read the organisation' – that is, being able to recognise patterns of organisational culture or 'tuning in' to the everyday norms, assumptions and customs that become part of the fabric of organisational life.

- *Using research evidence*
  The importance of 'evidence-based practice' has already been stressed. This is because the effectiveness of what social workers do needs to be open to question so that learning and development can take place. A basic component of evidence-based practice is the ability to use research appropriately, to weave relevant findings into the rationale underpinning our actions – what Everitt *et al.* (1992) call 'research-minded practice'.

- *Presentation skills*
  Perhaps in an ideal world presentation skills would not matter. That is, the value of what

someone has to say would be judged on its own merits, rather than being influenced by the skill with which it is put across. However, in our less than ideal world, we have to recognise that presentation skills do count for a lot. Being able to influence people and have a say in how policy is shaped and developed is likely to depend to a certain extent at least on presentation skills – putting arguments forward clearly, effectively and persuasively.

- *Using the law*
  The law, as we have seen, is a major influence on not only individual practice but also agency policy. This is an important point to recognise as it means that practitioners can use the law to influence policy development and implementation. For example, the point was made earlier that the implementation of the Human Rights Act 1998 raises major challenges for organisations and individuals alike. While new ways forward are being sought, opportunities for influence are likely to be more common than at other times – a point consistent with crisis intervention theory. That is, while current approaches can, in many cases, not be allowed to continue, a crisis point has been reached, and at times of crisis susceptibility to influence is considerably increased (Thompson, 1991).

Skill development is an important part of achieving and maintaining high standards of professional practice, in so far as social work takes place in a constantly changing and evolving environment – we need to keep developing just to make sure we do not become out of touch. This is an important point that will feature significantly in Chapter 5.

Exercise 4.7
In what ways might the challenge of implementing a new law present opportunities for practitioners to influence policy development and implementation? Consider, for example, the Children (Leaving Care) Act and/or the Carers and Disabled Children Act 2000.

Best value

The phrase, 'best value' is one that has begun to have a major impact on social work in recent years. It is a concept that has developed, indirectly at least, from the previous Conservative government's philosophy of 'rolling back the state', a lessening of reliance on state services. Part of this philosophy was the development of what came to be known as compulsory competitive tendering (CCT) – a system whereby certain services were put out to tender rather than provided directly by local government. The role of local government therefore shifted from provider of services to funder and regulator of services.

One of the aims behind the CCT initiative was the introduction of supposed business-world efficiency (brought about by market forces) into the public sector. However, a major criticism of CCT which quickly emerged was that, while it may possibly have been effective in terms of cost containment, it was not effective in ensuring optimal outcomes. That is, what CCT produced for the most part was the cheapest level of service rather than the optimal level of service. To a large extent the notion of 'best value' is a reaction to this state of affairs. Its underlying principle is that local authorities should balance cost against quality to achieve the best outcomes possible within available resources. That is, it is not simply a matter of going for the cheapest options as these may save money in the short term but lead to much greater problems (and thus expense) in the medium to long term. Nor is it a matter of going for the highest quality of service that can be achieved as this may mean that services have to be rationed later in the financial year because resource considerations have not been given adequate attention. The best value approach is therefore geared towards achieving *the best possible service outcomes within available resources*. It can therefore be described as an attempt to ensure that professional quality concerns are balanced against financial management requirements.

Since April 2000 local authorities have been obliged to plan to provide their services in accordance with the principles of best value. Best value can be understood in terms of what have come to be known as the 'Four Cs of Best Value'. These are:

- **Challenging** why and how the service is best provided

- **Comparing** performance with others (including non-local government providers)
- **Competing** the authority must show that it has embraced the principles of fair competition in deciding who should deliver the service
- **Consulting** local service users and residents on their expectations about the service

The first C is an interesting one, in so far as it reflects one of the key issues underpinning this book, namely the importance of systematic practice – keeping a clear focus and thus being explicit about what we are doing and why.

The views of Adams (1996), although predating the implementation of the Best Value initiative, are very relevant. He points out that auditing is the term used by the Audit Commission to describe processes of checking that public money is being spent economically, efficiently and effectively. He then goes on to draw an important distinction:

Different approaches to auditing predominate: conventional, focusing on quality imposition or maintenance; and progressive, focusing on quality enhancement or maximisation.

*The **conventional** approach fulfils more restricted financial goals and the managerialist requirement of controlling practice. It relies typically on a technical, tick-list approach. . . . The **progressive** approach to audit attempts to engage with the complexity of professional practice – not least the difficulties of decision-making and, despite standards and checklists, the lack of a single answer to problems. This approach also takes on board possible structural features of this, rather than pathologising them.* (pp. 145–6)

While the progressive approach may not be what the Audit Commission or the Government had in mind in introducing Best Value, it is clear that the Best Value approach offers considerable scope for moving away from the narrow technicalism of CCT towards the more professional approach of progressive audit. Best Value therefore offers opportunities for pressing the case for a broader, more professional approach rather than a narrow one which distorts reality by focusing primarily or even exclusively on financial indicators.

Children First and Quality Protects

Quality Protects is an initiative set up in response to criticisms of social work with children, young people and their families neglecting certain important issues, such as the importance of educational attainment. *Children First* is what could be described as the Welsh version of Quality Protects. It is a programme of measures geared towards raising standards of practice across the full range of what comprises the broad spectrum of social work with children, young people and their families.

Initially established as a three-year project due to end in 2002, it has since been extended to a five-year programme. It has a number of basic elements, including the following:

- *The assessment framework* As discussed in Chapter 2, the new assessment framework offers an overview of the issues that should be taken into account in assessing the needs and circumstances of children and young people.
- *Improved education for looked-after children* As a result of major concerns about the educational attainments of children and young people looked after by local authorities, there has been a marked shift towards making education a much higher priority. This is a challenge for both Social Services and Education Departments.
- *Improved health care for looked-after children* In parallel with the previous point, a great deal of concern has been voiced about children and young people not having their health needs adequately monitored or met when they become looked after (Mather *et al.*, 2000).
- *Management information systems* The development and monitoring of 'Management Action Plans' helps to develop a corporate approach in which relevant information is made available to inform planning and decision-making.
- *Corporate transformation* The money made available under these initiatives is designed for an overall corporate transformation of services for children, young people and their families rather than simply for specific projects.

A key aspect of the Quality Protects/Children First philosophy is, quite literally, the notion that quality protects – that is, children and young people's protection needs are best served by high-quality social work practice. To a large extent this is a reaction against the major focus on child protective services which developed during the 1980s and into the 1990s in which child protection interventions began to predominate at the expense, it can be argued, of preventative and supportive measures.

Exercise 4.8

How are developments like Best Value and Quality Protects/Children First influencing your work? What part can you play in shaping the response to such developments?

3. Tasks and challenges

Here we turn our attentions to considering the implications for practice in terms of the two elements of competence directly relevant to this chapter, namely:

D1 Contribute to working with neighbourhoods, communities and local agencies in the interests of safeguarding and promoting the welfare of all children.

This competence relates quite clearly to much of the material presented and explored in Chapter 3. However, the emphasis here is rather broader in so far as it relates to working at the level of law and policy. That is, an argument underpinning this chapter is that it is necessary to have a good grasp of law and policy issues in order to 'safeguard and promote the welfare of all children'. This is partly through recognising the importance of an approach which is both *corporate* (that is, spanning both individual and organisational concerns) and *participative* (involving service users and carers in planning, decision-making and policy development).

D2 Contribute to the development of local child care policy and practice.

Policy, as we have seen, is in many respects the bridge between the law as an overarching framework and actual practice. Practitioners can play a part in influencing policy development at a local level in a number of ways – for example, by raising issues through appropriate management and policy channels.

As individuals we may have little scope for making a difference to policy matters but, by contributing to the development of a collective role, individuals can and should have a say in the direction policy takes. This is particularly significant in the current climate of extensive and substantive change in which new initiatives abound.

Taking a more active part in influencing policy development and implementation is an important part of empowerment. This is because social work staff have far more contact with clients than managers do and are therefore in a better position to make sure that services and so on are appropriately focused. This can also be an important step in the direction of user involvement by establishing the value of devolving responsibility for policy as much as possible. This is not to say that practitioners and clients should carry primary responsibility for policy, but both groups are clearly important stakeholders in the overall policy field.

By examining how, as practitioners, we can have a say in the development and implementation of policy, we are also, of course, shaping models of best practice. What is particularly important in this regard is the emphasis on professionalism, and two aspects in particular, namely i) a commitment to high standards of practice; and ii) the use of a professional knowledge base.

The first aspect is significant because it involves a focus on achieving the highest standards of practice possible in the circumstances, rather than simply settling for 'good enough'. Of course, the problem with 'good enough' practice is that it is a poor source of motivation and does not provide fertile soil for learning (see Chapter 5).

The second aspect is significant because, as we have noted at various points in this book, the use of a professional knowledge base is a central part of reflective practice. Indeed, effective reflective practice hinges on being able to draw on a professional knowledge base and adapt this to the particular circumstances of the case – having the skill and flexibility to use such knowledge appropriately in differing circumstances. Using professional knowledge is partly a matter of developing evidence-based practice, but is also more broadly a process of developing models of best practice. This involves going beyond the letter of the law and its relatively narrow confines and branching out into the much wider field of professionalism. As we have seen, a focus on an explicit model of professional practice and accountability is to be encouraged, as this avoids the distortion of a mechanistic approach, and also allows for personal and professional development – the focus of Chapter 5.

4. Conclusion

This chapter has explored the central role of law and policy in shaping practice and the potential for our practice to have a bearing on policy development. It has emphasised that the law and related policy have a central role to play in shaping practice but it is generally not a direct, unmediated role – its influence passes through various 'filters', not least that of interpretation. This is an important message to emphasise as, sadly, there is so often an atmosphere of defeatism and self-disempowerment – factors which can both reflect and reinforce a culture of defensiveness and retrenchment.

The law is clearly an important starting point for practice but it is also clearly not the only one, and is certainly not the whole story. Effective, competent practitioners need at least a basic awareness of the law and its related policies but it is also important to recognise that such an awareness needs to be a *critical* one – that is, one which does not take matters at face value and seek to follow the law mechanistically as if it were simply a set of rules or prescriptions for practice. It is to be hoped that this chapter has helped to clarify the fundamental role of law and policy in guiding social work practice, but has also cast some light on the potential for practice to influence policy locally in the medium term and, at a collective level at least, to contribute to the development of the law in the longer term.

5. Points to ponder

➤ Do you see the law as something that is fixed and unyielding or are you able to identify the subtleties of legal and policy processes?

➤ Do you feel comfortable in engaging with law and policy issues? If not, what is holding you back?

➤ Are you able to recognise the values that are shaping law, policy and practice? How do these affect you and your practice?

➤ What are the factors that may lead agencies to practise defensively?

➤ Are you sufficiently familiar with the culture of human rights that the Human Rights Act 1998 is intended to promote?

➤ Do you feel confident about having a say in shaping local policy? If not, what is holding you back?

➤ Are you able to draw links between initiatives such as Children First or Best Value and your own professional practice?

6. Learning resources guide

There are several good basic textbooks that provide an overview of social work law, including: Ball (1996); Braye and Preston-Shoot (1997); Brayne and Martin (1997); Fishwick (1996) and Vernon (1998). Cull and Roche (2001) is a recent welcome addition to the literature, an edited collection covering a wide range of issues relating to law, policy and practice. Child care law in particular is well covered in Freeman (1992) and Stainton Rogers and Roche (1994).

The law and values are helpfully discussed in Braye and Preston-Shoot (1997) as well as in various chapters in the collection of readings in Cull and Roche (2001).

Foucault's theory of power is discussed in Rabinow (1986). See also Foucault (1980).

The Human Rights Act 1998 is covered thoroughly in Crompton and Thompson (2000), a training pack, while Wadham and Mountfield (1999) is a basic introductory textbook which includes the actual text of the Act. Drew (2000) is a short but helpful guide to the child care implications of the Act.

Child care policy has an extensive literature base. Fox Harding (1991) presents an interesting discussion of different models of child care policy and is a good starting point. See also Foley *et al.* (2001) and, albeit from an American perspective, Pecora *et al.* (2000).

The organisational context is discussed in Chapter 6 of Thompson (1998). Payne (2000) is also an important text in this regard.

Best value is a relatively new phenomenon and does not yet have a substantial literature base. However, information is available from the following website:

www.bestvalueinspections.gov.uk

Quality Protects and Children First are discussed in various publications available from the Department of Health and the National Assembly for Wales.

5. Professional development

1. Introduction

The overall theme of this final chapter is that of professional development, broken down into three key areas, as follows:

- maintaining our own learning and development through reflective practice;
- promoting learning by supporting the learning of others and generally contributing to a positive atmosphere conducive to learning; and
- handling work and life pressures in such ways that successfully negotiate some if not all of the factors that can act as obstacles to learning.

In some ways, this chapter underpins all that has preceded it. This is because, without continuing to learn and develop, promoting a positive atmosphere for learning and handling our pressures effectively, it is likely that the important issues discussed in the earlier chapters and previous unit will be of little significance. That is, the lessons to be learned from this final unit can be seen as fundamental to good practice – basic components of high-quality professional practice.

Professional development is something that has been given considerable backing over the years, and this is perhaps not surprising, given its crucial role in underpinning good practice. However, it is important to be realistic and to acknowledge that professional development is also something that can be neglected, left to falter as a result of work pressures or other such barriers. We should therefore not be complacent and assume that the role and significance of professional development are fully established. There are still many people who either fail to recognise its value or fail to capitalise upon that value. None the less, the importance of professional development is clearly part and parcel of this programme and is therefore a topic worthy of detailed examination.

2. The knowledge base

The knowledge base relating to professional development and related matters is once again an enormous one, and so our discussions are necessarily selective and limited in scope. We begin by examining what is involved in managing our own continuous professional development, drawing on one of the book's underpinning themes, namely that of reflective practice. This leads into a discussion of how we can contribute to the development of a positive learning environment, an atmosphere in which learning and development are encouraged and supported. In particular, we look at how the learning of others can be enhanced by steps we take to support and guide them in their learning. Finally, in terms of the knowledge base, we explore the important question of managing pressure and stress. This is an area in which a lot of myths and misunderstandings are to be found, and so an important aspect of the material presented here is a focus on clearing away such myths.

Maintaining our own learning and development

Social work is, of course, a complex and demanding occupation. What makes it so complex, amongst other things, is the constant flow of change (Lesňik, 1997). The more things change, the more learning we have to do just to keep up. And, of course, it is to be hoped that we will want to do more than just keep up by actually improving and developing over time. Similarly, the complexity of social work means that there is always scope for further learning. The worker who claims that they have learned all that they need to learn is guilty of either gross oversimplification and/or self-delusion. They are also entering some very professionally dangerous territory. The need to continue learning as we practise is therefore clearly an important part of maintaining high professional standards. This section looks at some of the key elements involved in maintaining that learning and development throughout your career.

Reflective practice revisited

The theme of reflective practice is one that has recurred throughout this book but it is here, in relation to learning and development, that it really comes into its own. This is because reflective practice provides an excellent foundation for learning. Consider, for example, the opposite. Routinised, unthinking, uncritical practice provides little or no opportunity for lessons to be learned, for new forms of practice to be developed and so on. In this respect, routinised (that is, non-reflective) forms of practice are a cul-de-sac when it comes to learning. If we simply do today what we did yesterday, then how does this equip us to do something better tomorrow? As the saying goes: 'If we always do what we've always done, we'll always get what we've always got'.

Reflective practice provides fertile ground for learning in a number of ways, not least the following:

- It involves drawing on theory, research and the professional knowledge base more broadly and therefore provides a constant stream of opportunities to gain new insights from that knowledge base.
- It encourages us to be creative, to move beyond formula solutions and look at a range of possible ways forward. This allows us to have a fresh and open approach to each new situation we encounter and thus be open to new ideas.
- It entails reflection-*on*-action, looking back over a piece of work in order to learn from it – evaluating our practice, not necessarily in a formal sense, but none the less in ways that enable us to benefit from the lessons of experience.
- It recognises the complexity and variability of the problems and situations social workers encounter and therefore helps to sensitise us to the rich diversity of the social world and the need to remain alert to its subtleties and intricacies. That is, it discourages us from oversimplifying the challenges we face.

Indeed, a focus on learning is a fundamental part of the philosophy of reflective practice, a core element underpinning this approach. As such, reflective practice sets the scene for continuous professional development and so it is to this that we now turn.

Continuous professional development and lifelong learning

The point was made above that we need to continue learning just to keep up, such is the nature and pace of change in social work. In this way a case can easily be made for the importance of continuous professional development (or CPD for short). Another term that is often used in this context is that of 'lifelong learning'. This is a notion used to challenge the traditional view of occupational learning as a period of study and/or apprenticeship as a precursor to practice. In this traditional model learning is concentrated in the early stages and features much less as time goes by, as if the person concerned has achieved a sufficient level of competence and therefore has limited learning needs. The philosophy of lifelong learning challenges this model and seeks to replace it with an approach which regards learning as an essential dimension of good practice *at all times*, regardless of the stage we are at in our career. Each day brings new challenges and new opportunities for learning (or new opportunities for getting increasingly out of touch if we turn our back on learning).

Exercise 5.1
What opportunities for learning present themselves to you as part of your day-to-day work? How fully do you draw upon those opportunities? Is there anything that stands in your way?

This emphasis on CPD or lifelong learning has (at least) two implications for our approach to learning and development:

1. At a personal level, each of us needs to be sensitive to opportunities for learning and feel confident enough to embrace them. We need to be sensitive to the obstacles to learning that can hold us back (see the discussion of these below) and be prepared

to address them in whatever ways we reasonably can.

2. At an organisational level, the use and style of training becomes significant. Indeed, CPD is part of a movement which is critical of traditional approaches to education and training.

Point 1 is an issue to which we shall return below when we explore strategies for promoting reflective learning. Similarly, Point 2 will be discussed in more detail under the heading of 'Promoting learning'.

The Chartered Institute of Personnel and Development (CIPD) is an organisation that sets a lot of store by continuous professional development. Part of the CIPD's approach to lifelong learning is a recognition of the importance of what is known as a 'learning organisation'. This refers to an organisation which has developed a culture in which learning is encouraged and supported at all levels. This important concept will feature as a significant part of our discussions below.

Strategies for promoting reflective learning

The pressures of a busy workload can easily lead to a situation where all our efforts are ploughed into getting the job done, leaving little time or energy for reflection and learning. The danger of slipping into a non-reflective approach to practice is therefore a very real one. In order to guard against this danger and make reflective learning a reality, it is therefore important that we should be equipped with a range of strategies that can be drawn upon to help us develop and maintain a reflective, learning-based approach to our work. The following are just some of the strategies that can be used in this regard:

- *reviewing practice* There are, of course, legal requirements to review statutory cases at predefined intervals. However, such formal reviews should be seen as a basic minimum, as far as reviewing practice is concerned. That is, we should also consider more informal reviews of our work on a more frequent basis so that we can not only keep a clear picture of developments and issues in our minds, but also explore opportunities for learning from our practice. It is commonly

assumed that we learn from experience. However, it is more accurate to say that we learn from what we do with that experience – from reflecting on it, relating it to our earlier learning and so on (see Kolb, 1984; Thompson, 2000a). Experience does not automatically produce learning, as it is possible to have many years' experience whilst learning relatively little from it. Reviewing our practice is clearly one important way of generating opportunities for learning.

- *evaluating practice* While review of practice is (or should be) an ongoing process, evaluation is a similar process that can be carried out at the end of a piece of work. It involves examining what worked and why; what could have worked better; and what lessons can be learned from the piece of work in question. In this way, evaluation of practice can clearly generate significant opportunities for learning.

- *exploring options* The point was made above that reflective practice involves moving beyond the idea that there is only one solution for every problem. In reality, there are various ways of dealing with the problems social work with children, young people and their families casts before us, each with its own advantages and disadvantages. The task, then, is not to find 'the right answer', but rather to explore a number of possible ways forward and work out which is the most appropriate in the circumstances. This broader, more creative approach may be difficult to develop for those who are not used to it, but the efforts involved in such development are well worth investing, given the benefits of this approach – not least the learning opportunities offered by exploring different options.

- *action learning sets* This is a term that refers to the establishment of a group to explore a particular topic or set of issues, with a view to facilitating learning through discussion, debate and analysis. Such groups can be a significant source of motivation and mutual support as well as a forum for sharing ideas, gaining fresh insights and so on.

- *working in partnership* The value of working in partnership is a theme that has received a great deal of emphasis in this programme. However, what is worth emphasising here is another aspect of its valuable role – as an aid to learning. Working closely with others – fellow professionals, parents, carers, children and young people, and so on – gives us the chance to widen our perspective, gain new insights and therefore to further our own understanding and skills. In other words, partnership offers us opportunities for learning through our interactions with others.

- *reading* This may seem an obvious point, but it is one that is worth making none the less. There is a vast and growing literature relating to social work with children, young people and their families, offering a great deal of potential for learning through extending and deepening our understanding of relevant theory and research. However, having the literature available is not sufficient in its own right – we also have to find the time and energy to read it, make sense of it and relate it to our own practice. In addition, for many people at least, there are barriers to reading that need to be overcome – not least an organisational culture which devalues reading in particular and the exploration of new ideas in general (see the discussion of the 'learning organisation' below).

This is, of course, by no means an exhaustive list, but it should be sufficient to demonstrate that we have available to us a considerable learning resource base when it comes to promoting our own professional development. However, we should be wary of making the false assumption that it is necessary to pursue a formal course of study for significant learning to take place. Being registered for a course can provide us with structured opportunities for learning, access to library resources and the academic support and guidance of one or more tutors. However, we can generally also create such foundations for learning through other means, if we are able to make the necessary steps to do so (see Exercise 5.2)

Exercise 5.2

What 'learning support resources' do you have access to (mentors, libraries, support groups and so on)? Do you use these resources to the full? Of not, what prevents you from doing so? What can you do to increase your (access to) learning support resources?

Recognising barriers to learning

While it is clearly important to be aware of the range of strategies that are available to promote reflective learning, we should also bear in mind the other side of the coin – the barriers that can stand in the way of learning. In this section we therefore identify some of the major barriers to learning. These are offered in the context of an awareness of the importance of recognising that 'forewarned is forearmed'. That is, it is to be hoped that, by having a higher level of awareness of barriers to learning, we should be in a much stronger position when it comes to removing them, circumnavigating them or at the very least lessening their effects.

Earlier the point was made that experience does not automatically produce learning – it is what we do with that experience that acts as the catalyst for learning and development. Learning may also not happen automatically because of one or more barriers which stand in its way. In order to maximise opportunities for learning it is therefore necessary to be able to:

- recognise the existence of a wide range of obstacles to learning;
- identify which may apply to you; and
- take the necessary steps to remove, avoid or minimise them.

Once again, what is offered here is not an exhaustive list, but rather enough to paint a picture of the types of obstacle that are likely to be around, and which are likely to require our attention if we are to do what we can to make learning as strong a feature of our practice as we can:

- *Anxiety* A significant barrier to learning is anxiety, especially where it has the effect of contributing to a lack of confidence. Anxiety tends to be generalised and non-specific, and so a well-recognised way of dealing with it is to translate it into fear – that is, to make it more specific by identifying what it is that we are afraid of. It is much easier to deal with a specific fear than a generalised anxiety. Is it failure that we are afraid of? Or perhaps there are other fears that are holding us back?

- *Complacency* If people feel there is little left for them to learn, then we should not be surprised when they learn little or nothing. That is, a complacent view of one's own level of knowledge and skills and/or a failure to recognise the need for continuous learning to stay abreast of developments can so easily lead to minimal or non-existent learning.
- *Habit* Force of habit can lead us into practising in routinised ways – following tramlines rather than creatively exploring options. Such reliance on habit is clearly counterproductive when it comes to learning. Habit may be very comforting at times and may be useful in dealing with routine, straightforward matters. However, applying a routine, habit-based approach to situations that are not simple and straightforward is not only unhelpful as far as learning is concerned, but also extremely dangerous as an approach to professional practice.

Promoting learning

In some respects, much of what has already been covered in relation to our own continuous professional development can also be applied to promoting or supporting the learning of others. What follows, then, should be seen as what needs to be done in addition to the ideas already presented.

Practice teaching and learning

An important role amongst any professional group is the preparation of the next generation of staff. In social work much of this role falls to practice teachers who play a major part in social work education. We are perhaps fortunate to have such a long and well-established tradition of practice teaching in social work, although what we perhaps lack is the expectation discernible in some other professional groups that such activities should be part and parcel of the duties of all professional staff, rather than simply those who choose to undertake these duties. None the less, there is clearly a strong tradition of practice learning to draw upon.

The point was made earlier that traditional approaches to training and development have come to be challenged over the years. This is because they have been criticised for relying on what Freire (1972) refers to as a 'banking model' of learning – that is, one which treats learners as empty vessels in which wiser, better informed people deposit knowledge. Of course this model is far from adequate as a basis for promoting learning but has none the less enjoyed a position of dominance. Consider, for example, the traditional reliance on simply imparting information (very often through lectures). We have in many ways moved beyond this traditional model in social work education, although it has by no means been eradicated altogether. One way in particular that we have progressed is in the movement from the traditional idea of the 'student supervisor' to that of the 'practice teacher' – a much more active role, with a clear focus on promoting learning.

This does not simply involve passing on our wisdom to the next generation of practitioners, as this is not possible. We can transfer information from one person to another but we cannot do the same with understanding. Rather, the task is to support the learner in developing his or her own understanding. That is, we can support others in taking forward their own learning but what we cannot do is give them learning as if it were a commodity to be passed from one person to the next.

This role of supporting and facilitating learning can be a very demanding one at times but it is also a very rewarding one, and can be a major source of learning for ourselves as well as those we are seeking to help.

Mentoring

Practice teaching is in many ways a form of mentoring, in the sense that mentoring involves offering advice and guidance as part of a process of promoting personal and professional development. However, there are also other forms of mentoring above and beyond practice teaching. For example the Post qualifying Award in Child Care has created the need for a number of people to act as assessors and/or mentors in establishing a firm foundation of practice-based staff to support the academic input relating to the underpinning knowledge base.

A mentor is, in effect, a learning guide. He or she is not a teacher in the conventional sense, n so far as the role does not involve a major focus on imparting knowledge or information. Rather, it is a case of acting as a facilitator of learning by helping the individual concerned to build on strengths, identify areas for development and barriers to progress and find the most effective way forward in terms of personal and professional development.

Exercise 5.3

In giving or receiving mentoring support, what do you see as the basic ingredients of a helpful or effective approach?

Supervision skills

Just as practice teaching incorporates elements of mentoring, so too does it include an element of supervision. However, supervision also goes far beyond practice teaching, as it is a central element in effective human resource management in so far as it involves supporting the organisation's most important and valuable resource – its people.

As noted in Chapter 3 where we discussed the importance of making best use of the supervision you (should) receive, supervision can be seen to have a number of functions. Following Morrison (2001), we can identify four main functions, as follows:

- *The executive function* This involves managerial accountability, ensuring that quality standards are achieved or surpassed and that policy requirements are met.
- *The educational function* Supervisors can, of course, play an important role in helping staff learn and develop.
- *The supportive function* Staff care is increasingly being recognised as an important managerial role, helping staff to deal with the range of pressures they face (see the discussion below).
- *Mediation* Acting as a neutral 'go-between' in terms of disputes or conflicts can be a very helpful supervisory activity and complements well the other three functions.

For present purposes it is the second function that we are concerned with, that of helping people learn. The important fundamental question to address is: how do we help others to learn?

Of course, there is no simple answer to this question, but there are a number of issues to take into consideration if we are to take seriously our role in supporting the learning of others:

- *Trust and relationship-building* If there is an atmosphere of mistrust and suspicion we should not be surprised to find that little learning takes place. Unfortunately, for many years a number of trainers and educators worked under the motto of 'no pain, no gain' and therefore adopted a highly confrontational approach to learning (for example, the now highly discredited 'race awareness' training – see Thompson, 1998). Such approaches failed to recognise that anxiety, mistrust and defensiveness are not a sound foundation on which to build learning. It is therefore clearly important to establish as far as reasonably possible an atmosphere of trust in which positive relationships can develop.
- *The balance of challenge and support* Inskip (1986) argues that learning is maximised when we have a balance of high support and high challenge. That is, if there is a low level of support, the trust and security needed for effective learning will be absent (see the previous point). At the other extreme, if there is high support but low challenge, learners run the risk of becoming complacent. They may enjoy the positive, supportive relationship, but if they are not being 'stretched' by an appropriate level of educational challenging, then their learning potential will be far from fulfilled. The most effective way to promote learning, then, is to combine a high level of support with a high level of challenge.
- *Promoting confidence and empowerment* As we have noted, learning can be an anxiety-provoking experience, partly because it involves taking risks. What is often needed, then, to promote learning in others, is the ability to boost confidence, to encourage and support learners in taking the risks that are necessary to move forward. This can be seen as a form of empowerment – helping learners take greater control over their lives, and in particular over the factors that contribute to the development of learning.
- *Identifying learning styles* Much work has been done on the notion of learning

processes and learning styles (see the 'Further reading' section below). The basic idea is that different people learn in different ways and so we can help people learn by identifying their preferred learning style(s). In doing so, we can help them recognise their strengths and thus build on them, but also recognise their areas for development to enable them to become more rounded learners.

- *Removing barriers* We discussed earlier the range of barriers that can stand in the way of learning. An important part of promoting learning can therefore be seen as i) identifying such barriers for the learner concerned; ii) identifying the necessary steps to remove, minimise or circumnavigate those barriers; and iii) working together to put those steps into action.

- *Promoting unlearning* An important aspect of developing anti-discriminatory practice is what can be called 'unlearning'. This refers to the need to recognise discriminatory assumptions that are part and parcel of the culture in which we have been brought up, and make sure that we are able to challenge and remove such assumptions from our own thinking and actions. Helping people to undergo such unlearning is a skilful and sensitive undertaking and needs to be done carefully and supportively (see the discussion above of the need to establish a balance between supportiveness and challenge).

Underpinning any attempts to promote learning in others should be a recognition of the importance of learning as a *self-directed process*. As Mezirow (1981) comments:

Although the diversity of experience labeled adult education includes any organized and sustained effort to facilitate learning and, as such, tends to mean many things to many people, a set of standards derived from the generic characteristics of adult development has emerged from research and professional practice in our collective definition of the function of an adult educator. It is almost universally recognized at least in theory, that central to the adult educator's function is a goal and method of self-directed learning.

Enhancing the learner's ability for self-direction in learning as a foundation for a distinctive philosophy of adult education has breadth and power. It represents the mode of learning characteristic of adulthood. (p. 21)

This returns us to the point made earlier about the role of empowerment – helping people gain greater control over their lives. We can see a strong relationship between learning and empowerment. This is because, as Mezirow implies, empowerment promotes learning and because promoting learning in general is an important element in the process of empowerment.

Promoting learning in others is not simply a matter for line managers and practice teachers. We should also recognise at least a potential role to play a part in supporting the learning of colleagues such as family aides, foster carers, project workers and so on. This can be an important role for both the learners concerned and for those who play such a role in promoting learning.

An important distinction to draw in relation to promoting self-directed learning is that between *intrinsic* and *extrinsic* motivation. The latter refers to external motivation – that is, when we are motivated to undertake an activity (such as learning) by something other than that activity (obtaining a qualification, for example). The former, by contrast, refers to motivation to undertake an activity which is part of the activity itself (wanting to learn because learning is its own source of motivation). While extrinsic motivation is clearly important and has a significant role to play, we should be able to recognise that intrinsic motivation is likely to be more powerful, more long-lasting and more effective (because of its links with self-directed learning).

Exercise 5.4

What motivates you to learn? Can you divide your motivation into intrinsic and extrinsic factors? What can you do to motivate others to learn? In particular, how can you encourage intrinsic motivation?

The 'learning organisation'

This is a concept that has developed in the management literature relating to human resource development – that is, the investment in the learning and professional development of an organisation's most important resource, its people. Developing a learning organisation involves promoting an atmosphere across the whole organisation in which learning is not only valued but also recognised as an essential part of a successful organisation that achieves its objectives and keeps in touch with important developments both within and outside that organisation.

Roderick (1993) describes in some detail what this entails. It is worth reproducing her comments in full:

Learning organisations do:

- *take every opportunity to learn both from experience and in general at individual, group and corporate level*
- *experiment with new ways of organising work and new ways of learning both within and outside the organisation*
- *establish a climate in which learning from each other is actively supported*
- *use the training function to facilitate the development and learning of all employees*
- *see a key role for managers as facilitators*
- *develop structures which encourage two-way communication as a means of promoting learning and development*
- *encourage questioning, experimentation and exploration of new ideas at all levels*
- *remove barriers and blockages to learning in both the individual and the environment*
- *encourage and foster continuous learning and self-development in all employees*
- *think about how to learn as well as what to learn.*

Learning organisations do not:

- *use command and control as the dominant method of management*
- *rely almost exclusively on formal conventional training as the primary source of learning and development within the organisation*
- *assume that past success is the key of future success*
- *take the view that the workforce is essentially passive and therefore incapable of autonomy and self-regulation*
- *take the view that new blood is the only means of achieving adaptive change in the belief that the existing workforce is too old to learn*
- *hold the belief that advanced information and manufacturing technologies are sufficient in themselves to guarantee success* (p. 13)

The process of developing a learning organisation is clearly a matter of implementing a strategy of culture change. It requires a concerted effort to change the dominant values and assumptions within the organisation if these run counter to a philosophy of continuous organisational learning. Of course, such a change of culture is not something that can be achieved over night. It involves a strong commitment of time and energy over a period of time.

Exercise 5.5

You may feel that your organisation is a long way from being a 'learning organisation' (most are!). However, this does not mean that progress cannot be made towards giving learning and development a higher profile across the board. Indeed, you may find it helpful to consider (alone or with colleagues) what can be done to develop these ideas further and move closer towards the status of being a learning organisation. For example, you may wish to consider how the barriers to learning we discussed earlier in relation to individuals can also be applied to organisational learning.

Handling pressure

It does not need to be emphasised that social work with children, young people and their families is a pressurised job. Indeed, it is an occupation that involves not only a large amount of pressure, but also a number of different pressures – and often pressures of a particularly intense and demanding nature. The ability to handle pressures is therefore clearly a fundamental part of the successful social worker's repertoire of skills. This section therefore explores what is involved in handling time and workload pressures, dealing with the emotional dimension of social work and fending off the dangers of stress.

Time and workload management: creating space for learning

Social work is one of those types of work where demand is likely to outstrip supply. The skills involved in making the best use of scarce resources of time and energy should therefore be at a premium. It is therefore surprising (and sad) that social work education has tended to neglect this aspect of the skills base required for effective social work practice.

A very significant danger is that we can become so engrossed in day-to-day pressures that we lose sight of what we are doing. This means that we can easily become prone to drift when pressures start to get the better of us. The great irony of this is that, when the need to practise systematically (that is, with a clear plan of what we are trying to achieve, how we are going to achieve it and how we will know when we have achieved it) is greatest, the danger of not doing so is also at its greatest.

There is a very real danger here that such a situation can lead to a vicious circle. That is, pressures can lead us into drift and a lack of focus. This, in turn, leads to a greater likelihood of time and effort being wasted (because we have lost our focus) and thus to even greater time and workload pressure. The extra pressure can then lead to a further loss of focus. And so the circle continues.

There is also a further dimension to this vicious circle. A key part of time and workload management is *motivation* (Thompson, 2002a). This is because, if we are motivated, if we feel on top of things, we are likely to achieve much more in the time available. This can produce the opposite of a vicious circle – a virtuous circle – in which the higher level of achievement brings greater job satisfaction which in turn brings more motivation. Drift and a lack of focus, by contrast, can destroy or at least undermine our sense of job satisfaction and thus reduce rather than enhance our level of motivation – leading to a situation where we achieve less in the time available and thus feel more pressurised. Drift again brings us into a vicious circle.

It should be clear, then, that a fundamental part of effective time and workload management is the need to maintain a clear focus through systematic practice. A lack of a systematic approach not only wastes time but also takes away something just as important if not more so – job satisfaction and thus motivation.

Handling feelings

Working with people who are experiencing pressures, problems, unmet needs, unresolved conflicts, abuse, discrimination, disadvantage and oppression is, of course, highly likely to involve a wide range of feelings for both service users and service providers. The emotional dimension of social work is therefore clearly an important one.

This is not to say that there is an expectation that social workers should be psychoanalysts alongside all their other roles, but there is clearly a danger in going to the other extreme of neglecting the emotional dimension, acting (or seeking to act) as if feelings did not have a part to play.

Handling the feelings dimension involves two elements. On the one hand, it is important that we are able to be 'emotionally literate' in reading and responding to the feelings of others. That is, we need to be sensitive to how children, young people and indeed the adults we work with are feeling and how they are expressing those feelings. This ties in with the idea that has taken off in some respects in recent management literature, that of emotional intelligence (see, for example, Goleman, 1996). This refers to the ability to deal with feelings by using interpersonal skills in order to enhance our effectiveness in working with people. In some ways, this is old wine in new bottles, in the sense that social work education has long recognised the importance of responding sensitively to emotional issues.

On the other hand, it is important that we recognise the emotional dimension as it affects us as workers. If we are not aware of our own emotional needs and the impact our work is having upon us, we may be ill-equipped to deal with the emotional pressures inherent in social work. For example, Morrison (1997) discusses the complex emotional entanglements that can occur in undertaking child protection work. The 'macho' approach of simply trying to deny that there is an emotional dimension to be taken into consideration is one that is fraught with a number of dangers and difficulties. The need to address openly and constructively the feelings dimension is therefore a very important consideration. Good supervision clearly has an important part to play but there are, of course, other steps that can be taken to ensure that feelings issues are not submerged under other aspects of the work or buried in an organisational culture that does not encourage openness.

Exercise 5.6

How comfortable do you feel with dealing with the emotional dimension of your work? Do you have any strategies or tried and trusted methods of dealing effectively and appropriately with feelings (your own and other people's)? How can you improve your ability to handle feelings sensitively and appropriately?

Stress management

In Chapter 1 a three-dimensional model of stress was introduced. That is, in addition to the traditional ideas of stressors (the sources of pressure that can contribute to stress) and coping methods, we must recognise the crucial significance of *support*. If the organisation we work for provides positive and helpful support, stressors can be kept in proportion and coping methods can be enhanced. If, on the other hand, the employing organisation provides insufficient or inappropriate support, stressors can loom large and coping methods can be undermined.

It is important to emphasise the role of support, as a tendency to neglect this dimension leads to a pathological model of stress. That is, if we take little or no account of the organisational dimension, we are left with a simplistic view which sees stress as a sign of a weak or inadequate individual. This can lead to (at least) three sets of problems:

- As with the problem of drift and time and workload management discussed above, a vicious circle can develop. If staff who are under stress are left to feel that the stress is as a result of their own failings, their confidence and thus coping abilities are likely to be undermined, thus leading to a higher level of stress.

- If stress is seen as a sign of weakness, staff may be unwilling to ask for support or raise stress as a problem, thus contributing to an atmosphere not characterised by openness – one in which it can be very difficult to speak freely about pressures and the need for support.
- An emphasis on the individual distracts attention from organisational issues – for example, an absence of support or an organisational culture which contributes to stress rather than to its alleviation.

It should be apparent, then, that our understanding of stress needs to be located in this broader context of organisational support.

The organisational dimension is also recognised in law. From a legal point of view, stress primarily comes under the heading of health and safety legislation. This is because employing organisations have a duty to safeguard their staff from undue hazards, and it has been established through case law precedent that stress counts as such a hazard. Supporting staff in dealing with their pressures is therefore not only an aspect of good management practice, it is also, in some respects at least, a legal requirement.

However, the health and safety legislation also makes it clear that individual employees have a responsibility for protecting themselves from hazards. The responsibility for avoiding stress is therefore a shared one. In view of this, what steps can we take as individuals to ensure that stress is not allowed to overwhelm us and cause us harm? There is no simple answer to this, as stress is a complex matter. However, the following points are worthy of consideration as part of a strategy of managing pressure and avoiding stress:

- *Identify the sources of pressure*
  Where are our pressures coming from? Here it is important to recognise that there is a subjective dimension to stress. That is, what one person finds stressful may present no problems at all to another person. A degree of self-awareness is therefore an asset. If we are not clear about what is causing pressure for us, we are going to be ill-equipped to deal with any such pressure.

- *Undertake a coping audit*
  How do we cope? We all have ways of dealing with our pressures. However, what is important to recognise is that some coping methods are not very helpful. For example, by becoming irritable I may give people a warning that they should stand back and give me some space – a positive outcome in the short term – but this may cause a great deal of resentment and thus further problems in the longer term. It is therefore helpful to be aware of the range of coping methods available to us and decide which are the most helpful, rather than make the mistake of assuming that all coping is good coping.
- *Explore, and use, sources of support*
  There are two main types of support – the formal, organisational mechanisms discussed above plus the more informal sources of support deriving from friends, family, colleagues and so on. Both types of support are important and valuable. However, we are sometimes unaware of some sources of support and may also be reluctant to use support at times (for example, because asking for support may be perceived as a sign of weakness). Recognising that asking for support is a sign of strength rather than weakness is therefore an important step forward.

There are, then, steps that individual staff can take to try to ensure that the inevitable pressures of social work with children, young people and their families does not overspill into harmful stress. However, there are also collective steps that can be taken – steps that involve the organisation as a whole as well as actual staff. These steps come under the heading of what has come to be known as staff care, and it is to this topic that we now turn.

Exercise 5.7

This exercise involves drawing up three lists. The first should be a list of 'stressors' – the things you can identify as sources of pressure for you. The second should be your 'coping audit' – the list of methods and techniques you draw upon to cope with pressures. The third should detail the sources of support you can draw upon. Once you have completed these lists (either alone or with colleagues),

look closely at them. Is there anything you can learn from gaining this overview? Are there any significant patterns that give you any clues as to how you might improve your stress management capabilities?

Staff care

The philosophy of customer care is one that has been established for a long time. It is based on the idea that customers (clients/consumers/service users) are important stakeholders in an organisation and so it is very important that they are listened to and their concerns taken seriously. Although not all organisations put this philosophy into practice, its value is none the less widely recognised.

The philosophy of staff care, by contrast, is not only far from being a feature of the majority of organisations, it is also nowhere near as well-established as a valuable approach to adopt. Indeed, as far as establishing staff care is concerned, we clearly have a long way to go.

Staff care refers to an approach to human resource management premised on the key principle that it is only through staff that success can be achieved. If staff are not adequately supported, then we should not be surprised to find that they achieve far less than their potential and may actually cause more problems than they solve – for example, as a result of a high error rate. But what support is it realistic to expect an organisation to provide? This is a significant question and a full answer would be a very long and detailed one, far beyond the scope of the space available here. I shall therefore restrict myself to the following points:

- *A reasonable workload*
  The importance of time and workload management was emphasised earlier. However, no amount of skill in this area will compensate for a workload that is unrealistically high – or, to put it another way, too much work is still too much work. Unfortunately, many organisations work on the mistaken premise that they can simply demand more and more work from their staff. In some cases, this approach can be seen as a form of bullying or harassment (see Thompson, 2000c). While a heavy, but realistic, workload may well motivate people to do well, it is likely that an unrealistic

workload will demotivate people, as unrealistic expectations are a well-established source of stress (Thompson *et al.*, 1994a).

- *Supervision*
  As noted earlier, supervision is an important source of support. Having the opportunity to discuss our work and the issues it raises can be a significant factor in safeguarding ourselves from stress. Indeed, supervision can be seen as a focal point for staff care.
- *Training and development*
  The point has already been made that the work we face is subject to change and development over time and so it is important that we too change and develop over time if we are not to become more and more out of touch with the demands upon us. A key part of staff care is therefore the provision of opportunities and resources for professional development. Indeed, staff care and training and development can be seen to go hand in hand. Training and development support is essential in promoting staff care and a commitment to staff care is necessary if opportunities for learning through training and development are to be maximised.
- *An ethos of permission*
  This is a term that refers to an aspect of organisational culture and describes an atmosphere within an organisation (or section of an organisation) which is characterised by openness and a sense of 'permission' to express feelings, admit mistakes, ask for help and so on. It is the opposite of a 'macho' or 'be tough' atmosphere which can be a significant barrier to pressure and stress issues being acknowledged and addressed (Pottage and Evans, 1992). If staff care is to be a reality rather than simply a rhetorical slogan, then the necessary steps to create and sustain an ethos of permission need to be identified and taken.

Organisations will vary enormously in terms of how far they promote staff care, and few if any will have nothing to learn when it comes to addressing these complex issues. Perhaps the greatest danger, though, is for staff care to acquire buzzword status and therefore be treated in a superficial and oversimplified manner. Staff care incorporates a set of complex issues which cut across human psychology, organisational culture and dynamics and social processes and institutions (the use of power, for example). A simplistic approach is therefore highly unlikely to be appropriate and may be quite dangerous at times.

Exercise 5.8

What elements of staff care are already well established in your organisation? What elements can you identify as being absent or insufficiently well developed? And, most importantly of all, what steps can you take i) as an individual employee; and ii) collectively with your colleagues, to promote staff care?

3. Tasks and challenges

In recognising the tasks and challenges we face, we need to be clear about the implications for practice in terms of the two elements of competence for this chapter, namely:

E1 Take responsibility for your own professional development.

The importance of self-directed learning has been emphasised. While there are many people who can be of assistance in promoting our personal and professional development, this does not alter the fact that each of us carries the primary responsibility for our own learning. And this is, of course, as it should be, for no one is in a better position to take the necessary steps to drive our own development forward. The challenge we face, therefore, is being able to i) motivate ourselves to keep learning, even when there may be pressures to 'just get on with the job' (we should remember that continuing to learn *is* part of the job) and have the courage to face any barriers to learning we may encounter; and ii) draw on the support for learning that is available in both formal terms (tutors, training and development staff, mentors and so on) and informal (discussions with colleagues, reading/personal study and so on). The 'Action plan for learning' which appears as an appendix to this chapter may prove helpful to you in planning your own professional development.

E2   Contribute to the professional development of others.

Part of the broad umbrella of professional responsibility is, of course, to make a contribution to the collective development of our profession by promoting the learning of others, exploring and developing the knowledge base, contributing to the development of an atmosphere conducive to learning and so on. In some respects, such work is an extension of existing social work skills (communication, relationship-building and so on), but also involves the development of new skills (making presentations perhaps).

There are various opportunities available for making a contribution to the professional development of others, and so it is to be hoped that you will be able to find at least one where you feel sufficiently comfortable to get involved. It should not be forgotten that there is no need to see this contribution as an individual effort. There is excellent scope for teaming up with others and supporting one another in tackling these issues. This form of group approach can help to build confidence and to keep anxiety at bay.

4. Conclusion

We live and work in a fast-changing world. New developments are never very far away. Consequently, if we do not keep up with developments through continuous learning, we will become increasingly out of touch. This chapter has explored a number of ways in which we can make learning a reality, both for ourselves and for others.

A focus on personal and professional development is clearly important for the reasons discussed here. However, we should also not forget that such a focus can help to maintain the heart of social work, to keep the human dimension to the fore by remembering that, in undertaking social work, we are working as people with people. A focus on development can help in making sure that we resist the tendency to lose sight of what social work is all about – or, as Kroll (1994) puts it, to make sure that we do not become dinosaurs:

I believe that agencies need to rethink what social work is all about – fast. In responding to the chaos created by poverty, homelessness, oppression of every kind, unemployment, rising crime, drug and alcohol abuse, AIDS, the disintegration of 'the nuclear family', child abuse in many forms, moral 'panics', and the increasing divorce rate, there is a move towards devices that control and manage rather than listen and explore. There is a tendency to over-simplify, often through the use of worker-or manager-led approaches that deny or ignore the complex needs of people for whom the service was designed in the first place. The thinking, feeling, contemplative and imaginative social worker who wants to spend time making an assessment, talking to clients, being uncertain and struggling with that feeling is in danger of becoming the social work equivalent of the dinosaur.

Yet the Children Act demands such workers, requires just these qualities and skills if all the complex tasks identified are to be accomplished. As a consequence, child centred agencies and their managers need to attend not only to case management but also to practice – the encouragement of skills development, of openness about the impact of the work, of further training, as well as the celebration and validation of expertise.
(p. 179)

This sets us all a major challenge, but a vitally important one for us to tackle individually and collectively as far as we are able.

5. Points to ponder

➤ Do you give your own development the time and attention it deserves or does the drive to 'get on with the job' get in the way?
➤ What part do you feel able to play in promoting the learning of others, either now or in the future?
➤ How well-developed are your time and workload management skills? Are there any ways that you might be able to develop these further?
➤ How confident do you feel about handling feelings – your own and other people's? Are there any ways in which you can develop your skills in this area?

➤ How aware of the dangers of stress are you? Are you able to accept that everyone can fall foul of stress at times and that this is not a sign of weakness?

6. Learning resources guide

A basic introduction to continuous professional development is to be found in Thompson (2002a) Chapter 8. Waldman (1999) is also a very useful guide.

Reflective practice is discussed in Thompson (2000a), Palmer *et al.* (2000) and Gould and Taylor (1996). The original works of Donald Schön are also worth consulting (Schön, 1983; 1987; 1992). Boud *et al.* (1985) and Boud *et al.* (1993) are also informative.

Reviewing and evaluating practice are discussed in Chapter 22 of Thompson (2002a), while Shaw (1996) offers a more in-depth discussion of evaluation.

Practice teaching is covered in Thompson *et al.* (1994b), Shardlow and Doel (1996) and Lawson (1998).

Morrison (2001) and Curtis and Metcalf (1992) provide good introductions to supervision. A broad managerial perspective is to be found in Betts (1993), while Gorell Barnes *et al.* (2000) adopt a systemic approach. Gilbert and Thompson (2002) is a training pack which covers both supervision and leadership.

Emotional intelligence is covered in Goleman (1996) and Cooper and Sawaf (1997). However, these texts and others in the same tradition have a very strong element of biological reductionism and should therefore be used with caution. These issues are also covered in Thompson and Harrison (2002), a training pack on learning culture, emotional and spiritual intelligence in organisations.

My own work has concentrated a great deal on stress. Thompson *et al.* (1994) provide a basic introduction to stress in social work, while Thompson *et al.* (1996) focus more on the training and management dimensions. Thompson (1999) offers a short practical guide to handling pressure and stress.

Time and workload management is covered in Thompson (2002a) Chapter 2. See also Eisenberg (1986), Murdock and Scutt (1993) and Turla and Hawkins (1983).

Conclusion

As we have noted, there can be no doubt that social work with children, young people and their families is demanding work. It is complex and multifaceted, often involving tension and conflict, and even outright hostility at times. Added to this is the pressure that comes from the recognition that the stakes are high, in the sense that the welfare and well-being of children and young people will often depend on the actions of one or more social workers and others in the multidisciplinary network. And, of course, we must not forget the problems associated with such work being potentially in the media spotlight, with various factions only too willing to pillory social workers, given half a chance. Clearly, it is not an easy job.

Given this situation, it does not take much to work out that the people who make a success of the job do so because they are i) committed to the values on which the work is based and the overall value of providing high-quality services to children, young people and their families; and ii) well-equipped for the tasks they face in terms of their professional knowledge base and the skills needed to rise to the challenge. In other words, it takes a special kind of person to be able to deal effectively and appropriately with the various demands that are part and parcel of the job.

It is to be hoped that studying this book will have made a positive contribution to supporting you in rising to the very real and significant challenges of social work with children, young people and their families. No book can provide 'all the answers', nor should a book attempt to do so. However, each of the chapters has offered a great many ideas about various aspects of the immense knowledge base that we can draw upon in seeking to make sure that our practice is well-informed and based on understanding, rather than guesswork, pot luck or untested assumptions.

Of necessity, the book has covered a lot of ground in a relatively short space and should therefore be seen as a gateway to further study rather than a substitute for it. It would be unrealistic to try to summarise here the knowledge base the book has covered. However, what is perhaps more appropriate (and certainly a lot easier) is for me to summarise the main 'messages' I have tried to put across in writing this book. What follows, then, is a brief restatement of some, but by no means all, of the main points I have tried to convey in the book as a whole:

1. Children and young people are not 'static'. They are involved in a process of development. Effective practice depends on having at least a basic understanding of child and adolescent development and taking such matters into account in our work, not least in our assessment.
2. Loss can often be a significant part of children's and young people's experience, although the important role it plays is frequently missed. Traditional approaches to the study of loss can be seen to be lacking in a number of ways, and so it is important to develop a more sophisticated understanding of it and its effects.
3. It is important to avoid 'drift' by being *systematic* – that is, by being clear about what we are doing and why we are doing it. It is relatively easy, in the pressurised world of social work, to lose sight of what we are trying to achieve and to be dragged off course. This is a temptation that we have to guard against very carefully.
4. Although the children and young people are clearly our primary concern, we should not forget that they are part of families, and that the family context is a complex matter. We have to be careful to ensure that we do not oversimplify the situation by allowing stereotypes or discriminatory assumptions to distort matters.

5. Planning is an essential underpinning of good practice. The process of planning allows all concerned to have a clear focus on what steps need to be taken to meet identified needs, solve problems and so on, to co-ordinate actions and to bring a degree of clarity and security to an otherwise unsettled situation.

6. While providing a supporting role to parents is a legitimate activity, we should beware of slipping into a paternalistic 'superparenting' model in which the social worker 'parents' the parents. We need to take account of the wider context, including rights, and not simply rely on a pathologising model of (inadequate) parenting.

7. Good practice is premised on partnership, including partnership with the children and young people themselves, their parents and other carers, the multidisciplinary network of professionals and the wider community. Partnership is premised on effective communication.

8. Social work takes place in an organisational context. The ability to appreciate how one's organisation works and to influence its culture is therefore something that is worth cultivating over time. This involves going beyond being able to access institutional resources to actually playing a part in shaping the organisation, its working practices and its ethos. This is necessarily a collective endeavour.

9. Social work is largely governed by law and policy, but not exclusively so. Professional practice involves working within the parameters of the legal and policy context, but not seeking to follow guidelines and established practices mechanically or unthinkingly.

10. Although opportunities for practitioners to shape child care policy and practice are limited, we should avoid being defeatist in assuming that there are no such opportunities. Defeatism only serves to hamper what little progress we can make in this regard.

11. Social work is constantly changing and developing, and so we need to be engaged in continuous professional development if we are to remain competent, well-informed practitioners. We should therefore seek opportunities for learning and development in whatever ways we can, as part of a commitment to reflective practice.

12. Coping with pressure and avoiding stress are essential safety mechanisms for surviving, and indeed, flourishing in this demanding field of work. We should therefore take seriously our own needs, develop a self-care plan and not be afraid to ask for support when we need it.

These twelve points are not intended as prescriptive rules to be followed unthinkingly, but rather as guidelines to encourage further reflection, discussion and learning. I hope that you will find them helpful as part of the process of continuous learning in striving for high-quality practice in difficult circumstances.

Appendix 1: Action plan for developing partnership skills

1. Communication

1.1 What are my existing strengths?
1.2 How can I build on them/extend them?
1.3 What aspects of communication do I need
    to develop?
1.4 How can I develop them?

2. Shared action planning

2.1 What are my existing strengths?
2.2 How can I build on them/extend them?
2.3 What aspects of communication do I need
    to develop?
2.4 How can I develop them?

3. Conflict resolution

3.1 What are my existing strengths?
3.2 How can I build on them/extend them?
3.3 What aspects of communication do I need
    to develop?
3.4 How can I develop them?

Appendix 2: Action plan for learning

1A   What do I need to know?
(the knowledge base)

1B   How will I find out?

2A   What do I need to do?
(the skills base)

2B   How will I learn?

3A   What else do I need to enable me to learn?

3B   How can I obtain it?

References

Adams, R. (1996) *Empowerment and Social Work*, 2nd edn, London, Macmillan – now Palgrave.

Adams, R. (1998) *Quality Social Work*, London, Macmillan – now Palgrave.

Adams, R., Dominelli, L. and Payne, M. (eds) (1998) *Social Work: Themes, Issues and Critical Debates*, London, Macmillan – now Palgrave.

Ainsworth, M.D.S., Blehar, M. Walters, E. and Walls, S. (1978) *Patterns of Attachment*, Hillsdale, NJ, Erlbaum.

Ainsworth, M.D.S. (1985) 'Patterns of Infant–mother Attachments: Antecedents and Effects on Development', *Bulletin of New York Academy of Medicine* 66(9).

Alcock, P. (1993) *Understanding Poverty*, London, Macmillan – now Palgrave.

Alderson, P., Brill, S., Chalmers, I., Fuller, R., Hinkley-Smith, P., Macdonald, G., Newman, T., Oakley, A., Roberts, H. and Ward, H. (1995) *What Works? Effective Social Interventions in Child Welfare*, Barkingside, Barnardo's.

Aldgate, J. and Colman, R. (1999) *Post Qualifying Award in Child Care: Conceptual Framework*, Leicester, University of Leicester.

Aldridge, M. (1994) *Making Social Work News*, London, Routledge.

Archard, D. (1993) *Children: Rights and Childhood*, London, Routledge.

Argyris, C. and Schön, D.A. (1974) *Theory and Practice*, San Francisco, CA, Jossey Bass.

Audit Commission (1994) *Seen But Not Heard*, London, HMSO.

Ball, C. (1996) *Law for Social Workers: An Introduction*, Aldershot, Arena.

Ball, C. (1997) 'The Law', in Davies (1997).

Ball, C., Preston-Shoot, M., Roberts, G. and Vernon, S. (1995) *Law for Social Workers in England and Wales: Guidance for Meeting the DipSW Requirements*, London, CCETSW.

Barber, J.G. (1991) *Beyond Casework*, London, Macmillan – now Palgrave.

Barker, V. (1994) *Promoting Partnerships Through Consultation*, Lyme Regis, Russell House Publishing.

Barnes, J. (1996) *Human Development, Language and Practice*, Cardiff, CCETSW Cymru.

Barnes, P. (ed.) (1995) *Personal, Social and Emotional Development of Children*, Oxford, Basil Blackwell.

Barrett, M. and McIntosh, M. (1991) *The Anti-Social Family*, 2nd edn, London, Verso.

Bate, P. (1992) 'The Impact of Organizational Culture on Approaches to Organizational Problem-Solving', in Salaman (1992).

Bates, J., Pugh, R. and Thompson, N. (eds) (1997) *Protecting Children: Challenges and Change*, Aldershot, Arena.

Beddoe, C. (1980) *Stress in Residential Work*, a Report to the RCA AGM 1980 by a working party Residential Care Association.

Belsky (1984) 'The Determinants of Parenting: A Process Model', *Child Development* 55, pp. 83–96.

Beresford, B., Sloper, P., Baldwin, S. and Newman T. (1996) *What Works in Services with a Disabled Child?*, Barkingside, Barnardo's.

Beresford, P. and Croft, S. (1992) *Citizen Involvement*, London, Macmillan – now Palgrave.

Betts, P.W. (1993) *Supervisory Management*, London, Pitman.

Biestek, F.P. (1961) *The Casework Relationship*, London, Allen and Unwin.

Billingsley, A. (1968) *Black Families in White America*, Englewood Cliffs, NJ, Prentice-Hall.

Bocock, R. (1983) *Sigmund Freud*, London, Tavistock.

Boud, D.J., Cohen, R. and Walker, D. (eds) (1993) *Using Experience for Learning*, Buckingham, Open University Press.

Boud, D.J., Keogh, R. and Walker, D. (eds) (1985) *Reflection: Turning Experience into Learning*, London, Kogan Page.

Bowlby, J. (1953) *Child Care and the Growth of Love*, Harmondsworth, Penguin.

Bradley, M. and Aldgate, J. (1994) 'Short-term Family Based Care for Children in Need', *Adoption and Fostering*, 18(4).

Brandon, M, Schofield, G. and Trinder, L. (1998) *Social Work with Children*, London, Macmillan – now Palgrave.

Branthwaite, A. (1985) 'Development of Social Identity and Self-concept', in Branthwaite and Rogers (1985).

Branthwaite, A. and Rogers, D. (eds) (1985) *Children Growing Up*, Milton Keynes, Open University Press.

Braye, S. and Preston-Shoot, M. (1997) *Practising Social Work Law*, 2nd edn, London, Macmillan – now Palgrave.

Braye, S. and Preston-Shoot, M. (1998) 'Social Work and the Law', in Adams *et al.* (1998).

Brayne, H. and Martin, G. (1997) *Law for Social Workers*, (5th edition), London, Blackstone Press.

Broad, B. (2001) *Kinship Care: The Placement Choice for Children and Young People*, Lyme Regis, Russell House Publishing.

Bronfenbrenner, U. (1986) 'Ecology of the Family as a Context for Human Development', *Developmental Psychology* 22, pp. 723–42.

Bryer, M. (1988) *Planning in Child Care: A Guide for Team Leaders and Their Teams*, London, BAAF.

Buchanan, A. (2000) ' . . . You're Walking on Eggs: Findings from Research into Parenting', in Wheal (2000).

Burgoon, M., Hunsaker, F.G. and Dawson, E.J. (1994) *Human Communication*, 3rd edn, London, Sage.

Burton, J. (1993) *The Handbook of Residential Care*, London, Routledge.

Butler, I and Roberts, G. (1997) *Social Work with Children and Families: Getting into Practice*, London, Jessica Kingsley.

Calder, M. with Peake, A., and Rose K. (2001a) *Mothers of Sexually Abused Children: A Framework for Assessment, Understanding and Support*, Lyme Regis, Russell House Publishing.

Calder, M. with Hanks, H., Epps, H.J., Print, B., Morrison, T. and Henniker, J. (2001b) *Juveniles and Children who Sexually Abuse: Frameworks for Assessment*, Lyme Regis, Russell House Publishing.

Coleman, J. and Roker, D. (eds) (2001) *Supporting Parents of Teenagers*, London, Jessica Kingsley.

Cooley, C.H. (1902) *Human Nature and the Social Order*, New York, Scribner.

Cooper, J. and Vernon, S. (1996) *Disability and the Law*, London, Jessica Kingsley.

Cooper, R. and Sawaf, A. (1997) *Executive EQ: Emotional Intelligence in Business*, London, Orion Business Books.

Corby, B. (2000) 'The Impact of Public Inquiries on the Perceptions of Residential Child Care', in Crimmens and Pitts (2000).

Corr, C.A., McNabe, C.M. and Corr, D.M. (1996) *Death and Dying, Life and Living*, (2nd edition), Pacific Grove, CA, Brooks/Cole.

Corrigan, P. and Leonard, P. (1978) *Social Work Practice Under Capitalism: A Marxist Approach,* London, Macmillan – now Palgrave.

Cowie, H. (1995) 'Child Care and Attachment', in Barnes (1995).

Cox, D. and Parish, A. (1989) *Working in Partnership*, Barkingside, Barnardo's.

Crimmens, D. and Pitts, J. (eds) (2000) *Positive Residential Practice: Learning the Lessons of the 1990s,* Lyme Regis, Russell House Publishing.

Crompton, I. and Thompson, N. (2000) *The Human Rights Act 1998: A Training Resource Pack*, Wrexham, Learning Curve Publishing.

Crompton, M. (1990) *Attending to Children: Direct Work in Social and Health Care*, London, Edward Arnold.

Cropper, A. (1997) 'Rethinking Practice: Learning from a Black Feminist Perspective', in Bates *et al.* (1997).

Cull, L-A. and Roche, J. (eds) (2001) *The Law and Social Work: Contemporary Issues for Practice*, Basingstoke, Palgrave.

Curtis, C. and Metcalf, J. (1992) *Becoming a Care Supervisor*, London, Churchill-Livingstone.

Daines, R., Lyond. K. and Parsloe, P. (1990) *Aiming for Partnership*, Barkingside, Barnardos.

Dallos, R. and McLaughlin, E. (eds) (1993) *Social Problems and The Family*, London, Sage.

Dallos, R. and Sapsford, R. (1997) 'Patterns of Diversity and Lived Realities', in Muncie *et al.* (1997).

Dalrymple, J. and Burke, B. (1995) *Anti-Oppressive Practice, Social Care and the Law*, Buckingham, Open University Press.

Daniel, B., Wassell, S. and Gilligan, R. (1999) *Child Development for Child Care and Protection Workers*, London, Jessica Kingsley.

Davenport, G.C. (1994) *An Introduction to Child Development*, 2nd edn, London, Collins.

Davies, M. (ed.) (1997) *The Blackwell Companion to Social Work*, Oxford, Blackwell.

Davies, E. (1994) *'They All Speak English Anyway':* *The Welsh Language and Anti-Oppressive Practice,* Cardiff, CCETSW Cymru.

Department of Health (1991a) *Children Act 1991 Guidance and Regulations Volume 4: Residential Care*, London, HMSO.

Department of Health (1991b) *Working Together Under the Children Act 1989*, London, HMSO.

Department of Health (1995a) *Inspection of Local Authority Fostering Services*, London, HMSO.

Department of Health (1995b) *Independent Fostering Agencies Study*, London, HMSO.

Department of Health Social Services Inspectorate (1995a) *Child Protection: Messages from Research,* London, HMSO.

Department of Health Social Services Inspectorate (1995b) *The Challenge of Partnership in Child Protection: Practice Guide*, London HMSO.

Department of Health, Department for Education and Employment and the Home Office (2000) *Framework for the Assessment of Children in Need and Their Families*, London, The Stationery Office.

Department of Health (2001) *The Children Act Now: Messages from Research,* London, The Stationery Office.

DHSS (1974) *Report of the Committe of Inquiry into the Care and Supervision of Maria Colwell*, London, HMSO.

Doka, K. (ed.) (1989) *Disenfranchised Grief: Recognizing Hidden Sorrow*, Lexington, MA, Lexington Books.

Donnison, D. (1998) *Policies for a Just Society*, London, Macmillan – now Palgrave.

Drew, S. (2000) *Children and the Human Rights Act*, London, Save the Children.

Durkin, K. (1995) *Developmental Social Psychology: From Infancy to Old Age*, Oxford, Basil Blackwell.

Dwivedi, K.N. (1996) 'Culture and Personality', in Dwivedi and Varma (1996).

Dwivedi, K.N. and Varma, V.P. (eds) (1996) *Meeting the Needs of Ethnic Minority Children: A Handbook for Professionals*, London, Jessica Kingsley.

Earnshaw, J. and Cooper, C. (1996) *Stress and Employer Liability*, London, IPD.

Egan, G. (1998) *The Skilled Helper: A Problem Management Approach to Helping*, 6th edn, Pacific Grove, CA, Brooks/Cole.

Eisenberg, R. (1986) *Organise Yourself*, London, Piatkus.

Erikson, E. (1977) *Childhood and Society*, London, Paladin.

Etzel, B. and Thomas, P. (1996) *Personal Information Management: Tools and Techniques for Achieving Professional Effectiveness*, London, Macmillan – now Palgrave.

Everitt, A., Hardiker, P., Littlewood, J. and Mullender, A. (1992) *Applied Research for Better Practice*, London, Macmillan – now Palgrave.

Everitt, A. and Hardiker, P. (1996) *Evaluating for Good Practice*, London, Macmillan – now Palgrave.

Factor, F., Chauhan, V. and Pitts, J. (eds) (2001) *The RHP Companion to Working with Young People*, Lyme Regis, Russell House Publishing.

Fahlberg, V. (1988) *Fitting the Pieces Together*, London, BAAF.

Fahlberg, V. (1994) *A Child's Journey Through Placement*, London, BAAF.

Family Rights Group (1991) *The Children Act 1989: Working in Partnership with Families – Reader*, London, HMSO.

Faulkner, D. (1995) 'Play, Self and the Social World', in Barnes (1995).

Fisher, R. and Ury, W. (1991) *Getting to Yes*, 2nd edn, Harmondsworth, Penguin.

Fishwick, C. (1996) *Community Care and Control*, 2nd edn, Birmingham, Pepar.

Foley, P., Roche, J. and Tucker, S. (eds) (2001) *Children in Society: Contemporary Theory, Policy and Practice*, Basingstoke, Palgrave.

Foucault, M. (1977) *Discipline and Punish*, London, Tavistock.

Foucault, M. (1980) *Power/Knowledge: Selected Interviews and Other Writings 1972–77* (ed. C. Gordon), Brighton, Harvester Press.

Fox Harding, L. (1991) *Perspectives in Child Care Policy*, London, Longman.

Fox Harding, L. (1996) *Family, State and Social Policy*, London, Macmillan – now Palgrave.

Francis, D. and Henderson, P. (1992) *Working with Rural Communities*, London, Macmillan – now Palgrave.

Franklin, B. (ed.) (2001) *The New Handbook of Children's Rights: Comparative Policy and Practice*, London, Routledge.

Freeman, M.D.A. (1992) *Children, their Families and the Law: Working with the Children Act*, London, Macmillan – now Palgrave.

Freire, P. (1972) *Pedagogy of the Oppressed*, Harmondsworth, Penguin.

Fry, E. (1994) *On Remand: Foster Care and the Youth Justice System*, London, NFCA.

Gambe, D., Gomes, J., Kapur, V., Rangel, M. and Stubbs, P. (1992) *Anti-Racist Social Work Education: Improving Practice with Children and Families*, Leeds, CCETSW.

Garrett, M. (1999) 'Questioning the New Orthodoxy: The Looking After Children System and its Discourse on Parenting', *Practice* 11(1).

German, G. (1996) 'Anti-racist Strategies for Educational Performance: Facilitating Successful Learning for All Children', in Dwivedi and Varma (1996).

Giddens, A. (ed.) (1992) *Human Societies: A Reader*, Cambridge, Polity Press.

Gilbert, P. and Thompson, N. (2002) *Supervision and Leadership Skills: A Training Resource Pack*, Wrexham, Learning Curve Publishing.

Gittins, D. (1993) *The Family in Question*, London, Macmillan – now Palgrave.

Godefroy, C.H. and Robert, L. (1998) *The Outstanding Negotiator: How to Develop Your Arguing Power*, 2nd edn, London, Piatkus.

Goleman, D. (1996) *Emotional Intelligence: Why it Can Matter More Than IQ*, London, Bloomsbury Publishing.

Gomm, R. (1993) 'Issues of Power in Health and Welfare', in Walmsley *et al.* (1993).

Gorell Barnes, G., Down, G. and McCann, D. (2000) *Systemic Supervision: A Portable Guide for Supervision Training*, London, Jessica Kingsley.

Gould, N. and Taylor, I. (eds) (1996) *Reflective Learning for Social Work*, Aldershot, Arena.

Greenberg, M., Ciccetti, D. and Cummings, M. (eds) (1990) *Attachment in the Pre-School Years*, Chicago, University of Chicago Press.

Guirdham, M. (1999) *Communicating Across Cultures*, London, Macmillan – now Palgrave.

Hackett, S. (2001) *Facing the Future: A Guide for Parents of Young People who Have Sexually Abused*, Lyme Regis, Russell House Publishing.

Hall, S. (1997a) 'The Work of Representation', in Hall (1997b).

Hall, S. (ed.) (1997b) *Representation: Cultural Representations and Signifying Practices*, London, Sage.

Harrison, R., Mann, G., Murphy, M., Taylor, A. and Thompson, N. (2002) *Partnership Made Painless*, Lyme Regis, Russell House Publishing.

Hawtin, M., Hughes, G. and Percy-Smith, J. (1994) *Community Profiling: Auditing Social Needs*, Buckingham, Open University Press.

Hayden, C., Goddard, J., Gorin, S. and Van Der Spek, N. (1999) *State Child Care: Looking After Children?*, London, Jessica Kingsley.

Hill, M. and Aldgate, J. (eds) (1996) *Child Welfare Services: Developments in Law, Policy, Practice and Research*, London, Jessica Kingsley.

Hindess, B. (1988) *Choice, Rationality and Social Theory*, London, Unwin Hyman.

Horwath, J. (ed.) (2001) *The Child's World: Assessing Children in Need*, London, Jessica Kingsley.

Howe, D. (1987) *An Introduction to Social Work Theory*, Aldershot, Ashgate.

Howe, D. (1995) *Attachment Theory for Social Work Practice*, London, Macmillan – now Palgrave.

Howe, D., Brandon, M., Hinings, D. and Schofield, G. (1999) *Attachment Theory, Child Maltreatment and Family Support*, London, Macmillan – now Palgrave.

Hucsynski, A. and Buchanan, D. (2001) *Organizational Behaviour*, 4th edn, London, Prentice-Hall.

Hume, C., Lowe, F. and Rose, G. (2000) 'Building in the Lessons: A New Start for Residential Care in Lewisham', in Crimmens and Pitts (2000).

Humphries, B. (ed.) (1996) *Empowerment: A Critical Perspective*, Birmingham, Venture Press.

Huws Williams, R. Williams, H. and Davies, E. (eds) (1994) *Social Work and the Welsh Language,* Cardiff, University of Wales Press.

Inskipp, F. (1986) *A Manual for Trainers*, Alexia Publications.

Isaac, B. (1991) 'Negotiation in Partnership Work', in Family Rights Group (1991).

Jackson, S. and Kilroe, S. (eds) (1996) *Looking After Children – Good Parenting: Good Outcomes*, London, HMSO.

Jackson, S. and Thomas, N. (1999) *On the Move Again? What Works in Creating Stability for Looked After Children,* Barkingside, Barnardo's.

Johansen, S. (1999) 'Working in Partnership: Social Workers and Carers', in Wheal (1999).

Johnson, N. (1987) *The Welfare State in Transition*, Brighton, Wheatsheaf.

Johnson, N. (1990) *Reconstructing the Welfare State: A Decade of Change 1980–1990*, Hemel Hempstead, Harvester Wheatsheaf.

Kahan, B. (1994) *Growing Up in Groups*, London, HMSO.

Kemshall, H. and Pritchard, J. (eds) (1995) *Good Practice in Risk Assessment and Risk Management*, London, Jessica Kingsley.

Kennedy, G. (1998) *The New Negotiating Edge: The Behavioural Approach for Results and Relationships,* London, Nicholas Brealey.

Knight, T. and Caveney, S. (1998) 'Assessment and Action Records: Will They Promote Good Parenting', *British Journal of Social Work* 20(1).

Kolb, D.A. (1984) *Experiential Learning*, Englewood Cliffs, NJ, Prentice-Hall.

Kolb, D.A., Rubin, I.M. and MacIntyre, J.M. (1979) *Organizational Psychology*, Englewood Cliffs, NJ, Prentice-Hall.

Kroll, B. (1994) *Chasing Rainbows: Children, Divorce and Loss*, Lyme Regis, Russell House Publishing.

Kübler-Ross, E. (1970) *On Death and Dying*, London, Routledge.

Lambert, T. (1996) *The Power of Influence: Intensive Influencing Skills at Work*, London, Nicholas Brealey.

Langan, M. and Day, L. (eds) (1992) *Women, Oppression and Social Work*: *Issues in Anti-Discriminatory Practice*, London, Routledge.

Lau, A. (1996) 'Family Therapy and Ethnic Minorities', in Dwivedi and Varma (1996).

Lawson, H. (ed.) (1998) *Practice Teaching – Changing Social Work*, London, Jessica Kingsley.

Lesňik, B. (ed.) (1997) *Change in Social Work*, Aldershot, Arena.

Lindstein, T. and Meteyard, B. (1996) *What Works in Family Mediation,* Lyme Regis, Russell House Publishing.

Lloyd, E. (ed.) (1999) *Parenting Matters: What Works in Parenting Education?*, Barkingside, Barnardo's.

London Borough of Brent (1985) *A Child in Trust: Report of the Panel of Inquiry Investigating the Circumstances Surrounding the Death of Jasmine Beckford*, London, London Borough of Brent.

Lupton, C., North, N. and Khan, P. (2001) *Working Together or Pulling Apart? The National Health Service and Child Protection Networks*, Bristol, the Policy Press.

Macdonald, G. and Sheldon, B. (1992) 'Contemporary Studies of the Effectiveness of Social Work', *British Journal of Social Work* 22(6).

Macdonald, K.I. and Macdonald, G.M. (1999) 'Perceptions of Risk', in Parsloe (1999).

Main, M. and Soloman, J. (1990) 'Procedures for Identifying Infants as Disorganized/ Disorientated During the Ainsworth Strange Situation', in Greenberg *et al.* (1990).

Maslow, A. (1973) *The Farther Reaches of Human Nature*, Harmondsworth, Penguin.

Mather, M. with Batty, D. and Payne, H. (2000) *Doctors for Children in Public Care*: *A Resource Guide Advocating, Protecting and Promoting Health,* London, BAAF.

Mather, M., Humphrey, J. and Robson, J. (1997) 'The Statutory Medical and Health Needs of Looked After Children', *Adoption and Fostering* 21(2).

Mayo, M. (1994) *Communities and Caring: The Mixed Economy of Welfare*, London, Macmillan – now Palgrave.

Mezirow, J. (1981) 'A Critical Theory of Adult Learning and Education', *Adult Education* 32(1).

Middleton, L. (1999) *Disabled Children: Challenging Social Exclusion,* Oxford, Blackwell.

Millham, S., Bullock, R. and Hosie, K. (1980) *Learning to Care: The Training of Staff for Residential Social Work with Young People,* Farnborough, Gower.

Mills, C.W. (1970) *The Sociological Imagination*, Harmondsworth, Penguin.

Milner, J. and O'Byrne, P. (1998) *Assessment in Social Work,* London, Macmillan – now Palgrave.

Mitchell, J. (1974) *Psychoanalysis and Feminism*, Harmondsworth, Penguin.

Moore, J. (1992) *The ABC of Child Protection*, Aldershot, Ashgate.

Morrison, T. (1997) 'Emotionally Competent Organizations: Fact, Fiction or Necessity?', in Bates *et al.* (1997).

Morrison, T. (2001) *Supervision in Social Care,* 2nd edn, Brighton, Pavilion.

Moss, B. and Tzilivakis, G. (2002) *Conflict Management: A Training Resource Pack,* Wrexham, Learning Curve Publishing.

Mullins, L.J. (1996) *Management and Organisational Behaviour,* 4th edn, London, Pitman.

Muncie, J. and Langan, M. (1997) 'Introduction: Public Definitions and Private Lives', in Muncie *et al.* (1997).

Muncie, J., Wetherell, M., Langan, M., Dallos, R. and Cochrane, A. (eds) (1997) *Understanding the Family,* 3rd edn, London, Sage.

Murdock, A. and Scutt, C. (1993) *Personal Effectiveness,* Oxford, Butterworth-Heinemann.

Murphy, M. (1995) *Working Together in Child Protection,* Aldershot, Arena.

National Assembly for Wales (2000) *Working Together to Safeguard Children: A Guide to Inter-Agency Working to Safeguard and Promote the Welfare of Children,* Cardiff, NAW.

National Foster Care Association/National Assembly for Wales (1999) *Code of Practice on the Recruitment, Assessment, Approval, Training, Management and Support of Foster Carers,* London and Cardiff, NFCA/NAW.

Neimeyer, R.A. and Anderson, A. (2002) 'Meaning Reconstruction Theory', in Thompson (2002b).

Neimeyer, R.A., Keesee, N.J. and Fortner, B.V. (1998) 'Loss and Meaning Reconstruction: Propositions and Procedures', in Rubin *et al.* (1998).

Nias, J. (ed.) (1993) *The Human Nature of Learning,* Buckingham, Open University Press.

O'Sullivan, T. (1999) *Decision-Making in Social Work,* London, Macmillan – now Palgrave.

Oates, J. (1994) *The Foundations of Child Development,* Oxford, Basil Blackwell.

Oliver, M. (1990) *The Politics of Disablement,* London, Macmillan – now Palgrave.

Oliver, M. and Sapey, M. (1999) *Social Work with Disabled People,* 2nd edn, London, Macmillan – now Palgrave.

Palmer, A., Burns, S. and Bulman, C. (eds) (1994) *Reflective Practice in Nursing: The Growth of the Professional Practitioner,* Oxford, Blackwell.

Parkes, C.M. (1970) 'The First Year of Bereavement: A Longitudinal Study of the Reaction of London Widows to the Death of their Husbands', *Psychiatry,* 33, pp. 444–67.

Parkes, C.M. (1995) *Bereavement: Studies of Grief in Adult Life,* 3rd edn, Harmondsworth, Penguin.

Parkes, C.M., Langauni, P. and Young, B. (1997) *Death and Bereavement Across Cultures,* London, Routledge.

Parsloe. P. (ed.) (1999) *Risk Assessment in Social Care and Social Work,* London, Jessica Kingsley.

Parton, N. (1991) *Governing the Family: Child Care, Child Protection and the State,* London, Macmillan – now Palgrave.

Parton, N., Thorpe, D. and Wattam, C. (eds) (1997) *Child Protection: Risk and the Moral Order,* London, Macmillan – now Palgrave.

Payne, M. (2000) *Anti-Bureaucratic Social Work,* Birmingham, Venture Press.

Payne, M. (1997) *Modern Social Work Theory,* 2nd edn, London, Macmillan – now Palgrave.

Pecora, P.J., Whittaker, J.K., Maluccio, A.N. and Barth, R.P. with Plotnick, R.D. (2000) *The Child Welfare Challenge: Policy, Practice and Research,* 2nd edn, New York, Aldine de Gruyter.

Philpot, T. (ed.) (1989) *On Second Thoughts: Reassessments of the Literature of Social Work,* Wallington, Reed Business Publishing.

Piaget, J. and Inhelder, B. (1966) *The Psychology of the Child,* London, Routledge.

Pithers, D. (1987) 'Understanding Love and Loss: Child Care and the Growth of Love, by John Bowlby', in Philpot (1987).

Postle, K. and Ford, P. (2000) 'Using Mediation Skills in Family Work', in Wheal (2000).

Pottage, D. and Evans, M. (1992) *Workbased Stress: Prescription is Not the Cure,* London, NISW.

Pugh, G. (1996) 'Seen But Not Heard: Addressing the Needs of Children Who Foster', *Adoption and Fostering* 20(1).

Rabinow, P. (ed.) (1986) *The Foucault Reader,* Harmondsworth, Penguin.

Ramsay, D. (1996) 'Recruiting and Retaining Foster Carers: Implications of a Professional Service in Fife', *Adoption and Fostering* 20(1).

Reid, I. (1992) 'Social Class and Education', in Giddens (1992).

Rhodes, P. (1993) 'Charitable Vocation or "Proper Job"? The Role of Payment in Foster Care', *Adoption and Fostering* 17(1).

Riches, G. and Dawson, P. (2000) *An Intimate Loneliness: Supporting Bereaved Parents and Siblings,* Buckingham, Open University Press.

Robertson Elliot, F. (1996) *Gender, Family and Society,* London, Macmillan – now Palgrave.

Robinson, L. (1995) *Psychology for Social Workers: Black Perspectives,* London, Routledge.

Roderick, C. (1993) 'Becoming a Learning Organisation', *Training and Development,* March.

Rubin, S., Malkinson, R. and Witztum, E. (eds) (1998) *Traumatic and Nontraumatic Bereavement,* Madison, CT, International Universities Press.

Ruegger, M. (2001) *Hearing the Voice of the Child: The Representation of Children's Interests in Public Law Proceedings,* Lyme Regis, Russell House Publishing.

Rutter, M. (1975) *Helping Troubled Children,* Harmondsworth, Penguin.

Rutter, M. (1981) *Maternal Deprivation Reassessed,* 2nd edn, Harmondsworth, Penguin.

Rutter, M. (1985) 'Family and School Influences on Behavioural Development', *Journal of Child Psychology and Psychiatry* 26, pp. 349–68.

Salaman, G. (ed.) (1992) *Human Resource Strategies*, London, Sage.

Sargent, K. (1999) 'Assessing Risks for Children', in Parsloe (1999).

Sartre, J-P. (1963) *Search for a Method*, New York, Vintage.

Schaffer, H.R. (1998) *Making Decisions About Children*, 2nd edn, Oxford, Blackwell.

Schein, E.H. (1992) 'Coming to a New Awareness of Organizational Culture' in Salaman (1992).

Schön, D. (1983) *The Reflective Practitioner,* London, Temple Smith.

Schön, D.A. (1987) *Educating the Reflective Practitioner*, San Francisco, CA, Jossey Bass.

Schön, D.A. (1992) 'The Crisis of Professional Knowledge and the Pursuit of an Epistemology of Practice', *Journal of Interprofessional Care* 6(1).

Sellick, C. (1992) *Supporting Short-term Foster Carers*, Aldershot, Avebury.

Sellick, C. (1996b) 'Short-term Foster Care', in Hill and Aldgate (1996).

Sellick, C. and Thoburn, J. (1996) *What Works in Family Placement?*, Barkingside, Barnardo's.

Shardlow, S. and Doel, M. (1996) *Practice Learning and Teaching*, London, Macmillan – now Palgrave.

Shaw, I. (1996) *Evaluating in Practice*, Aldershot, Arena.

Sheldon, B. and Chilvers, R. (2000) *Evidence-based Social Care: A Study of Prospects and Problems*, Lyme Regis, Russell House Publishing.

Sibeon, R. (1996) *Contemporary Sociology and Policy Analysis: The New Sociology of Policy Analysis*, Eastham, Tudor Press.

Sibeon, R. (1999) 'Anti-Reductionist Sociology', *Sociology* 33(2).

Siencyn, S.W. (1995) *A Sound Understanding: An Introduction to Language Awareness*, Cardiff, CCETSW Cymru.

Sinclair, R., Garrett, L. and Berridge, D. (1995) *Social Work and Assessment with Adolescents,* London, NCB.

Singh, R. (1997) *The Future of Human Rights in the United Kingdom*: *Essays on Law and Practice,* Oxford, Hart Publishing.

Skaff, L. (1988) 'Child Maltreatment Coordinating Committees for Effective Service Delivery', *Child Welfare LXVII(3)*.

Smith, S.C. and Pennells, M. (eds) (1995) *Interventions with Bereaved Children*, London, Jessica Kingsley.

Social Services Inspectorate (1995) *The Challenge of Partnership in Child Protection: Practice Guide*, London, HMSO.

Squirrell, G. (1999) *Developing Social Skills*, Lyme Regis, Russell House Publishing.

Stainton Rogers, W. and Roche, J. (1994) *Children's Welfare and Children's Rights: A Practical Guide to the Law*, London, Hodder and Stoughton.

Stein, M. (1997) *What Works in Leaving Care?*, Barkingside, Barnardo's.

Stevens, R. (1983) *Freud and Psychoanalysis*, Milton Keynes, Open University Press.

Stewart, A. (1994) 'The Grief of the Abused Male', paper presented at the Helping the Bereaved Male conference, London, Ontario, Canada.

Stewart, J.K., Yea, M.D. and Brown, R. (1989) 'Changing Social Work Roles in Family Centres: A Social Psychological Analysis', *British Journal of Social Work* 20(3).

Stone, M. (1990) *Child Protection Work: A Professional Guide,* Birmingham, Venture Press.

Stroebe, M.S., Hansson, R.O. and Stroebe, W. (1993a) 'Contemporary Themes and Controversies in Bereavement Research', in Stroebe *et al.* (1993b).

Stroebe, M.S. and Schut, H. (1999) 'The Dual Process Model of Coping with Bereavement: Rationale and Description', *Death Studies*, 23(3).

Stroebe, M.S., Stroebe, W. and Hansson, R.O. (eds) (1993b) *Handbook of Bereavement: Theory, Research and Intervention*, Cambridge, Cambridge University Press.

Subhra, G. (2001) 'Reclaiming the Evaluation Agenda', in Factor *et al.* (2001).

Sullivan, T. (1999) *Decision-making in Social Work*, London, Macmillan – now Palgrave.

Thomas, N. (2000) *Children, Family and the State Decision-Making and Child Participation*, London, Macmillan – now Palgrave.

Thomas, N. (2001) 'Listening to Children', in Foley *et al.* (2001).

Thomas, N. and O'Kane, C. (1998) *Children and Decision-Making*, Swansea, University of Wales.

Thompson, N. (1991) *Crisis Intervention Revisited*, Birmingham, Pepar.

Thompson, N. (1992) *Existentialism and Social Work,* Aldershot, Avebury.

Thompson, N. (1995) 'Men and Anti-Sexism', *British Journal of Social Work*, 25(4).

Thompson, N. (1997) 'Responding to Loss', in Bates *et al.* (1997).

Thompson, N. (1998) *Promoting Equality: Challenging Discrimination and Oppression in the Human Services*, London, Macmillan – now Palgrave.

Thompson, N. (1999) *Stress Matters*, Birmingham, Pepar.

Thompson, N. (2000a) *Theory and Practice in Human Services,* 2nd edn, Buckingham, Open University Press.

Thompson, N. (2000b) *Understanding Social Work: Preparing for Practice*, Basingstoke, Palgrave.

Thompson, N. (2000c) *Tackling Bullying and Harassment in the Workplace*, Birmingham, Pepar.

Thompson, N. (2001) *Anti-Discriminatory Practice*, 3rd edn, Basingstoke, Palgrave.

Thompson, N. (2002a) *People Skills*, 2nd edn, Basingstoke, Palgrave.

Thompson, N. (ed.) (2002b) *Loss and Grief: A Guide for Human Services Practitioners*, Basingstoke, Palgrave.

Thompson, N. and Bates, J. (1995) 'In-Service Training: Myth and Reality', *Curriculum* 16(1).

Thompson, N. and Bates, J. (1996) *Learning from Other Disciplines: Lessons from Nurse Education and Management Theory* , Norwich, University of East Anglia Social Work Monographs.

Thompson, N. and Bates, J. (1998) 'Avoiding Dangerous Practice', *Care: the Journal of Practice and Development* 6(3).

Thompson, N. and Harrison, R. (2002) *The Intelligent Organisation: A Training Resource Pack*, Wrexham, Learning Curve Publishing.

Thompson, N., Murphy, M. and Stradling, S. (1994a) *Dealing with Stress,* London, Macmillan – now Palgrave.

Thompson, N., Murphy, M. and Stradling, S. (1996) *Meeting the Stress Challenge*, Lyme Regis, Russell House Publishing.

Thompson, N., Osada, M. and Anderson, B. (1994b) *Practice Teaching in Social Work*, 2nd edn, Birmingham, Pepar.

Thompson, N. and Thompson, S. (2002) *Understanding Social Care: A Guide to the Underpinning Knowledge Requirements of the S/NVQ Awards in Care at Level 4,* Lyme Regis, Russell House Publishing.

Thorpe, M. (2000) 'Working with Families with Sick and Disabled Parents', in Wheal (2000).

TOPSS (2000) *National Occupational Standards for Child Care at Post Qualifying Level*, London, TOPSS.

Triseliotis, J., Sellick, C. and Short, R. (1995) *Foster Care: Theory and Practice*, London, Batsford.

Turla, P. and Hawkins, K.L. (1983) *Time Management Made Easy*, London, Panther.

Utting, W. (1991) *Children in the Public Care*, London, HMSO.

Vernon, S. (1998) *Social Work and the Law*, 3rd edn, London, Butterworth.

Wadham, J. and Mountfield, H. (1999) *Blackstone's Guide to the Human Rights Act 1998*, London, Blackstone Press.

Waldman, J. (1998) *Help Yourself to Learning at Work*, Lyme Regis, Russell House Publishing.

Walmsley, J., Reynolds, J., Shakespeare, P. and Woolfe, R. (eds) (1993) *Health, Welfare and Practice: Reflecting on Roles and Relationships*, London, Sage.

Waterhouse, R. (2000) *Lost in Care*, London, The Stationery Office.

Waterhouse, S. (1992) 'How Foster Carers View Contact', *Adoption and Fostering* 16(2).

Westcott, H. and Cross, M. (1996) *This Far and No Further: Towards Ending the Abuse of Disabled Children*, Birmingham, Venture Press.

Wetherell, M. (1997) 'Social Structure, Ideology and Family Dynamics: The Case of Parenting', in Muncie *et al.* (1997).

Wheal, A. (1995) *The Foster Carer's Handbook*, Lyme Regis, Russell House Publishing.

Wheal, A. (1998) *Adolescence: Positive Approaches for Working with Young People*, Lyme Regis, Russell House Publishing.

Wheal, A. (ed.) (1999) *The RHP Companion to Foster Care*, Lyme Regis, Russell House Publishing.

Wheal, A. (ed.) (2000) *Working with Parents*, Lyme Regis, Russell House Publishing.

Wilkinson, R. (1996) *Unhealthy Societies: The Afflictions of Inequality*, London, Routledge.

Williams, B. (1997) 'Rights versus Risks: Issues in Work with Prisoners', in Kemshall and Pritchard (1997).

Worden, W.J. (1991) *Grief Counselling and Grief Therapy: A Handbook for the Mental Health Practitioner*, 2nd edn, London, Routledge.

Index